£19·99

Women and American Politics

Women, Power and Politics

Anne Stevens

palgrave
macmillan

First published 2007 by
PALGRAVE MACMILLAN
Houndmills, Basingstoke, Hampshire RG21 6XS and
175 Fifth Avenue, New York, N.Y. 10010
Companies and representatives throughout the world

PALGRAVE MACMILLAN is the global academic imprint of the Palgrave Macmillan division of St. Martin's Press, LLC and of Palgrave Macmillan Ltd. Macmillan® is a registered trademark in the United States, United Kingdom and other countries. Palgrave is a registered trademark in the European Union and other countries.

ISBN-13: 978–0–230–50780–7 hardback
ISBN-10: 0–230–50780–8   hardback
ISBN-13: 978–0–230–50781–4 paperback
ISBN-10: 0–230–50781–6   paperback

This book is printed on paper suitable for recycling and made from fully managed and sustained forest sources. Logging, pulping and manufacturing processes are expected to conform to the environmental regulations of the country of origin.

A catalogue record for this book is available from the British Library.

Library of Congress Cataloging-in-Publication Data

Stevens, Anne, 1942–
   Women, power and politics / Anne Stevens.
      p. cm.
   Includes index.
   ISBN 0–230–50780–8 (alk. paper)
      1. Women in politics—OECD countries. 2. Women and democracy. I. Title
HQ1236.S736 2007
   320.082—dc22   2007021656

10   9   8   7   6   5   4   3   2   1
16   15   14   13   12   11   10   09   08   07

Printed and bound in China

For Hilary, Lucy and Mary
with love and admiration

Contents

Contents

List of Boxes, Figures and Tables

Boxes

Acknowledgements

Some twenty years ago Professor Siân Reynolds brought together a group of women academics to offer a lecture series (subsequently published as *Women, State and Revolution*) marking the introduction of a number of courses with a focus on women into the European Studies syllabus of the University of Sussex. My experience of participating in those lectures, and subsequently of teaching such courses there and in two other universities, reinforced my understanding of how women can work together and what the study of issues relating to women has to offer both researchers and students. I acknowledge with gratitude and affection the example and encouragement of Professor Reynolds and the other women with whom I have worked, especially at Sussex and Aston. Moreover, all her successors, including me, owe a considerable debt to the work of Professor Vicky Randall, a pioneering author in this area whose encouragement, when I first broached this project, I much appreciated.

My then Vice-Chancellor, Professor Michael Wright, and my Head of School, Dr Pamela Moores, agreed to release me for a year from some teaching and all general administrative obligations, thereby enabling me to find the time to write the book. To them and to my colleagues and students at Aston University who bore so tolerantly with my frequent absences, I express my thanks.

I am especially grateful to Dr Janneke Jansen for information and to Dr Sarah Childs, Professor Françoise Dreyfus, Professor Elizabeth Meehan, Mary Stevens and two anonymous reviewers, who read parts or all of the text in draft and provided very valuable comments.

Dr Handley Stevens has lived with the production of the book, borne with my presence and my absence, supported and assisted me in innumerable ways both domestic and professional, and read and commented on my draft. I hope he has some inkling of just how grateful I am for everything. My publisher Steven Kennedy and I disagree over whether this book is the result of the application on his part of a strong arm or soft soap. What is certain is that it would not have been begun or finished without his steadfast support, wise and well-informed advice and unfailing encouragement and friendship. For all these I am enormously grateful. It has been a renewed pleasure to work with Valery Rose as the copy-editor.

For the errors, shortcomings and weaknesses of this book, I alone am responsible.

Anne Stevens
London and Birmingham

List of Abbreviations and Acronyms

ALP	Australian Labour Party
CDU	Christlich Demokratische Union (Christian Democratic Union, Germany)
CEDAW	Convention on the Elimination of All Forms of Discrimination Against Women
CFDT	Confédération Française Démocratique du Travail
EC	European Communities
ECJ	European Court of Justice
EEOC	Equal Employment Opportunity Commission (USA)
EFILWC	European Foundation for the Improvement of Living and Working Conditions
EMILY	'Early Money is Like Yeast'
EOC	Equal Opportunities Commission (United Kingdom)
ERA	Equal Rights Amendment
EU	European Union
FDP	Freie Demokratische Partei (Free Democratic Party, Germany)
GLC	Greater London Council
HALDE	Haute Autorité de Lutte Contre les Discriminations et pour l'Egalité (Office for the Struggle against Discrimination and for Equality, France)
IDEA	International Institute for Democracy and Electoral Assistance
ILO	International Labour Organization
IPU	Inter Parliamentary Union
MEP	Member of the European Parliament
MP	Member of Parliament
MSP	Member of the Scottish Parliament
NGO	Non-governmental organisation
NIWC	Northern Ireland Women's Coalition
OECD	Organization for Economic Co-operation and Development
PR	Proportional representation

Introduction

The position of women in the societies of economically advanced liberal democracies has changed considerably within my lifetime. There have been interlinked changes both in their economic status and in the scope and extent of their political participation. This book sets out to trace the contours of their current position in the politics and power structures of such societies. It argues that the changes that have occurred have been important, far-reaching and in general beneficial in enhancing the conditions, status and power of women within society, but that these developments and their outcomes have not necessarily been well understood, have often been acquired with difficulty, and may still need defending. In doing so it looks at the trends that have resulted in the current situation, and at the explanatory factors which help us to see why the position is as it now is. These explanatory factors include observable social changes in, for example, the economic activity of women and in the attitudes of both men and women towards the place of women in society. They also include normative (moral, philosophical) opinions and statements about what the place and role of women in society ought to be.

The Five Aims of this Book

My first aim in this book is to provide an overview and comparison of women's political circumstances in the contemporary world and their broad social and economic context. For reasons of coherence and clarity I focus on the economically advanced liberal democracies – primarily those that are members of the Organisation for Economic Co-operation and Development (OECD). The role and position of women in poorer and/or authoritarian countries has many similarities with those in the advanced countries but also raises many other issues to which I did not feel able to do justice within the scope of a single study. While this is not intended as a detailed comparative study of particular countries I have selected 15 countries which I have used as my main examples throughout especially in figures and tables, which I have selected to cover a range of small and large states with different political arrangements and traditions:

these are Australia, Belgium, Canada, Czech Republic, France, Germany, Hungary, Italy, Netherlands, Norway, Poland, Spain, Sweden, the United Kingdom (UK), and the United States of America (USA). In general, I refer to OECD countries as a convenient term for economically advanced industrial and post-industrial liberal democracies.

The second aim of the book is to provide an accessible introduction to issues of women's political behaviour and position covering a range of countries. In recent years research and publication in this area have proliferated, particularly in the United States, for a number of reasons:

- From the 1960s onwards, the emergence of so-called 'second-wave' feminism (see Chapter 8) focused attention on the position of women in relation to the political process.
- Scholars interested in the factors promoting economic development in less developed economies began to focus on the contribution of women to both political and economic development. The United Nations designated 1975 International Women's Year, and designated 1976–85 the 'United Nations Decade for Women: Equality, Development and Peace'. World conferences on Women took place in 1975, 1980, 1985 and 1995, all of them increasing the attention paid to women's issues.
- The United States media adopted the slogan 'the year of the woman' to describe the electoral campaigns of 1992. Women doubled their numbers in Congress (from 5 to 10 per cent), coming 'forward to run in record numbers and . . . supported by record numbers of women' (Duerst-Lahti and Verstegen 1995: 221).
- The 1990s also saw intensified debate about strategies to increase the representation of women in representative assemblies, in the context partly of the example set by the Scandinavian countries (Denmark, Finland, Norway and Sweden) where women in the early 1980s already made up between 24 (Denmark) and 35 (Norway) per cent of Members of Parliament, and partly of the impassioned debate in France, from 1982 onwards, about the imposition by law of quotas by sex for electoral candidacies.
- The study of politics was increasingly recognised, especially by female researchers, teachers and students, as being the province of men, who all too often systematically ignored the actions and presence (or absence) of women, or adopted stereotypical and often poorly supported views of their nature (Lovenduski 1998; Randall 2002: 113–14; Mackay 2004: 99). Even though the still predominantly male political science profession (Bennie 2002) has been slow to adopt their insights, women have increasingly sought to redress the balance, to

revise and extend political theories, to find new approaches and concepts, and to utilise evidence in new ways or find new evidence.

Influenced by these factors researchers, many of them women and often motivated by feminist ideals, sought to identify, measure and explain the nature of women's political activities and the impact of women's activity upon the polity as a whole. Much of this research appears as specialised papers and learned journal articles, and as detailed monographs, for example those published by members of the Research Network on Gender Politics and the State (Mazur and Stetson 1995; Mazur 2001; Stetson 2001; Mazur 2002; Outshoorn 2004; Lovenduski et al. 2005). But for students and informed general readers this literature is not always user-friendly. There have been excellent attempts to provide introductory overviews, for example by Julie Dolan, Melissa Deckman and Michele Swers (Dolan et al. 2006) and by Catherine Achin and Sandrine Lévêque (Achin and Lévêque 2006) but these focus on only one country (the USA and France, respectively). It is in the hope of opening up concepts and explanations and encouraging a critical appreciation of the position in the reader's own country in the light of developments elsewhere that this book's discussion ranges across a number of countries.

A third aim is to assist readers to explore and develop a critical appreciation of concepts that are central to the discussion of the place of women within politics and power structures. Many of the key concepts used are indeed central to any informed and analytical discussion of modern-day political life. The double objective is therefore both to suggest that the political activity of women can and should be discussed, considered and researched as an integral part of the analysis of the operation of politics and of power within society, and to suggest that considering these concepts as they apply to various aspects of the position of women may cast a fresh and illuminating light upon them.

As Dolan et al. observe (2006, p. 3), 'Women do not always see eye to eye on what is best for women'. Women, as individuals or groups with very different approaches and policy solutions, can all claim to be expressing the best and fundamental interests of women. In some cases these diversities – for example, the contrasts between women's movements and demands in English-speaking countries and in Eastern Europe (see Penn 2005) – are the outcome of very different histories and contexts. Often, however, these differences reflect underlying dilemmas about differences and similarities between men and women (see pp. 6–9). The impact of these dilemmas, and the nature of the political choices which spring from various approaches to them, is a theme that runs throughout this book. Therefore a fourth aim is to emphasise the diversity of women's viewpoints. The choice of a transnational approach is also intended to point up both shared interests and diverse interpretations and approaches.

The current status and position of women within the societies of OECD countries, and particularly within their political and public life – the current power balance between men and women – is far from being deep-rooted or stable. There have been over the past half century or so major changes in some long-established patterns and traditions of political activity and interaction. Many of these have involved changes in the role of women within political life: the increasing proportion of women in legislative assemblies (see Chapters 4 and 5) being one example. Nevertheless, traditional and stereotypical views about appropriate feminine and masculine behaviour cast long shadows, as the discussion of policies on 'work–life balance' in Chapter 9 suggests. I start from the assumption that enhancing the social, economic and political status of women, and thereby increasing their empowerment, within economically advanced liberal democracies, is a desirable and beneficial change. But such changes have never been easy or automatic – 'women's political engagement occurs against long odds' (Nelson et al. 1994: 21) – they have frequently involved high levels of courage and determination on the part of the people, both men and women, involved in effecting and implementing them, and they cannot be taken for granted.

In seeking to achieve these aims the book falls within the category of feminist political science. Feminism is an ideology and attitude – a political position – that developed as a 'critical and disruptive social movement' aiming first and foremost to effect social change and 'enhance women's status and power' (Randall 2002: 110). While feminism is thus first and foremost a set of ideas that results in action, it also gives rise to perspectives that can illuminate and inform the analysis of political life and of the activity of states and governments. However, the perspectives derived from feminist attitudes come in numerous and even conflicting versions, so that feminist political science may most 'appropriately be viewed as a kind of developing dialogue around a common but evolving agenda' (Randall 2002: 109). That agenda includes the re-examination of concepts, images and theories that have long been central to understanding and explaining political life. These concepts, images and theories have been biased and skewed when they have been underpinned by masculine assumptions that those who participate in political life all, regardless of their sex, share masculine attributes and behaviours (Lovenduski 1998: 333). One aim of this book is thus to prompt its readers to engage in the dialogue about what politics is, and how it should be studied, analysed and explained.

The Terms of the Debate: Sex and Gender

Any discussion of women and politics involves the use of terminology that has in recent years given rise to very substantial debates. The debates arise from the 'baggage' that so many words carry with them because of the ways in which they are commonly used, the situations and structures to which they refer, and the connotations involved. Since, in this book's title, and in its aims, as set out above, there is an implication that women are in at least some respects distinctive and different from men, the distinctions between men and women, male and female, masculine and feminine are clearly central to our discussion. In general we recognise people as belonging to one or other of the two categories, and indeed, identification as being either male or female (in all but very rare cases readily and correctly) is the first event that occurs in most people's lives. This book starts from the assumption that there are minimal basic biological differences between men and women which we recognise in everyday life and which make it meaningful to talk about men and women and apply the adjectives male and female to members of the respective groups.

Difficulties arise, however, as soon as any kind of inference or conclusion is drawn about what consignment to one of the two groups actually means or implies. How important and relevant is the distinction in political contexts? The concept of what is 'natural' to people, of what constitutes 'human nature', is fundamental to political scientists' thinking about both how people actually do behave and how they ought to behave. But do the physiological differences between men and women actually have any consequences for determining what any person's 'nature' is? During the 1980s, much discussion focused on separating the concept of sex, as a characteristic of a person in the same way as their age or their race, from the concept of gender, which referred to the construction that society put on what it meant to be a man or a woman. One's gender was taken to be the facets of one's identity that one acquires from social expectations of what being male or female entails: and these facets of identity were categorised as masculine or feminine. Moreover, gender is seen as being expressed in relationships and hierarchies; being feminine (or masculine) can be seen as something that we 'do' and as being accompanied by particular types of values. And the values that prevail in economically advanced modern societies have tended to define what 'masculine' and 'feminine' mean in ways that sustain and largely perpetuate masculine domination and gender inequality. So relationships between the masculine and the feminine in these societies produce 'gender differentiation, gender inequalities, and gender hierarchy' (Orloff 1996: 52). Public power having historically been in the hands of men, 'males, who are much more aligned with masculinity than any female could be' are able to use their ability to 'perform masculinity' to their advantage and to legitimise their dominance (Duerst-Lahti and Kelly 1995: 19; see also Jones 1993: 81; Lovenduski 1998: 339; Borrelli 2000: 187).

The concept of gender as something performed and experienced in relationships is a valuable one in illuminating the ways that politics operates within structures and institutions even if, as Ann Oakley has suggested, too much academic writing has tended to imply that gender is an attribute that only women possess: 'gender was invented to help explain women's position: men neither wonder about theirs nor need to explain it' (Oakley 1997: 30). This book draws heavily on the work of researchers who have asked crucial questions not just about whether men and women are present in any particular political situation (which would be a question about sex) but about how their interactions shape and are shaped by the gender relationships within that situation (see Lovenduski 1998: 338–9; Randall 2002: 124).

Essentialism versus autonomy

One of the pitfalls which the concept of gender seeks to avoid is what is known as 'essentialism'. Essentialism is the attribution of some characteristic to a group of people which asserts that it is of the essence of all members of that group 'naturally' or 'inevitably' to possess it. For example, because women are capable of being mothers, it is argued, they are therefore 'naturally' more mothering and caring than men. And thence extrapolations may follow which have political consequences. For example, on the one hand, it might follow that because women are naturally caring and mothering, their place is in the home or the private sphere (see Chapter 2) and they are 'naturally' unsuited to politics. On the other hand, it might follow that because they are caring they are 'naturally' more virtuous and politics might be better in their hands (see Chapter 8).

Suggesting that historical, social or cultural influences produced specific gender characteristics in all women is essentialist just as much as suggesting that those characteristics are the consequence of anatomy and physiology (Squires 1999: 66). That they had fallen into this trap is essentially the criticism levelled at those theorists who sought to assert 'that all women share a distinctive experience of life' which can form the basis for a political standpoint (Hartsock 1998; Randall 2002: 115). We need to be cautious about making assertions about what people do or want or need in ways that apply to all members of one or other sex at all times. Equally, just as we need to be cautious about statements about 'people', which so often turn out to be just about men (see Chapter 2) so we need to beware of statements about women which turn out to be about *some* women, usually white, middle-class, educated women. This is called 'universalism' or universalisation. From the 1980s onwards this approach was challenged as women who were conscious of the factors that gave them particular experiences, wants and needs – for instance their ethnicity, race and sexuality – rejected such generalisations. The difficulty is on the one hand to avoid making universal generalisations which are asserted to be valid for all times and places, and on the other to accept that if anything at all is to be said about women and men as categories then some level both of essentialism and of universalisation is unavoidable. In confining its discussion to the societies of the OECD countries this book seeks to make some level of generalisation possible while on the other hand recognising the enormous diversities which exist within them.

If none of us can avoid thinking of ourselves, and being seen by others, as a woman or a man, the question arises of the extent to which we can be autonomous – free to 'be ourselves'? Can a woman escape from the constraints of 'her socialization as a female human being and . . . the biological fact of living in a female body' which, at least potentially, menstruates, becomes pregnant, suckles (Diamond and Hartsock 1998: 194–5)? It may be that the concept of the socially and politically autonomous person, free to be an agent, is a masculine construction 'which privileges men's behaviour and norms' (Squires 1999: 68; see also Chapters 2 and 4 below). It may equally be that we need a concept of women's autonomy in order to make any claims on their behalf. The discussion in this book takes the line that Judith Squires attributes to 'the majority of [feminist] theorists' who 'have adopted some form of essentialism in order to reflect upon women as a category and have endorsed some form of autonomy in order to campaign for women's legal and political rights' (Squires 1999: 69).

Difference and equality

Are women and men so alike as to be entitled to social and political equal treatment, or are the differences between them such as to require different approaches and potentially different treatment within society and politics? These questions are of substantial contemporary political relevance since different stances in relation to them can produce quite different answers to (amongst many other issues) questions of political citizenship (see Chapter 2), representation (see Chapter 5) and policy (see Chapter 9).

Those who hold firmly to demands for equality maintain that within the public and political spheres apparent differences between men and women are the consequence of social phenomena, notably of patriarchy, which is understood to mean the system, characteristic of all modern societies, in which men systematically control and dominate women, so that political, social and economic resources are unequally divided between men and women, with men getting more (Kimmel 2000: 2). They do not deny all differences between people, but assert that such differences may well be as great between men as between men and women, and difference is never a reason for treating a person unequally. Human and political rights should be gender-neutral.

Others argue that women are biologically and psychically different from men in ways that deserve to be reflected within the organisation of society and politics. The point is not an equality which simply treats women as if they were men, but that women's qualities, contribution and situation should be positively recognised, fully incorporated into a completely reshaped organisation of society, valued as highly as those of men and celebrated.

There are many practical ramifications of these positions, although political debate is very seldom sufficiently clearly articulated to bring them to the surface. An obvious example is the way in which maternity should be treated by employment and benefit law. There has been increasing pressure for equality to take the form of a more equal division and sharing of childcare responsibilities between parents, expressed, for example in moves towards parental leave for both parents which cannot all be taken by one parent. However, the dilemma remains as to whether pregnancy and childbirth are to be treated as being a normal experience for a woman, and indeed a necessary contribution to the continuance of society, that require a different handling from the way in which any experience undergone by a man might be tackled. Or are they to be regarded as assimilable to sickness in a man (although they are not sickness or disease) since both do involve physical events and symptoms and require absence from work?

The dilemmas are many: those who argue that men and women are intrinsically different are challenged by other thinkers to define where the difference starts and how far it extends. On the other hand perhaps it is relevant and useful to remember that at least some aspects of men's and women's experiences *do* differ (men cannot become pregnant) and to recognise such differences where they are relevant to discussion and analysis (Randall 2002). Similarly, if we claim that men and women are equal does that mean that we are saying that they are, or must become, the same? Perhaps, on the contrary, the point is the importance of attaching equal social value to, and ensuring equal political and economic participation by, people with many sorts of identity. The theme runs throughout this book, and the stance that I seek to adopt is put simply and succinctly by Joni Lovenduski: 'Equality is needed if difference is to be compensated and difference must be recognised if equality is to be achieved' (Lovenduski 2005: 30).

The Terms of the Debate: Power and Politics

Definitions of politics abound, but all agree that politics is a human activity – something people do – involving relationships with one or more other people and therefore can exist only within a social setting –a collectivity or community of two or more people. Because the position of women in society is a matter of their relationships – with men and with other women – politics is crucial to it. The particular aspect of relationships which we call 'politics' involves the use of power. The concept of power has been defined in markedly different ways by scholars starting from various approaches (positivist, pluralist, Marxist, feminist). One widely used definition, in its simplest form, says that power has to do with the ability of a person or group to cause events to occur, or indeed not to occur, in the ways which she, he or they want, even if the preferences of others involved are different. This notion of power recognises that where power is, there is always the possibility of conflict. The physical, emotional and psychological needs of individuals and groups are not always and inevitably compatible. Stephen Lukes's highly influential and radical definition moves the argument forward in a way which is particularly relevant to the position of women. He points out that it is 'the supreme and most insidious exercise of power to prevent people . . . from *having* grievances by shaping their perceptions, cognitions and preferences in such a way that they accept their role in the existing order of things' because they take it that either there is no alternative, or it is natural, or it is beneficial (Lukes 1974: 24, my emphasis). The conflict may be a 'latent' or potential one which will emerge only as people come to a better understanding of what their real interests are. To do that, people need to be rational and, as we have already seen, autonomous (Heywood 1994: 85). It is the strategies, some of them very deep-rooted, (Dahlerup 1984: pp. 42–47; Marchbank 2005: 4) adopted to avoid, suppress, prevent, deal with and resolve potential and actual conflict that constitute politics.

The outcome of such conflicts and strategies are decisions, usually collective decisions which are accepted as binding on all members of the collectivity, and which therefore shape society. Because such decisions are collective, they are reached within structures and procedures. Some of these are very formal, while others (see Chapter 7) may be informal and even transitory. Because they are so crucial in shaping society, this book concerns the position of women within such structures, working with a definition of politics that encompasses public activities. I do not deny that power, conflict and strategies for resolution can potentially be present in even the most intimate and personal relationships. When those intimate relationships exist between men and women, the persistence of gender values that favour masculine domination (see above p. 25) makes the presence of power, and hence political, factors in those relationships very likely. The recognition that this is so by the feminists of the 1960s and 1970s who coined the phrase that 'the personal is political' was an insightful and illuminating contribution to discussions of the position of women. However, the issues that then arise are rather different from those relating to public activity and are not discussed.

This book considers the general position of women as citizens within that sphere in Chapter 2 and women in relation to the formal mechanisms of representational politics in Chapters 3, 4 and 5. The influence of women on decision-making is considered in Chapters 6 and 7. Chapter 6 looks at their position as members of the political and policy-making elite, while by contrast Chapter 7 argues that women's public political activity and influence has not been, and is not, confined to those institutions conventionally considered as part of any polity's political structures. Chapter 8 considers the thorny question of whether the activity of women within the public sphere results in a distinctive impact, and in particular in one which results in social improvement, including enhancement in the conditions, status and power of women. Chapter 9 presents a substantial case study of the key area of equal employment policy which illuminates the ongoing themes of the nature, direction and difficulty of change and the book concludes with a brief overview of these themes.

1

The Social and Economic Status of Women

The position of women in the political life of OECD countries and the changes that have occurred over recent decades are closely linked to changes in their economic and social position. A circle of cause and effect is to some extent at play: political changes may place women in a position to influence the economic and social conditions of their lives. And developments in society and the economy underpin women's claim to enhanced political status. This chapter seeks to set the context for subsequent discussion of political developments by outlining some relevant features of the social and economic structures of contemporary society. Even though some gaps between men and women in performance and position are narrowing or have even been reversed, the overall picture is one of substantial difference rather than similarity. There is an element of circularity in what we observe. The position of women in society can be seen as stemming, to an important extent, from widespread, if frequently tacit, unacknowledged and even unconscious, assumptions and stereotypes about appropriate activity and behaviour for members of the two sexes. And in return such gender roles are imposed and reinforced by social and economic structures. The strength of this circle makes it possible to say, as Dolan, Deckman and Swers do of the USA, that gender roles continue to structure society today (Dolan et al. 2006: 6).

The concept of the sexual division of labour helps to explain the way in which modern societies have evolved. The traditional division confined women largely to the domestic sphere and to the reproduction and nurture of children as their primary role, while generally affording a much greater share of both power and resources to men. However this division is being undermined in complex ways (Walby 1997: 2). In particular, modern market-driven capitalism tends to treat everyone alike, whether as a factor of production (a worker) or a consumer. Moreover, scientific advance has given women a much greater capacity to control their own fertility. The consequences, over the second half of the last century and into the new one, have been marked changes in both gender cultures (i.e., the underlying assumptions about what men and women are and do) and gender orders (i.e., the social structures, such as the labour market and the welfare state which condition relationships between men and women; see Pfau-Effinger 1998: 150). Together these form what may be called the gender arrangement (Pfau-Effinger 1998: 150) or the gender contract (Duncan 1996: 95–6; MacInnes 1998: 232). This can vary substantially between countries and even within them (MacInnes 1998: 232). It provides, however, the framework within which political action takes place in the OECD countries, and some of its main contours are set out below.

Women in the Population

Although often referred to as a minority in political terms, largely because they are under-represented in political institutions, women in fact constitute a majority of the population in those countries on which this book focuses, outnumbering men by between two and ten percentage points. Much of the explanation lies in the greater longevity of women. In these countries in 2003 there were between 180 and 265 women over the age of 80 for every 100 men whereas, amongst children aged between 5 and 9 years, boys outnumbered girls in every country (United Nations Statistics Division 2006).

Women in Households

Many of the formal political practices and public policies of advanced democracies are constructed around the assumption that people live in households, and that these are composed of members of both sexes, usually with a couple bound together by marriage, and with some dependent household members, usually children but also the very aged. However, these assumptions are becoming increasingly disconnected from reality (Eurostat 2006a; UNECE 2006). In 2000, in most of the relevant countries for which data is available, over twenty per cent of households consisted of only one person: for example in the United States some 26 per cent of households consisted of only one person. Only in Spain was the figure, at 11 per cent, much lower. In the United States in 2000, of those households that did comprise a couple, 28 per cent included no children, while in the EU in 2005 two-thirds of all households were without children and in most EU countries over ten per cent of households with children are single-parent households. Over the previous 20 years the proportions of one-person households had risen by between 3.5 (Spain) and 12 (the Netherlands) percentage points.

In 2000, out of 14 of the OECD countries under study, only in the United States were over half (54 per cent) of all women currently married to a surviving partner. In Norway, Sweden and the United Kingdom, the proportion was under 40 per cent. In 2005 marriage was the context for the birth of only two-thirds of children in the EU. Many stable households exist without marriage. One politically prominent example is Ségolène Royal, Socialist candidate for the presidency of France in 2007, and her partner François Hollande, the secretary general of the Socialist party, who are not married. They have four children. The position of women within households today reflects the changes in the gender order which modernisation is inducing and points to new relationships which are underpinning the changing place of women in politics.

Women in Education and Employment

In many advanced liberal democracies, women's claims to political status and rights have been intimately linked to demands for education. Over two centuries ago one of the first feminist thinkers, Mary Wollstonecraft, made a compelling argument that the deficiencies in women that men perceived as natural, and she to some extent admitted, and that were held to render them unfit for participation in political life, were actually deficiencies in their education. If they were afforded the same education as men, they would be as capable of participating rationally in public life. The history of women's struggle for political rights, especially in the nineteenth century, was closely related to the struggle for educational rights. In OECD countries at the beginning of the twenty-first century, that struggle has largely been successful. Educational opportunities at tertiary (university) level have expanded rapidly within advanced democracies, and women's participation has kept up with this expansion. This expansion of tertiary education, and of the proportion of women within it, has occurred within the lifetime of many women today. According to OECD statistics, amongst the major western European and English-speaking countries, only in Canada, Sweden and the USA do more than a quarter of people between the ages of 55 and 64 have university degrees, and only in Canada and Sweden are more of those who do women than men. But amongst people aged between 25 and 34 in those same countries, at least a quarter have degrees and everywhere except in

Germany and the Netherlands half or more of those who do are women. Poland and Hungary rank with Norway in having the highest female share (63 per cent) amongst those graduating in 2004. Women are thus, at the start of the twenty-first century, taking up opportunities for tertiary education at a slightly higher rate than men. However, there are marked variations in the proportion of women within each disciplinary field. In the relevant countries women made up between two-thirds and four-fifths of all humanities graduates, but nowhere more than one-third of graduates in engineering and only in Italy and Sweden more than one-third of graduates in mathematics. Such differences contribute to variations between the sexes in the career paths upon which young people advance, and may be particularly important in societies where technical and scientific qualifications tend to lead to careers with higher social standing or better remuneration. There is considerable evidence that the higher the level of a women's education, the more likely she is to reject the traditional patriarchal gender arrangement (MacInnes 1998: 245). Growing political participation by women is one of the consequences.

The proportion of women who are engaged in paid employment is also now substantial, but they are still slightly more likely than men to be unemployed and in many countries notably higher proportions of women than men work part-time (see Table 1.1). There are substantial variations in proportions. The legacy of the Communist regimes of Central and Eastern Europe, where it was a political obligation for all, men and women, to work full-time, is one of the explanations for the very low levels of part-time work by both men and women in these countries; full-time employment continues to be important to women's sense of identity and self-worth (Einhorn 2006: 165).

Women are far from being equally distributed across the workforce. They are strongly clustered in certain occupations, where they typically make up a high proportion of employees. In the 27 states comprising the European Union (EU 27) more than 75 per cent of all employed people work in occupations whose workforce is more than 60 per cent male or 60 per cent female (European Foundation for the Improvement of Living and Working Conditions 2006). This produces what is known as vertical segregation:

> In the OECD area, the vast majority of the female workforce – at least three-quarters – is concentrated in just 19 out of 114 occupations. These 19 occupations tend to be strongly female-dominated, with women representing 70% of total employment on average. Large numbers of women, across all OECD countries, are found working as

Table 1.1 Employment, unemployment and part-time employment rates by sex

Country	Women in employment[1]	Men in employment[1]	Women's unemployment rate[2]	Men's unemployment rate[2]	Part-time women[3]	Part-time men[3]
Australia	54.7	69.1	5.1	5.0	41*	16*
Belgium	53.8	68.3	9.5	7.6	21.7	4.9
Canada	69.2	78.5	6.46	7.02	21.29	8.50
Czech Republic	56.3	73.3	9.8	6.5	4.5	1.2
France	57.6	68.8	10.8	8.8	17.6	3.7
Germany	59.6	71.2	10.3	8.9	25.8	4.9
Hungary	51	63.1	7.4	7	2.9	1.5
Italy	45.3	69.9	10.1	6.2	11.6	3
Netherlands	66.4	79.9	5.1	4.4	49.8	17.4
Norway	71.7	77.8	4.4	4.8	31.5	10.2
Poland	46.8	58.9	19.1	16.6	6.2	4.1
Spain	51.2	75.2	12.2	6.1	12.3	3.2
Sweden	70.4	74.4	7.7	7.9	26.6	7.5
UK	65.9	77.2	4.3	5.1	27.6	7.1
USA (2004)	65.4	77.2	5.1	5.1	19*	8*

Notes:
1 Percentage as a proportion of the total age cohort 15–64 (except Australia, where cohort is population over age of 15).
2 Percentage of the 'economically active' population actively seeking work.
3 Percentage of the total age cohort (see note 1) declaring themselves in part-time employment (*except Australia and USA where proportion is percentage of total employment in 2004).

Source: Compiled and calculated from data in Eurostat (2006); Statistics Canada (2006); United Nations Statistics Division (2006a) table 5b.

15

salespersons, domestic helpers and cleaners, secretaries, personal care and related workers. Slightly lower down in terms of female concentration ranking are primary and secondary school teachers . . . [In contrast,] on average, three quarters of male wage and salary employees are employed in 30 out of 114 occupations, in which the male share of employment averages 73%. Drivers, construction workers, mechanics and, at a higher skill level, physical and engineering science technicians are typical occupations for men in most of the countries examined.   (OECD 2002: 88)

Such gender segregation is very pervasive: it was a characteristic even of the Communist bloc countries of Europe before the 1990s, despite formal commitments to sexual equality.

Mining, metallurgy, chemicals, machine building, construction and transport were overwhelmingly male-dominated sectors of the economy (apart from their large clerical, administrative and research sections) while light industry, communications and services remained female-dominated . . . [T]his gender-based segregation of the labour force has been, if anything, exacerbated in the course of the [post-1990] transformation process'.   (Einhorn 2006: 157)

Moreover, there is little evidence of substantial change over time in occupational segregation, though some evidence now suggests that 'the younger generations, who are better educated, appear to be more occupationally integrated than the older ones' (OECD 2002: 92). Given the persistence of sexual divisions of labour within employment, it is perhaps unsurprising that they persist in politics as well (see Chapters 4 and 5).

Another type of segregation, horizontal segregation, occurs where, as is also frequently the case, women employees are clustered at the lower levels of any organisation. In the UK only 34 per cent of managers, senior officials and professionals are women (EOC 2005: 5). In the former East Germany, after unification, 'women were being edged out of "slimmed down" corporate hierarchies' as the consequence of the 'import of a Western structural model that favoured male managers' (Einhorn 2006: 158–9). The positions of women in commercial and industrial elites and in political elites mirror and reinforce each other, and the issues are further explored in Chapter 6.

As Table 1.2 shows, women's pay still lags behind men's pay although the data must be understood as a very broad-brush generalisation and tend to show year on year variations up and down (EFILWC 2006b: 2). Data for

Table 1.2   Gender pay ratios (women's average (mean) pay as a proportion of men's)

	1999	2005
Australia	81 (2000)	81
Belgium	79.6	82.8
Canada	71	70
Czech Republic	78	74.9
France	75.8	85.8
Germany	73	74
Hungary	79	85
Italy	94	81.2
Netherlands	76	80.7
Norway	86	84.5
Poland	85	83
Spain	77.8	80.7
Sweden	82	83
UK	82	82.9
USA	76.5	80.3 (2004)

Note:
1   For all EU countries and Norway, the data refer to hourly rates for all paid employees aged 16–64 that are 'at work 15+ hours per week'. For the USA and Australia the data refer to weekly rates for full-time workers aged 16 and above, and for Canada to full-time, full-year workers.

Sources: Calculated from data in Institute for Women's Policy Research (2005); European Industrial Relations Observatory (2006); Australian Bureau of Statistics (2000/6); Statistics Canada (2006).

the pre-2004 EU-15 in the early 2000s, taken at a more disaggregated level, show that the pay gap varies by age – being very small in the 16–24 age group and largest in the 55–64 age group. It also varies by education and skill level. There is a rather smaller difference on average between what low-skilled, low-paid men and women earn than between the earnings of high skilled, high-paid men and women. But women remain clustered amongst the lowest paid workers – in the 27 EU countries, half of them fall into the lower pay bands and only 20 per cent of women, as against 40 per cent of men, have earnings in the higher bands (EFILWC 2006a). Societies which have big differences in income levels between the highest and the lowest paid tend also to have big gender pay gaps (European Commission 2003: 14; Grimshaw and Rubery 2001: 19).

The reasons for the gender pay gap have been much debated. Occupational segregation is undoubtedly one factor: if women are largely absent from highly paid sectors of employment and heavily concentrated within lower paid sectors, then their average pay across the board is likely to be lower than men's. Typically occupations where there is a high proportion of women are poorly remunerated. In the UK, '[t]he 2001 census confirmed that women remain concentrated in the five lowest paid employment sectors' (EOC 2005: 5). Moreover in sales, cleaning and catering, where there are high concentrations of female employment and low wages, wage scales are short, so there is little scope for upward mobility within the occupation (Grimshaw and Rubery 1997: 28). Unequal treatment can thus arise from the gender of jobs, rather than of workers.

Paradoxically the gender pay gap is frequently higher in highly skilled occupations and managerial positions, largely because women tend to be clustered at the lower levels of managerial responsibility; men occupy the very senior and very highly paid positions while the introduction of minimum wage legislation in many countries may have been a factor in bringing women's earnings at the lowest skill levels closer to those of men (Dex et al. 2000: 86–7; Rubery et al. 2002: 100).

In so far as statistical analyses have been able to suggest probabilities for the causes of the gender pay gap, one major factor has been differences in earnings between men and women with family responsibilities: there is a debate about the extent to which this is the result of lifestyle choices by women. They may deliberately opt to pursue less demanding and well remunerated careers and to avoid taking on higher responsibilities; the inevitable result of this will be that on average they do not at any one time earn as much as men who started out with similar qualifications (OECD 2002: 92). Equally they may choose to take breaks in their careers, so that they fail to acquire the work experience and seniority, and hence the remuneration, of similarly qualified men (see for example Hakim 2004). One estimate for the 1990s suggests that 'in the UK women lose over 50 per cent of lifetime earnings as a result of quitting the labour market to have children. This loss is composed in almost equal parts of lost years of work, reduced hours after returning to work and lower hourly earnings following their return to work' (Grimshaw and Rubery 2001: 29). The UK is an extreme case; similar estimates for other European countries showed much smaller losses, though in all cases lower pay on return was one factor. Part of the debate revolves around the extent to which such an outcome is in fact a free choice or is forced upon women by the social attitudes which make them perforce the primary carers in their families, and render such caring incompatible with high-earning activities. But it also seems that women nevertheless receive lower earnings than comparable men with comparable career breaks, such as occur, for example, in some countries when military service is undertaken (European Commission 2003: fn 17). In relation to education and employment we seem to be observing a social construction of gender roles which we may expect to find echoed and repeated in relation to political activity.

Women's Use of Time

Women's use of time differs from that of men. On average women spend more hours per week than men do on maintaining the household and caring for household members, even when they are equally occupied in paid employment. It has been estimated that, in the United States over the last 30 years, the amount of time spent on housework by women has reduced from four to three times that spent by men (in the 1990s, an average of eighteen and a half hours per week against just over six and three-quarters) but '[d]espite a slight reallocation of housework activities from wives to husbands in recent years, most of the housework as well as the care of children within the home are still primarily the responsibility of the woman' (Keith and Malone 2005: 224–5). Time use surveys, carried out between 1998 and 2001 covering 13 current and future members of the EU, show that men devote a higher proportion of their time to remunerated work or study than women do (see Table 4.4). Women, on the other hand, devote a higher proportion of their time to domestic work, except in Norway and Denmark, where proportions are roughly equal. On average women spend approximately one hour a day more than men in domestic work. In Sweden, Norway, Denmark and the United Kingdom, the total time spent on average in the combination of remunerated work or study and domestic work by men and women is roughly equal; in Belgium, Finland and France, women spend up to half an hour a day more on the combination of these activities, while in Estonia, Slovenia and Hungary, the difference is as much as an hour. The presence of children in the household increases the total time taken up by the combination of remunerated work and domestic work for both men and women. This increase is greater when the youngest child is under the age of seven. However, the differences in this total time for the two activities combined persist, most notably in Hungary, Estonia and Slovenia where, even where there are children in the household, men's total time for the combination is about an hour less than women's. These differences reflect social expectations about gender roles in relation to work and domestic work (including childcare). In so far as these result in differences in the disposable time that men and women have potentially available for activity outside employment and the household, they may also have an impact upon the scope and nature of political participation and activity.

Conclusion

The discussion in this chapter has pointed up ongoing variations in social roles. It has shown that although women are converging with or even overtaking men in some areas of education and qualification, their experience in paid employment, in remuneration, and in their use of time is still markedly different. The statistical and empirical evidence of measurable differences indicate the continued existence of deeper differences in gender cultures: in lifestyle, social expectation, patterns of labour, duties and responsibilities, status and esteem. It is these differences and patterns that interact with the structures of the state, especially the welfare state (see Chapter 2), the labour market, and households to produce the gender arrangement of each country. By and large in the societies of the OECD countries they influence this has privileged the masculine. The old order is being undermined; through the requirements of modern capitalism for an educated female workforce (Walby 1997: 1), through the development of liberal democratic political ideas (see Chapter 2), and through women's growing, though far from complete, capacity to control their fertility and hence to some extent to determine their social role (MacInnes 1998: 234–5). However, such change is resisted by those who may find their previously unquestioned privileges and status challenged, as the continuing gender pay gap suggests. The outcome is political struggle and conflict, resulting in both substantial advances and backlash and resistance. Political conviction, activity and participation are closely linked to economic and material interests, along with social experience, so they form a key element of the overall gender arrangement of any society. They both influence and are influenced by the factors considered in this chapter, and the aspects of women's political experience described in the subsequent chapters must be considered in this framework.

2
Women as Citizens

All countries in the 'western' or 'first' world with which this book is concerned aspire to and promote democracy. Being a democracy is, for example, one of the conditions for membership of the European Union, while the promotion of democracy has become a central feature of the United States' foreign policy. Democracies open up the possibility of political participation to all adult citizens. Because full participation requires one to be a citizen, citizenship is considered sufficiently important for access to it to be subject to very particular legal conditions. In many countries celebratory ceremonies are organised to mark such access by people who acquire a new citizenship in adulthood. Another indication of the importance of citizenship was the creation, simultaneously with the creation of the European Union by the Maastricht Treaty of 1992, of EU citizenship. This was seen as a key symbol of the move to a new stage of ever-closer union and in practice it provides access to a limited set of additional political rights, including voting rights in some (but not all) elections, wherever in the EU the citizen happens to be resident. The earliest democracy, in ancient Athens, specifically excluded women, alongside foreigners and slaves, from citizenship. Nowadays most democratically-minded people would agree with Anne Phillips when she says 'societies cannot confidently establish which policies are most just without the equal involvement of women and men, young and old – of the less as well as the more powerful members of society' (Phillips 2002: 132, quoted by Einhorn 2006: 9).

Common usage tends to equate citizenship with nationality, and regard it as a straightforward demarcation between those who 'belong' within any community and those who are 'immigrants' or 'foreigners'. However, as the EU example, which goes beyond simple nationality, suggests, citizenship is complex. It is linked to both nationality and system of government. So citizenship can be understood in two rather different ways: there is a formal notion of a legal relationship to a particular geographically defined state, and a more social notion of full participation and inclusion in the life of the community. Another way of describing these understandings would describe the first as conceiving of citizenship as a status, and the second as seeing it as an activity (Squires 1999: 167). Being a citizen (status) means having formal civil and political rights. But being a citizen – acting as a citizen – also means having the social and economic rights that make full participation possible (Lister 2003: 35; Einhorn 2006: 179).

This chapter argues that the notion of citizenship, its rights and obligations, has posed, and continues to pose, particular dilemmas for women. It explores the issues that arise when women participate fully in the public arena of political life, noting in this area the long shadows cast by traditional and stereotypical views of women's place. The chapter then considers the ways in which citizenship is defined and the implications for women of the ways in which citizenship rights have been achieved and defined. The chapter underlines the continuation of many tensions and suggests that we should not take for granted that the achievement of citizenship and democracy resolves problems. Indeed, when the strongly constraining framework of totalitarian Communism was removed in Eastern Europe, traditionalist ideas about masculinity and femininity helped to shape new practices and assumptions, creating what some commentators have criticised as 'masculine democracies' (Einhorn 2006: 9). Citizenship is thus a matter of key importance for women's role in politics, and is central to the political rights and participation of women explored in the following two chapters.

Public and Private

Citizenship is a precondition of participation in public politics. The norms of behaviour and the institutions – in the sense of structures and routines for shaping them – of public politics (see above, p. 10) shape interactions between people who may not know each other at all, and certainly may have no degree of intimacy between them. Consequently politics has been (at least implicitly) assumed to occur within a sphere that was impersonal and public and separate from other parts of life, which were personal, intimate and private. Hence, when they talk about politics, many scholars and political scientists have tended to use language and ideas which relate to the public domain, since that is where they have perceived and recognised the existence of power (Stacey and Price 1981: 5, citing Dahl, Urry and Wakeford, Stanworth and Giddens).

Many of the political theories that underpin modern liberal democracies hold that individuals inherently possess certain rights, stemming from justice and the requirement to treat and respect people as equals. 'To respect persons is to recognise that they possess an inviolability that even the welfare of society as a whole cannot override' (Dietz 1998: 380; Rawls 1999: 513). So in order to distinguish an area of the life of any individual which is based within society and not subject to regulation and surveillance by the political, that is public, authorities, the concept of a private sphere has been developed. Where the private sphere is unduly limited, proponents of liberal democracy see restrictions on the ability of people to become and be truly themselves and risks of totalitarianism (Turner 1990: 201). From the point of view of women, however, the distinction between public and private poses problems. First, there is very often an elision between the notion of the private sphere and the notion of the family. Secondly, the distinction has in the past been used to support the notions that not only do women have crucial roles within the private domain, but that these should be their only roles and they should be kept out of the public sphere.

Will Kymlicka (Kymlicka 2002: 388–90) points out that liberal thought has developed two distinctions: one beginning in the seventeenth century with John Locke that distinguished between the political and the social, and a nineteenth-century distinction between the social and the personal. Since then the liberal notion of what allows people to be themselves has included the personal areas where emotions come into play – marriage, families, childcare. It is therefore scarcely surprising that 'private' and 'domestic' have been equated. So another distinction has emerged – between the public and the domestic. 'Here the public comprises both the state and civil society and the private is defined institutionally as the relations and activities of domestic life' (Squires 1999: 26). These interlocking spheres are represented in Figure 2.1.

However, the conventional distinctions have been used not only to guard the domestic against incursions from the state – the public – but also 'to keep those who "belong" in that realm – women – from the life of the public' (Dietz 1998: 381). Discourse about the public sphere assumed that each individual undertaking transactions within it was a rational and autonomous individual capable of making free choices – or if he (implicitly always he) was not, that was because he was dominated or oppressed. But people may have emotional and physical dependencies, needs and connections. These are then consigned to the private sphere, and it becomes the role of women to deal with them (McLaughlin 2003: 29). However, the family is not a single monolithic unit (Walby 1997: 170). Men and women within it may have conflicting interests, as the long struggles over the rights of married women to own property or control their own bodies (see below) have demonstrated. Turner observes that 'in modern societies with an emphasis on achievement . . . in public competition for material success, the private is seen as the space of personal leisure and enhancement'

Figure 2.1   Three spheres of public and private

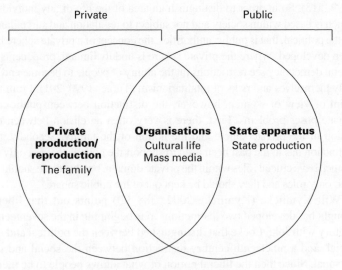

Source: Developed and adapted from Dahlerup (1992: 107).

(Turner 1990: 211). If this is so, then it cannot be equated with the family or household, which is not a place of leisure since a great deal of work takes place there, if mostly unpaid and mostly by women (Walby 1997: 170). Nevertheless it is precisely the identification of the family or the household, which is seen as the space in which women either should be, or are, primarily active, with the private, which has often hindered women from taking their place as full participants in political life. There are paradoxes here: 'the private sphere [in the sense of the family or household] is often contradictory for women because it is both a site of caring and mothering and a site of oppression and dependency' (Siim 2000: 19).

Notions of Citizenship

Equally important, however, from the point of view of the position of women within politics, is any linking of the notion of the public sphere, and only the public sphere, with citizenship. Such linkage derives in part from the history of citizenship, the modern version of which began to emerge during the Enlightenment of the seventeenth and eighteenth centuries with the implication that it involved the possession of rights and responsibilities that were common to all citizens. From the late eighteenth and the nineteenth centuries, the growth of nationalism within nation-states meant that citizenship with its civic and military rights and responsibilities was equally linked to nationality (Meehan 1993: 17). The use by the French Revolutionaries of the word 'citizen' as the common term of address was deeply symbolic of a new order, embracing the abolition of privileges, the assertion of rights and the obligation to defend militarily the values of the Revolution. However this concept of citizenship and the republic was grounded in the exclusion of women (Reynolds 1986).

One of the characteristics of the linking of citizenship to the public sphere is the extent to which all citizens are assumed to be alike. If citizenship is a status, then this implies that all enjoy equal rights. If citizenship is rather, or additionally, an activity, then all share not only rights but also responsibilities for achieving the common good, which implies a shared viewpoint of what that should be. Iris Marion Young says that the linking of citizenship to the public realm was, for modern men 'a flight from sexual difference, from having to recognise another kind of existence they could not entirely understand' (Young 1998: 404). Pressures for a homogenous citizenry lead to the exclusion of certain groups because they are divisive and disruptive since they are seen as being unable to adopt the general point of view. In this sense citizenship as activity may be inimical to citizenship as status. Some groups are excluded from citizenship as activity because their culture, histories, life experiences, socialisation and perception of social relationships give them a different take on public issues from that of the dominant majority (Young 1998: 408 and 421).

Citizenship can be expressed as a series of dichotomies. The citizen is abstract, rational, impartial, dispassionate; capable of making political decisions, such as casting a vote, in the service of the general interest, or, as a jury member, in determining guilt or innocence on the basis of empirical evidence. Such a citizen will be independent and potentially even heroic in upholding their own rights and the freedoms of the community. And such a citizen is not embodied, emotional, subject to desire or passion, tied down or preoccupied by the private, the mundane, the routine and domestic. Yet this is precisely what women are taken to be, and in many cases, necessarily are (Lister 2003: 71).

A universal citizenship which requires everyone to be 'just like a (white, prosperous) man' is, thus, not unbiased or neutral. Young argues for a citizenship in which everyone is included and participates, but which pays attention to differences rather than requiring the adoption of a shared and homogenous point of view. For Ruth Lister the problem with this approach is that it corrals people into groups and fragments the solidarity of people who are already disadvantaged (Lister 2003: 81). She sees a creative tension between universalism and diversity. Like Young she argues for retaining the ideal of inclusion and participation as a yard-stick against which the inclusion of differences, especially gender differences, can be measured. But the old values which supplied the content of universalism need to be challenged, and in particular the division between public and private which has allowed men to retain the masculine bias of the public sphere (Lister 2003: 199 and 202).

How the tension between the universal and the particular, and the relationship between the public and the private, work out is not always and everywhere the same. In Scandinavia, for example, the concepts and language of citizenship have evolved to 'express a "balance" between the public and private arena and between citizens and the state' (Siim 2000: 21) that has enabled women to take a more prominent place in the representative institutions of the state than elsewhere. Birte Siim compares three models of citizenship (British, French, Danish) as they relate to women and finds that in each case there are different key aspects, related to the rights that go with citizenship as a status.

Aspects of Citizenship: Civil Rights

The status of being a citizen brings with it the enjoyment of formal civil and political rights. Liberal democratic theory sees these as the crucial element of citizenship: civil rights comprise 'rights necessary for individual freedom' (Marshall and Bottomore 1992: 8), including rights to liberty of the person, freedom of speech, to justice and to own property. That quintessential product of the Enlightenment, the American Declaration of Independence (1776), summed up the view of the rights of men that has generally prevailed in modern western societies since then: life, liberty and the pursuit of happiness. The right to life can be more broadly interpreted as the right to dispose freely of one's own body, and to own and dispose of property. The right to liberty includes the right to freedom of movement, to just trials and not to be imprisoned, while the right to pursue happiness can encompass rights to think, say and believe whatever one chooses, and to associate freely with others.

Phrased in these general terms, the claim that these rights should be secured to all citizens may seem uncontentious and obvious. But for women they have been, and, to some extent still are, far from being so, as Abigail Adams noticed, protesting when she wrote to her husband on 7 May 1776 that 'whilst you are proclaiming peace and goodwill to men, emancipating all nations, you insist upon retaining an absolute power over wives' (Rossi 1974: 13). Modern formulations of these rights, for example in national constitutions or in the United Nations Universal Declaration of Human Rights (1948) and the European Convention on Human Rights (1950) insist that the rights they set out are universal. They speak of 'everyone' and 'all' where the Declaration of Independence specifies 'all men'. Moreover, most codified constitutions provide for equal rights for women, as have the French and German Constitutions since the 1940s. The struggle for the Equal Rights Amendment to the Constitution of the United States in the late 1970s and early 1980s (see Box 2.1) shows,

---

Box 2.1   The Equal Rights Amendment

The Equal Rights Amendment to the Constitution of the United States was first drafted in 1923. It reads 'Equality of rights under the law shall not be denied or abridged by the United States or by any state on account of sex'. It was introduced in every subsequent congress and passed by both the Senate and the House of Representatives in 1972. Constitutional amendments require ratification by a three-quarters majority of the states of the Union. As had occurred with previous amendments in the twentieth century, a seven-year time limit for ratification was specified by the proposing legislation. Within a year, nineteen states had ratified the amendment. In 1977, Indiana was the thirty-fifth and last state to ratify the amendment. Three more ratifications were required and did not occur. In the face of a large (100,000 marchers) demonstration co-ordinated by the National Organisation of Women in 1979 the deadline was extended by three years, but the necessary ratifications were not achieved.

For its proponents the ERA was a necessary step to ensure that, women having gained the vote, full equality was clearly entrenched. Whilst its proponents generally chose to represent it as a radical step towards true equality, it is hard to point to tangible and direct benefits it would have delivered (Mansbridge 2006: 34–5). Its opponents, including substantial numbers of women, were able 'to capitalize on fears concerning the impact of the ERA and the larger feminist movement on the status of home-makers, the welfare of the nuclear family, the obligation of the husband to support his wife and family in marriage and in cases of divorce and the moral fabric of society' (Dolan et al. 2006: 38). They argued, moreover, that it risked jeopardising legislation which protected women at work, and would expose women to conscription. Political momentum for an Equal Rights Amendment has since 1982 largely disappeared, both because of the effectiveness of the opposition (Mansbridge 2006: 36) and because the status and position of women has been enhanced in other ways as the political system has recognised their role as voters (see Chapters 3, 4 and 5) and the Courts have interpreted and applied existing laws, such as the 1963 Equal Pay Act and the 1964 Civil Rights Act (see Chapter 9), in ways which assist them.

however, that explicit formulations of equal rights have even rather recently been markedly controversial.

However, the trajectories of men and women as they move towards citizenship have varied. The development of citizenship rights for both men and women in the developed industrial and post-industrial world involved struggle and political campaigning, but the struggles and campaigns were different. And women have additionally faced, to a much greater extent than men, the problems posed by the implications of the status of marriage for them. The legacy of this history still has an influence and, despite a social liberal rhetoric of equality, variation can be perceived between men and women.

The principal issues at stake are issues of equality in some areas and of difference in others. Thus the debate between equality and difference can be discerned in ongoing discussion about whether, even within the formal frameworks of citizenship, the response should be continuing recognition of group differences between men and women, or perhaps a new formulation of the concept of citizenship which avoids focusing too exclusively on formal rights and on a notion of equality which assimilates everyone to a standard (male) model (Voet 1998: 44).

Equality and difference: criminal law

The right to be dealt with fairly and justly by the legal system and the courts is a central plank in modern liberal definitions of civil rights. Western cultures, unlike some others, have not in general afforded women a lesser status than men in their dealings with the justice system and the courts. Indeed Rian Voet asserts categorically that 'within western liberal democracies women have enough equal rights'. She does, however, go on to add that that women are still 'second-class' citizens, and, given that they have such rights' 'now they need to use them' (Voet 1998: 72–3).

Nor is practice always as equal as the formal language may imply. A comprehensive study of the British legal system undertaken by a Commission on Women and the Criminal Justice System in 2003–4 on behalf of the Fawcett Society observed, 'Women are shoe-horned into a system which frequently does not meet their needs nor take account of their different life experiences . . . men's lives and men's behaviour are the norm around which criminal jurisprudence, law and procedure have evolved and women are forced to fit awkwardly into this model' (Fawcett Society 2004: 2).

There are specific types of crime of which women are disproportionately the victims, most notably violence and assault within the home (domestic violence) and rape (Fawcett Society 2004: 2). The treatment of victims of rape by the judicial system has been a particular concern. Since it is a crime where there may be a perceived stigma in becoming a victim, the law in the UK, for example, now provides that the victim's identity must be protected. However, this is counterbalanced by a parallel require-ment that the alleged perpetrator's name must also not be revealed, contrary to normal practice in criminal law cases where the identity of the alleged malefactor is revealed. There is moreover particular concern that in an adversarial system the victim may be subject to aggressive ques-tioning about her sexual history, on the grounds that this may reveal that she is in fact likely (as the perpetrator may allege) to have consented to his actions. 'There is much evidence to show that rape complainants have felt they are the ones "on trial" and not the defendant' (Fawcett Society 2004: 29). An Australian study reported, 'In particular, the nature of the questions put to sexual offence victim-complainants are humiliating in a way not shared by the questions put in other assault trials' (Heath 2005).

The use of the complainant's sexual history in cross-examination was prohibited in most of Australia, for instance, during the 1970s and 1980s and partially restricted in the UK by law in 1999 but the problem persists, as, in both countries, does the tendency to dismiss cases if it can be shown that alcohol was used by the victim-complainant (Heath 2005) and espe-cially if the complainant was sufficiently intoxicated at the time of the alleged offence for her evidence of lack of consent to be cast into doubt. These factors partly explain why, of 11,766 rape allegations made in the UK in 2002, only 655 led to a conviction (*The Guardian*, 15 March 2006) while in Australia they varied between ten and three per cent of cases reported. Even within an apparently gender-neutral system of civil rights, can it be said that women are afforded equal and appropriate treatment?

This question also arises when women are the offenders. Gender stereotypes have tended to characterise women as innocent and law-abid-ing, and indeed United Kingdom figures showed that women represented only 21 per cent of known offenders in 2003 and 2004 (Home Office 2005: 59, Table 3.6): 'There is a perception that women who transgress gender roles by committing "male" offences such as burglary may be dealt with more harshly' as a consequence of a 'double deviance' from both social norms and ascribed gender roles (Fawcett Society 2004: 31). It is suggested that women 'are starting higher up the sentencing ladder and thus reaching prison sooner than men' so that women in prison had fewer previous convictions than men. In the United States in 1998, 35 per cent of female prison inmates had no previous convictions compared with 23 per cent of male inmates (Greenfield and Snell 1999: 8). The citizen as alleged or actual offender is not 'gender neutral'. Again, the argument is that even in the public space a woman is an embodied individual who does not enjoy identical treatment to men.

Equality of rights: disposal of person and property

In most European legal traditions, women were for many centuries 'in legal theory . . . relegated to the private sphere' (Robinson 1988), coming under the control of their father until they were adult and then their husband. Amongst adult women, the distinction between single women and married women was until relatively recently a crucial one and in most countries it was undertaking marriage that produced a diminution in civil rights for adult women. The legacy of fascism made Spain the 'exception that proves the rule': until the new post-fascist constitution of 1978, all women enjoyed a legal status under the Civil Code which 'equalled that of the mentally incapacitated [male]' (Radcliff 2001: 504). No woman could sign a contract, apply for a job or travel without permission from her father or husband. In modern legal systems marriage is regarded as an institution or status entered into by consent. It cannot be described as a contract, since the parties are not free to choose the terms under which they enter into it. Rather its conditions are prescribed by law. It does normally convey certain rights in relation to the spouse, for example in inheritance and occupation of the marital home, and it has been the acquisition of these, as well as its 'sacred, magical' characteristics (O'Donovan 1993: 44) that has led same-sex couples excluded from it to campaign for the right to enter into it. Such campaigns have resulted in the legalisation of same-sex marriage in Spain, Belgium, the Netherlands, Canada and the state of Massachusetts. France and the United Kingdom have introduced civil partnership laws which incorporate the same legal rights as marriage.

However, despite the rights attached, marriage between dual-sex couples was until relatively recently a status which in many countries severely limited the rights of the female partner. In common-law countries, such as the United Kingdom, from the early modern period onwards, the legal view was that marriage gave the husband control of his wife's body, her property, her physical liberty and her behaviour, since he might, with moderation, inflict physical punishment. Equally legal systems in the countries of mainland Europe, within the Roman-law tradition and influenced by the French Napoleonic law code gave married women a subordinate status. For example, before reforms were obtained in France, women there were unable to live where they chose or to take paid employment without their husband's consent.

Campaigns to reform the law and improve women's civil rights began in some countries as early as the nineteenth century, but progress was slow and long. Many decades separated the legal moves of the second half of the nineteenth century in the United States and the United Kingdom which allowed married women to control their own property from similar moves in, for example, the Republic of Ireland (1957) and France (1965). The acquisition of an income by undertaking paid employment was also much constrained. In the Roman-law tradition countries, although there were generally not outright bans on the employment of married women (see p. 42), the husband's permission was required at least until the reforms of the post-war period (Germany in the late 1950s, France in 1975; see Duchen 1994: 175–9; Laubier 1990: 146; Kolinsky 1989: 48–9).

And even when reform was undertaken, some anomalies persisted (see Box 2.2). Until well into the second half of the twentieth century, many banks and financial institutions persisted in requiring all women to find a male guarantor – father, brother or spouse – for a mortgage or loan. Anti-discrimination laws (see Chapter 9) have led to the eradication of many such practices but the historical legacy remains important if only because, as Ursula Vogel (quoted in Lister 2003: 69) points out, it contributed to an image of women as dependent, subordinated and not fully capable of citizenship.

The rights of married women in relation to their own bodies were, and in some cases still are, equally circumscribed. Recent years have seen some advances: in the early 1990s the states of the United States, Canada, Ireland and the United Kingdom all saw legislation or legal rulings that ensured that marital rape was criminalised. However, a report to the Council of Europe in 2004 noted that many member states had not yet made marital rape a criminal offence (Council of Europe Parliamentary Assembly Document 10273: paragraph 26).

Men in western societies acquired a substantial body of civil rights – rights to justice and to own property – before the achievement of political rights. The right of all men to participate fully in the political life of the state, an aspiration of the revolutionaries of the late eighteenth century, was acquired only gradually as autocratic and absolute rule was replaced by liberal democratic systems. However, for women the position has largely been reversed. Civil as well as political rights have had to be fought for and the acquisition of political rights has often been seen not only as an end in itself but as an essential means of securing equality in other spheres of rights. This chapter now turns to the acquisition of political rights.

Box 2.2   The Prime Minister's Tax Return

Until 1971, the United Kingdom income tax laws taxed married couples as a unit, and their joint income as if it were earned by only one person, which meant that the wife of a well-paid and wealthy husband could find herself paying a high rate of tax on her entire income. This was supposedly offset by the married man's allowance, introduced in 1918, in recognition of 'the legal and moral obligations he has to support his wife' (quoted in O'Donovan 1985: 139). After 1971, couples were allowed to opt to forgo the married man's allowance and have their earned income taxed as that of two separate individuals, but the wife's investment income was still deemed to belong to her husband, so that it was not eligible in its own right for any tax-free allowances. In addition the husband remained responsible for completing and signing the annual tax declaration, so that a wife was required to declare her earnings to her husband but there was no reciprocal obligation (O'Donovan 1985: 141).

In 1988, when Mrs Thatcher, a married woman, was prime minister of the United Kingdom, the then chancellor of the exchequer, Nigel Lawson, announced that separate individualised taxation would be introduced and the married man's allowance discontinued. These provisions came into force in the early 1990s. By then Mrs Thatcher was no longer prime minister. Throughout her term of office, although she had the power to take the United Kingdom to war in the Falkland Islands, she did not have the power to keep her income and investments confidential to herself or sign her own tax return.

Aspects of Citizenship: Political Rights

The unprecedented and hugely influential widening of the right to vote to most adult men in France in 1792 gave, albeit briefly, practical expression to the principles and claims which political thinkers had been developing for over a century. Very few thinkers at that time, however, were prepared even to consider that such principles and claims might extend to women (for some exceptions see Box 2.3). Women were classed, alongside male domestic servants, as being subject to the commands of another and, like the mentally ill, consequently unable to exercise a free choice. The National Assembly specifically rejected votes for women and banned political activity by them (Levy et al. 1979): women's political clubs were closed in 1793 and the care of the home was to be the full extent of women's civic duties (Reynolds 1986: 113). They were thus precisely excluded from citizenship, an exclusion that was reinforced by the 'warrior-hero' image of the citizen-in-arms, going to war to defend

---

Box 2.3   The Rights of Woman

Condorcet, aristocrat and supporter of the 1789 revolution, published, in July 1790, his essay *Sur l'admission des femmes aux droits de cité*. 'But the rights of men result solely from the fact that they are sentient beings, capable of acquiring ideas of morality and reasoning about those ideas. Women then, having these same qualities, have necessarily the same rights' [my translation]. Olympe de Gouges, also a supporter of the moderate revolution, composed a *Déclaration des droits de la femme et de la citoyenne* (Declaration of the Rights of Woman and the Female Citizen) in 1791, adopting and adapting the phrasing of the *Declaration of the Rights of Man*. The role of the polity, her *Déclaration* asserted, is to defend the natural rights of every man and woman, and the nation, in which sovereignty resides, is the coming together of Man and Woman. Women must have a voice in the Assembly and the right to hold office. 1791 also saw the composition of Mary Wollstonecraft's *Vindication of the Rights of Woman* (published in 1792). Having published in 1790 a vigorous defence of the Revolution as a *Vindication of the Rights of Men*, she moved on to draw the implication that these rights must also apply to women. Her argument is a general one about women's education and position in society, but she argues in her conclusion that women should be 'allowed to be free in a physical, civil and moral sense' (Wollstonecraft 1975: 319).

These voices were rare and transient: Condorcet and Olympe de Gouges both died during the Revolution, and Mary Wollstonecraft died in childbirth in 1797.

---

the revolution and the nation (Reynolds 1986: 111; Lister 2003: 72; for similar arguments in Switzerland up until the 1970s, see Ludi 2005).

General adult male suffrage in France was rescinded in 1795 and not reinstated until 1848 but by the end of the nineteenth century most of the OECD countries had granted the right to vote in national elections to all men. Women, however, were excluded, except (between 1776 and 1807) in some counties of New Jersey where women held the right to vote subject to the same property qualification as men. Since married women could not own property in their own names, the vote was restricted to property-owning unmarried women (Flexner 1976: 167).

During the nineteenth century, an intellectual case for political rights for women emerged more strongly. It was underpinned principally by three strands of thought, though they were not all equally, or indeed at all, influential in all cases. One was Protestantism, especially the evangelical Protestant denominations and sects which flourished in the nineteenth century that supported notions of the equality before God of men and women, and their responsibility as individuals for their moral stance and actions (Lovenduski 1986: 11; Anderson and Zinsser 1990: 356). Such ideas came to support an intellectual case for women's rights, including the right to vote.

The second strand stemmed from the growth of liberal ideas about individual rights. In the United Kingdom this intellectual case was cogently put by Harriet Taylor in 1851 and influentially restated after her death by her husband, the liberal philosopher John Stuart Mill, in *On the Subjection of Women*, published in 1869. What should prevail, he argued, was 'a principle of perfect equality, admitting no power or privilege on the one side, nor disability on the other' (Mill 1985: 219). Mill's views have been criticised by later feminists, in particular for not taking his logic to radical conclusions. He did not challenge the view that, in marrying, women 'voluntarily' surrendered their individual rights. His caution was echoed in the views of those who claimed the right for women to vote not on the basis of inalienable individual rights but of the rights attached to property, possession of which, at that time, gave men voting rights (Delmar 1986: 20; Levine 1987: 60; see Box 2.4). When Mill in 1866 presented a petition for votes for women to the Westminster parliament, his stepdaughter Helen Taylor argued for it on the grounds that 'property represented by an individual is the true political unit among us . . . by holding property women take on the rights and duties of property . . . it is

---

Box 2.4   Mary Smith's Petition

Extract from Hansard (daily record of proceedings in the United Kingdom House of Commons), 3 August 1832

> Mr Hunt said he had a petition to present which might be a subject of mirth to some honourable gentlemen but it was one deserving of attention. It came from a lady of rank and fortune, Mary Smith of Stanmore in the County of York. The petitioner stated that she paid taxes and therefore did not see why she should not have a share in the election of a representative; she also stated that women were liable to all the penalties of the law, not excepting death, and ought to have a voice in the fixing of them . . . the prayer of the petitioner was that every unmarried woman, possessing the necessary property qualification, should be entitled to vote for members of parliament.

Source: Mason (1912: 22).

on the supposition that property requires representation that a property qualification is fixed by the law' (quoted in Delmar 1986: 20).

This argument initially had more purchase in the United Kingdom in relation to local rather than national affairs. In 1869 unmarried women and widows who were ratepayers were given the right to vote in elections for town councils. Local affairs were likely to involve areas of concern that were considered consonant with an essentially familial and caring role for women, and the 1869 act also allowed the same women to vote for, and stand for election as, members of the boards overseeing the operation of the poor law. In 1870, the same arrangements were instituted for the new school boards overseeing elementary education. All these rights were extended to married women in 1894. Similarly in the United States' a number of state constitutions provided for votes for women at state level well before this was achieved at federal level. The first to do so was Wyoming, on its entry into the Union in 1869.

The third strand of ideas underpinning the case for political rights for women was based in socialist thought. The socialist case had been developed by the German August Bebel and by Friedrich Engels, resident in England, who published widely read analyses (see Rossi 1974: 478–505), that upheld the claim for rights for women but argued in essence that women's rights would only be secured when the oppressive capitalist system was overthrown, and energies should therefore be devoted to the achievement of socialism. Indeed the socialist movement consistently adopted a policy 'of placing the class struggle before women's demands' (Hilden 1986: 244). Campaigning for rights for women could only be a distraction of energy and resources from the more crucial business of achieving class-based revolution, following which the matter would be solved anyway within the new classless, post-revolutionary society. For example, in pre-First World War Russia, Marxist women, such as Alexandra Kollontai, campaigned against the liberal feminists, seeking to win women away from the campaign for women's rights and to the cause of socialist revolution (Williams 1986: 64–5).

Political campaigns for women's rights, including the right to vote, developed alongside the intellectual framework. In the early twentieth century, the struggle for the right to vote became, for a few decades, a defining and crystallizing focus for the movement of women's rights, even if it was never 'in any simple way the object of feminist aspirations' (Delmar 1986: 21). As noted above, the campaigns often emerged as a consequence of engagement in struggles for social justice more broadly. Whilst progress was made in many spheres, such as education and property rights, winning the right to vote proved particularly slow, costly and difficult. In the United Kingdom, the campaign for women's suffrage thus developed in the context of the emergence of a broader, middle-class women's movement campaigning across a number of areas, including education and married women's property. In the British colony of New Zealand, the campaign was based on Taylor and Mill's liberal principles and was also linked to general social causes, in particular temperance. It resulted in votes for women in 1893, making New Zealand the first country to achieve universal suffrage (see nzhistorynet). In the United States the women who, rapidly, almost spontaneously, organised a convention to discuss the rights of women at Seneca Falls in New York State in 1848, which marked the start of a long campaign for votes for women, were mostly Quakers, and had been active in the anti-slavery and temperance movements.

The notion that women ought to be able to contribute by their votes to policy choices and developments was influential in the suffrage campaigns in English-speaking countries. Anglo-American notions of representative democracy are, Rosanvallon claims (Rosanvallon 1992: 405), less anxious than is the Republican tradition, found for example in France, about the divisiveness of pluralism and more willing to admit utilitarian arguments about what women's contributions would bring and the need to ensure their specific concerns were voiced (Scott 2005: 36). The nineteenth-century French notion of what a Republic should be 'was built on a set of principles which wrote women out of the small share of public life they had previously been allotted and firmly back into private life' (Reynolds 1986: 113), recognising the dichotomies discussed above that locate women within the private, natural sphere (Rosanvallon 1992: 395). But if they therefore could not claim equality, the 'universalism' of the Republic also blocked claims for rights based on 'difference', which Anglo-American democracy was more willing to admit. One of the consequences was the absence in France of a mass middle-class, liberal campaign for the vote. The debate between universalism and specificity, equality and difference, resurfaced again in France in the 1990s in the debate around the *parité* legislation (see Chapter 5).

Whilst arguments about the value of women's distinctive policy emphases were important in the English-speaking world, in many parts of Europe liberal ideas became linked, during the nineteenth century, with nationalist demands. The Revolutions of 1848 brought these together, and women were politically active, especially in Germany, at this period. However, perhaps in recognition of their subversive potential, the reassertion of authoritarian government after the failure of the 1848 movements included a Prussian law forbidding political activity by women, rescinded only in 1908 (Lovenduski 1986: 31). In Finland the association of women with the nationalist struggle resulted in Finnish women being the first in Europe to gain the vote, in 1906.

Perhaps the overturning of a gender status quo is more acceptable as an element of a major reshaping of a political regime. Such upheavals brought women the right to vote, for instance, in Austria and Germany in 1918, and France and Italy in 1944–5 (Achin and Lévêque 2006: 13).

The gendered status quo was in general resolutely defended. Telling examples include the deliberate insertion of the word 'male' into the United Kingdom Reform Act of 1832 that extended the right to vote amongst men (Pateman 1994: 333). The 15th amendment to the United States Constitution, in 1870, granted the right to vote to male former slaves, but not to black or white women (Pateman 1994: 334). In France there was powerful resistance, amongst radicals, socialists and liberals, both men and women, to according the vote to women, on the grounds that women's naturally greater propensity to religion would afford undue and intolerable influence to the anti-republican and anti-socialist church (Reynolds 1986: 114–17). It is important to remember that the acquisition by women of the right to vote aroused fierce resistance and the struggle was always harsh and even sometimes violent, with opposition, if expressed in somewhat different arguments, coming from both the Left and from the Right.

Over a period of some eighty years, from 1893, when New Zealand women acquired this right, until 1971, when it was won in Switzerland, equality of voting rights has gradually become 'taken for granted' as a component of modern liberal democracies, so that, for example, the according of the right to vote to women in Kuwait in 2006 could be seen as a sign of modernisation. As Anne Phillips points out, 'the starting point for modern theories of democracy is consent' and the principles of choice and assent are nowadays interpreted as necessarily involving votes for all (Phillips 1991: 23). So citizenship as status has largely been secured for women. But there are still barriers to citizenship as an activity for women.

Social Rights for Women

Formal status rights ought not to be taken for granted: there are still countries where, as in South Africa or Eastern Europe, they have been formally acquired by all citizens only in the last quarter of a century (Lister 2003: 35) and many more where they are not fully available, certainly not for women. But they may be of little use to women if they lack the substantive rights that make full social and political participation possible. It is possible to argue that these rights are less central than civil and political rights: what matters is a passive right to be able to conduct one's life socially – within society – without interference from the state. Perhaps what matters is individual freedom to compete within an efficient economy. However, in Central and Eastern Europe the emphasis on the creation of a competitive privatised market has resulted, it can be argued, in 'the erosion of both social and political rights' (Einhorn 2006: 180). Civil and political rights are of minimal use if a citizen is unable to exercise them. This implies that all citizens should have at least the right to maintain their health as far as possible and to a minimal income. These rights need to be guaranteed in some way by the state. Barbara Einhorn speaks of entitlements, as a way of expressing the notion that:

> social and economic rights can be successfully exercised in conjunction with civil and political rights only if underpinned by the relevant state legislation and public as well as private social/welfare provision . . . the language of entitlements construes the individual as belonging both to a wider society that acknowledges collective responsibility for its members and to a polity that accepts a certain level of rights as being conducive to active citizenship.   (Einhorn 2006: 183)

Such rights/entitlements have had to be fought for. As Walby points out, the extensive welfare states that exist in Europe, that provide healthcare, maternity welfare, child benefits and in some countries extensive childcare, were a key demand of the Labour movement (trade unions and socialist parties) throughout the twentieth century. They were 'part of the collective strategy of the working class, from which women not only benefited but in which they took a leading role' (Walby 1997: 177). The trajectory in the United States in relation to such rights has been very different, not least because of the absence of a strong and lasting political labour movement.

While the view that a minimal level of support and resources should be assured to every member of the community is very widely held, even amongst the most convinced proponents of the need for the free operation of market forces (Friedman and Friedman 1980: 150–3), there is much less consensus about what the nature of such a right should be. For example, is the right to a minimal income a right that should be guaranteed to each individual separately, or to each household? Do social rights tend to lead to dependency and inflated expectations? Should they be dependent upon participation in labour outside the family or household – at the very minimum 'workfare' of some type? In other words, should these rights reflect citizenship as status, or as participation (Voet 1998: 79)?

The impact of the welfare state

The development of the welfare state, the regimes into which it is configured in different countries, and the way in which gender regimes interact with them have a substantial, but varied, impact upon the position of women. First, welfare state regimes which Gøsta Esping-Andersen defined as being the particular interrelationships between state, market and the family constructed in any country to ensure acceptable social rights and conditions (Bussemaker and van Kersbergen 1999: 17; Esping-Andersen 1999: 34–5), differ. These differences allow for the categorisation of welfare regimes into various types. In the provision of access to medical services and to income maintenance, liberal regimes (for example, Australia, Canada, the UK and the USA) mostly provide limited and means-tested 'safety-net' benefits on a basis of need; conservative regimes (much of Western Europe including France, Germany, Netherlands and Italy) base their provision more strongly upon active participation in the labour force and often involve the social partners (state, employers and labour unions) jointly in its administration; and social democratic regimes (essentially Scandinavia) base their provision on a framework of universal social rights (Esping-Andersen 1999: 34–5; Charles 2000: 10).

Second, however, the picture of the welfare state that this categorisation formulates does not adequately show how women are situated as citizens within these regimes (Sainsbury 1999: 76). First, the focus in all three welfare regimes is on labour force participation and on how situations where income is not provided through the market are dealt with. So people are viewed solely as workers. Women, however, are more likely than men to spend a proportion of their adult life outside paid employment, and thus outside the purview of these categories. Secondly, the categorisations fail to distinguish adequately between the incomes and resources of households and of individuals (Lister 2003: 172). Third, all women are someone's daughter, and many are also someone's wife and/or someone's mother. All these relationships have traditionally involved care-giving responsibilities at various stages in women's lifestyles. The extent to which caring responsibilities are allocated to the family or alternatively undertaken by the state through public provision varies across countries. In response to such criticisms Esping-Andersen has suggested that some welfare regimes, mostly within the conservative category, can be described as 'familialistic' – 'in which public policy assumes – indeed insists – that households [effectively the female members of households] must carry the principal responsibility for their members' welfare'(Esping-Andersen 1999: 51). Other regimes are 'de-familializing' where the system 'seeks to unburden the household and diminish individuals' welfare dependence on kinship' (Esping-Andersen 1999: 51). Tidy classifications tend to fragment: for example, whilst all the liberal countries make low provision for support for childcare, there are substantial variations within both the other groupings. Moreover, high levels of support enabling mothers of young children to access the labour market are not necessarily accompanied by similar levels of support of care for the elderly. France and Belgium are cases in point (Sainsbury 1999: 246).

Women in the OECD countries have achieved substantial progress in their rights to health and education. The question remains, however, whether the shape of the welfare state has in fact perpetuated women's subordinate position. On the one hand it has, under all regimes, provided at least a safety-net level of support for women's autonomy, for example for lone mothers, and it has also been the source of a considerable range of employment for women, albeit generally outside positions of author-ity. On the other hand, it is argued, welfare states were constructed around a particular version of the 'familialistic' system – the 'male bread-winner' model. As a model this starts from the premise, related to the public–private divide that we identified in relation to civil and political rights, that people exist within households, and that within those house-holds participation in public economic activity and the labour market, thereby procuring a household income, is the male role, and home-making and caring is the female role: 'Female dependence was inscribed in the model' (Lewis 2001: 153–4). The stronger the influence of this model, the greater the economic dependency of women, either on male partners or on the state. '[T]he social citizenship rights of married or cohabiting women are mediated by their male partners, so that in practice they cease to be rights at all' (Lister 2003: 172).

This argument has been criticised. As Siim points out, it certainly captures a crucial feature of the development of the welfare states in the United Kingdom and Germany (Siim 2000: 16). But there are marked differences between countries which share an apparently male-breadwin-ner model, for example in the way that paid employment by married women has been controlled (see below and Box 2.5). In France, for exam-ple, from the nineteenth century onwards, there was extensive support for children via family allowance and childcare provision, with a relatively high level of female participation in the labour market. The assumption was not 'that women are necessarily dependent, nor that men always have "families to keep"; rather [the policies] presume the dependence of children alone' and distribute resources from wage earners without children to those with them (Pedersen 1993, cited in Siim 2000: 57).

Rather than adopt the concept of strong, medium and weak male breadwinner states, Diane Sainsbury has analysed states on the basis of a concept of gender policy regimes (Sainsbury 1999: 77). She identifies three such regimes – the male breadwinner regime, the separate gender roles regime and the individual carer–earner regime. The first two involve a strong separation between husbands as breadwinners and wives as carers, reflected in the arrangements for entitlement to benefits, for taxation, and for a preference for masculine patterns of employment. They differ primarily in the extent to which they recognise that carers may have some independent entitlement to benefits in recognition of the caring role. The carer–earner model, on the other hand, assumes an equal division of responsibilities for both earning and caring, with the individualisation of both taxation and benefits, based solely on citizenship or residence. Such a model equally implies a strong state picking up much of the work of caring on a public basis, rather than confining it to private arrangements.

Tensions and contradictions: caring and earning

Each of these gender policy regimes has effects upon women. Only the individual carer–earner regime implies a general equality of social rights between men and women. But even within this model there are crucial tensions which, as in so many areas, can be conceptualised as tensions between equality and difference: the first tension is that between the rights that 'accrue or should accrue respectively to citizen–the mother or carer and citizen–the worker or wage earner' (Lister 2003: 176). Citizenship involves membership of a community. Membership implies that no individual citizen will be left isolated, abandoned and uncared for. But caring in turn demands effort and work. Moreover, it is frequently intimate in nature. In practice much of it takes place within the private sphere and falls to women. How is this to be recognised and handled? If women's care-giving roles in society are valued and catered for, might this not fix even more firmly the notion that care is women's work, not men's? Should the aim of policy be to validate female caring, since to be cared for is part of a citizen's social rights and the provision of the care a crucial part of citizenship as a practice, or to liberate women from it, both by better collective (state) provision and by ensuring that men share more equally in it?

The other side of the policy coin is thus the question of whether women should undertake paid employment, and on essentially the same terms as men, in order to have the stake in society that citizens should have? This was certainly the case in the state-socialist regimes of Central and Eastern Europe, where Communism was held to have brought the emancipation of women, which was defined as their 'involvement in social production, that is their labour force participation' (Einhorn 1992: 128). Emancipation in this sense (it did not amount to liberation from the double burden of shouldering the vast majority of domestic duties) was imposed by state socialism, and as a result by 1983, for example, nearly all working age women (around 90 per cent) were economically active in Poland and Hungary and East Germany (Einhorn 1992: 129; Matland and Montgomery 2003: 36).

Elsewhere (and in Eastern Europe before the advent of Communism), the right to participate appropriately in the labour market had to be fought for by women, and the battles are not yet over (see Chapter 9). The impact of the development of capitalism and the industrial revolution was to enforce a separation of public and private for middle-class women, who 'retreated from industrial labour', and for working-class women who were increasingly segregated from men and paid at lower rates (Frader 1998: 300 and 308; and see Box 2.5). In many countries marriage had an impact. In the UK a marriage bar (a policy of not employing married women, so that marriage meant the loss of previous employment) existed for women working in the public services (teaching, the civil service: see Box 2.5) and in many private companies until after the Second World War. Its abolition had been a demand of some feminist groups for some time, though not unresisted by other women. Women in the UK civil service, for example, many unmarried because of the loss of a generation of men in the First World War, feared being pushed out and undercut by women whose income would be a subsidiary one and who would not have the same incentive to push for equal pay. In the United States nearly half of all school districts operated a marriage bar until the Second World War, as did some of the large companies that employed women clerks (Goldin 1990: 160–79). In Australia, the bar for the Commonwealth of Australia public service was not removed until 1966 (Parliament of Australia 2006). In Ireland the prohibition on the employment of married women in the public services lasted until 1973 (Galligan 1998: 30). In other countries, for example France and Germany, regulation of married

---

**Box 2.5   Three Generations of Women in Employment:
Anecdotes from the Author's Family**

In the early years of the twentieth century, the author's grandmother was employed in the Post Office Savings Bank in London. The female employees were strictly segregated and not allowed out of the building during their lunch hour. But they might take fresh air on the flat roof. The author's grandfather used to travel from his office elsewhere at lunchtime to walk in the road below and wave at his fiancée on the roof.

In 1939, the author's mother, upon marriage, was obliged to leave her teaching job. Providing her with a testimonial – a reference for a future employer – the headmistress of the school expressed the wish that she would never have to make use of it. Future employment could, it was presumed, only occur if she were either widowed or divorced.

In the late 1970s, the author took up employment in a university and contributed to the national pension fund for university teachers. Her contributions were identical to those of her male colleagues, but her benefits were not. If they died their spouse and dependent children would receive a pension, regardless of their circumstances. If she died her spouse and children would receive a pension only if they could prove that they had been substantially dependent upon her earnings.

---

women's paid employment was delegated to the private sphere since married women required the consent of their husbands to undertake it.

From this point of view, women's access to full social citizenship requires formal equality of opportunity on a basis of equal treatment. This encompasses equal pay for equal work, a concept usually refined (as in current European Union legislation) to require equal pay for work of equal value. This latter concept immediately raises issues of both comparators and values (see Chapter 9). It also requires anti-discrimination laws that specify that, other things being equal, a woman should not receive different treatment because of her sex. Where the emphasis is on formal equality, then equality of outcome becomes less salient. The opportunities are there: whether or not they are utilised is a matter of choice and merit. The argument then centres on whether the opportunities are genuinely open. As Barbara Einhorn argues:

> the neo-liberal market paradigm empowers the male economic actor as the citizen with the capacity to exchange contracts in the marketplace. Without social entitlements, for example to adequate and affordable childcare, in a context where women are still seen as

primarily responsible for looking after children, they do not have an equal capacity to access the public spheres of either the market or the polity.   (Einhorn 2005: 7)

The sharp diminution in the provision of collective childcare in Eastern Europe since the fall of Communist regimes has thus set back the rights of women as citizens.

The social citizenship which the equality approach implies is sustained by anti-discrimination legislation (see Chapter 9). Within the European Union there have been increasing efforts to extend the vision of equality, rather than difference, to areas of social policy. Moreover, and here again the equality versus difference dilemma surfaces, the provision of equal treatment for those who seek or undertake paid employment may need to involve ensuring that opportunities even to do that are equal.

Citizenship and Obligations

Whether as status or as practice, citizenship is frequently interpreted as conveying not just rights but also obligations. In one of its earliest European expressions, under the French Revolution, the notion of obligation was strong. If the status of citizenship brought with it emancipation from the straitjacket of a privileged society and equal access for men to justice, property and the decision-making process, it was also a vulnerable status. Physical defence of the values of the Revolution against those who sought to overthrow them, and of the country against invasion by foreign enemies, was an obligation. The citizen as 'warrior-hero' was a powerful symbol. The fact that, despite the adoption of symbols of warrior females (Britannia for the UK and Marianne for France) as national icons, women were not considered capable of participating in the military functions of the citizen, and not subject to conscription into the armed forces, as men were in many European countries for long periods of the nineteenth and twentieth centuries, was an argument often used in favour of their exclusion from citizenship.

More recent views of the obligations of citizenship have tended to concentrate upon two types of obligation: an obligation of loyalty to shared values, or at least to 'public reasonableness' in debating what they should be (see Kymlicka 2000: 8–9), and an obligation of economic participation. The dilemma of reconciling specific practices, often affecting women, with the obligations imposed by shared community values can be acute. As Siim observes, 'there is an increasing tension between

the old republican ideals of civic virtues and the growth of cultural pluralism, heterogeneity and difference' (Siim 2000: 26). Policies of universalist assimilation on the one hand and multiculturalism on the other
constitute two very different approaches that can be found in neighbour-
ing countries. Neither fully resolves the tensions which arise particularly
where cultural and ethnic practices interface with the framework of citizenship. Two examples will illustrate how this can impinge particularly
on women when cultural values about appropriate behaviour come into
conflict with citizenship norms. Most people in the industrialised world
would see the prohibition of female genital mutilation as a necessary
protection of the civil rights of women not to suffer violent assault. Ten
OECD countries – Australia, Belgium, Canada, Denmark, New Zealand,
Norway, Spain, Sweden, the United Kingdom, and the United States –
have specific laws outlawing the practice and an eleventh, France, has
used other criminal legislation to prosecute perpetrators (see Center for
Reproductive Rights 2007).

A much more contentious issue is the question of whether citizenship
for women involves an obligation to emancipate themselves from what
many see as a religious or cultural requirement that they conceal at least
their hair under a headscarf or *hijab*, or indeed wear even more concealing clothing, or whether on the other hand the civil and human rights of
citizens encompass the right to wear whatever clothing one chooses. In
Turkey, Kemal Ataturk in the 1920s took the view that the public life of
the state does require a progressive and modernising emancipation. He
understood this to involve the abandonment of traditional clothing, and
imposed a principle of secularisation, repeated in the constitution
approved in 1982, which prohibits the wearing of the headscarf in state
institutions such as government offices and universities. In France and in
some German states, the wearing of the headscarf in state schools has
been banned on the grounds that it is a religious symbol that contravenes
the separation between the secular state and religion. Complying with
this ban can be seen as fulfilment of an obligation of loyalty to the constitutional values of the state. At least in France, however, much discussion
has suggested that it is also seen as fulfilment of an obligation to live as
an emancipated woman. One of the issues at stake here is the content
which is given to the notion of emancipation: is the wearing of the *hijab*
and generally concealing clothing always a symbol of female
subservience to male control, even when it is adopted as an apparently
free choice, or can it be an expression of emancipation from male expectations that women should present themselves visibly as embodied and
potentially sexually attractive persons?

A second obligation with a special bearing on women is the obligation to participate in paid work. Such an obligation has increasingly, especially amongst neo-conservatives in anglophone countries, come to be seen as the key counterpart to social rights. This has been expressed in the tendency to move to 'workfare'. The work obligation is, however, one that is genuinely a matter of choice for those with adequate personal means. There is a gender issue even here, since men are much more likely than women to accrue the substantial pensions that can facilitate early retirement. Moreover, the obligation to undertake paid work can be seen as in direct conflict with the obligation to care. At the same time the obligation to participate is seen as the means to gain full citizenship status, and as fundamental to the autonomy which that offers (Lister 2003: 20–1).

Lister argues powerfully that the dilemmas can be resolved through adjustments in both public and private spheres. It is possible to envisage what form such adjustments might take, although one should not underestimate the changes in policy and society and the market which they would require. The aim might be to alter the gendered division of labour in the private sphere, to ensure that obligations to care and to work were equally embraced by both men and women, to move towards an individual carer–earner policy regime, and 'to promote "time to care" both through the right to take (limited) time out of the labour market and through policies to facilitate the synchronisation of employment and care' (Lister 2003: 20). Similarly, Sevenhuijsen suggests that 'government[s] should see [their] primary task as enabling men to build intimate and caring relationships with women and children by making this possible in terms of time, space and primary resources' (Sevenhuijsen 1998: 111). However, as with policies to promote 'work–life balance' (see Chapter 9) – which is perhaps another formulation of 'time-to-care' – the impact will be minimal and may even serve to disadvantage women until and unless all society – not only policy-makers, but employers and families – accept that care for the young and the old, the ailing and the disabled is as compelling an obligation for all citizens individually as is that to participate in paid work and create wealth.

Conclusion

An analysis of the concept of citizenship has illuminated many of the dilemmas faced by women and men who seek a just, equitable and appropriate balance within the collective life of modern societies. The distinction between public and private spheres is both crucial and problematic: crucial because any erosion of the distinction may undermine individuality and permit totalitarian domination; problematic because the equation of the private with the domestic and the association of the domestic with women has traditionally kept them outside public life. Women's battles to achieve full status as citizens and the right to participate in public life have taken different forms from those of men, since men in general achieved legal and economic rights before they were all granted full political rights, while for women political rights have often been a necessary weapon in their struggle for civil and economic rights. It is the exercise of these rights – the role of women as voters and as representatives – that is explored in the next three chapters.

The achievement of women in this area may be seen in the fact that it is now a mark of modernity that women must be recognised as full citizens. But such recognition does not resolve all the dilemmas and paradoxes, especially those associated with the concept of citizenship as an activity, where the issues of equality or difference between the two sexes emerge very clearly. A broader, and less gendered, understanding of the obligations of individuals as citizens of democratic polities, with rights, obligations and entitlements, might produce some solutions. But achieving that will depend at least in part on women increasingly finding a voice in the public realm, and it is to this that the next chapter turns.

3
Women as Voters

The possession of a right to vote is within modern liberal democracies a defining characteristic of a person who participates in the polity – a political actor. 'Liberal democracy sets up voting as the main, or even only, mechanism through which we can voice our needs and interests' (Phillips 1991: 41). However, voting is an isolated act, carried out by an individual. As Chapter 2 argued, liberal theories of democracy characterise the political actor as an abstract individual, with no personal characteristics other than citizenship and the possession of certain rights. But, as we have seen, feminist critics point out that the 'individual' is not gender-neutral. The argument between equality and difference is crucial here, as is the question of whether women have distinctive interests which need to be expressed through their vote. This argument frequently formed part of the case for votes for women, for the campaigners often saw the vote as a key means by which action over issues they regarded as urgent could be induced. Have women in fact made use of their vote? And does an examination of the ways in which they vote suggest that their priorities and choices differ from those of men? These are issues which have to be handled with care, not least because until the 1980s '[c]onventional wisdom treated gender as a distinction without political importance and scholarship confirmed the conventional wisdom' (Kaufmann and Petrocik 1999: 864; see also Bourque and Grossholtz 1984).

Voting Turnout

For many women, and some men, the struggle for voting rights had been long and hard. It had been sustained by hopes, indeed expectations, that women's votes would ensure policy change. The vote had been seen as a means to a number of ends, such as better conditions for children and the poor, and the promotion of anti-alcohol temperance policies. Some, such as Millicent Fawcett, a leader of the non-violent suffragist movement in the United Kingdom, for whom winning the right to vote 'was, I think, the greatest moment of my life' (Fawcett 1925: 247), nonetheless recognised that the right to vote was only part of much broader changes in the position of, and opportunities for, women (Anderson and Zinsser 1990: 367). Others were bitterly disappointed when it transpired that this and other civil rights, such as the right to serve on a jury, once acquired, were rapidly taken for granted and not vigorously exercised. Evidence on voting patterns has not been systematically collected over a long period in a wide range of countries (see http://www.idea.int/vt/index.cfm). The International Institute for Democracy and Electoral Assistance (IDEA) has begun to develop a database of gender disaggregated turnout statistics over a long time period, but it is still limited to a handful of countries, including a few North European ones. Data collection does present a problem. Normally, as in the UK, official records are kept of the total numbers of voters, but these are not disaggregated by sex. In three towns in France during the 1950s, an experiment utilised separate ballot boxes for men and women (Mossuz-Lavau and Sineau 1983: 233, fn 22) but that is highly unusual and would in most countries require changes in the law. So knowledge of the behaviour of men and women has usually to be gathered by asking people, and the veracity of their answers may vary: for example, surveys find more people saying that they have voted than the actual polling figures confirm.

Nevertheless, studies in North America and Western Europe in the first few decades after they gained the vote found that women were less likely to turn out to vote than men (Lovenduski et al. 2004: 11, citing Merriam and Gosnell 1924; Gosnell 1930; Andersen 1996). In the postwar decades, women in many West European countries and in the United States turned out to vote in lower proportions than men. Research by IDEA shows that in four Scandinavian countries and Germany voter turnout by women was between five and ten percentage points lower than men's between 1945 and the early 1960s. In France in the 1950s the proportion of women voting was consistently around 7 to 9 percentage points lower than the proportion of men (Mossuz-Lavau and Sineau 1983: 26). In the United Kingdom general election in 1964 the proportion of women who voted was over 4 percentage points lower than the proportion of men who did so. Similarly in the United States in the 1950s, turnout amongst women was ten percentage points lower than amongst men (Evans 1981: 40). However, this trend has not continued. By the early 1980s the proportions had equalised in France and the United Kingdom (Mossuz-Lavau and Sineau 1983: 26; Lovenduski et al. 2004: 29). Indeed in Germany, Scandinavia and France since the mid-1990s, a higher proportion of women than men have voted. This has been the case in the United States since 1980 and in the presidential election of 2004 the turnout by women in the USA exceeded that by men by the highest ever margin, since 60.1 per cent of women eligible to vote did so (67.3 million women reported voting), compared with 56.3 per cent of men (58.5 million) (Center for American Women and Politics 2005a).

Explanations for gender differences in turnout to vote and their steady erosion in post-industrial democracies have focused on a range of factors. But it must be recognised that explanations in the past frequently tended to focus on generalisations based on unverified stereotypes. Thus in the early 1960s it could be alleged, with little testing of the underlying hypotheses, that, compared to men, women were somewhat more frequently 'apathetic, parochial, conservative, and sensitive to personality, emotional, and aesthetic aspects of political life and electoral campaigns' (Almond and Verba 1963: 325, quoted in Campbell 2002). This was thought to explain lower turnout, even if, as Campbell (Campbell 2002) points out, it could plausibly have been due to factors other than lack of interest, for example the demands of children or poorer access than men to transport to polling stations. Although this aspect has not been extensively researched there is some evidence, from those United Kingdom local elections where measures to increase the convenience of voting have been trialled, to suggest that the automatic provision of postal votes to all electors results not only in an overall increase in turnout, but also in a substantially greater (13 percentage points higher) proportion of women than men actually voting (Lovenduski et al. 2004: 51).

Change has occurred: as we have seen, women's propensity to vote now equals or exceeds that of men. The changes are reflected in generational differences. An analysis by Pippa Norris of the Comparative Study of Electoral Systems, which utilised survey data dating from the late 1990s from 15 Anglo-American and European democracies (and three others), found that women over 65 were significantly less likely to vote than men of the same age, as were women with low educational attainment compared with men who had reached the same level (see Figure 3.1). However long-term trends, 'fuelled by generational change, may have removed many factors that had inhibited women's voting participation in the past' (Inglehart and Norris 2003: 105). The data seem to confirm that women have increasingly become as willing as men to turn out to vote, and Norris predicts that as the older generation disappears women as a whole are likely to display no smaller a propensity to vote than men (Norris 2002: 101). Indeed the trends in the USA and some other countries suggest they may increasingly overtake men.

Figure 3.1   Non-voting in 15 democracies by sex and age and sex and education: proportions in each category who reported *not* voting in general elections, 1996–1999

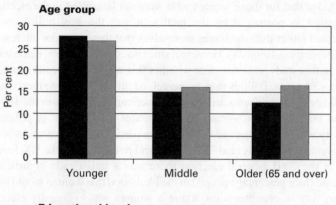

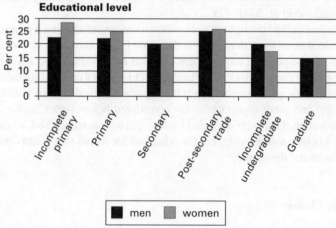

Source: Data from Comparative Election Survey (1996–2001) summarised in Norris 2002, Table 24.

One explanation for the increase in the proportion of women as compared to men who cast their votes may be the widening of women's educational opportunities and attainment and their increased participation in the workforce (Norris 2002: 97). Another explanation may relate to interest in politics. Following the 2001 election in Britain a survey of men and women who had not voted found that women were slightly more likely than men to say that they had not done so because they were 'not interested' (Lovenduski et al. 2004: 30) but the difference was small. Moreover, even the concept of 'not interested' requires some unpacking. A study of women in the context of the 1997 UK general election concluded that for those women who were not interested in the election campaign as portrayed by the media 'it was the way politics was presented rather than the issues themselves that they were not interested in' (Stephenson 1998: 24). However, since no comparison was made with men in this study, it is not clear whether this was a specifically gender-based viewpoint. Politics may be perceived differently by women when candidates or incumbents are female. American researchers in the 1990s found that American women have a greater involvement in political activity where they can see other women participating as candidates or representatives (Burns et al. 2001: 353) and researchers in the UK found that in the 2001 general election there was a statistically significant increase (four percentage points) in the likelihood that women would turn out to vote in constituencies where a woman was eventually elected (Lovenduski et al. 2004: 47).

Having gained the right to vote, women are now exercising it as much as, indeed often more than, men as they slowly gain economic and social status, as the political environment contains more women and if voting can be made more convenient. Turning out to vote is a crucial foundation of democratic participation, but it is only one manifestation of political activity, and other components are considered below (see Chapter 7). Moreover, as those who struggled for the right to vote recognised, it is not only whether women vote, but for what and for whom that is important within liberal democracy.

Voter Choice

The ability of women to organise around political and social issues was clearly demonstrated in many countries by the nineteenth century campaigns that are often characterised as 'first-wave feminism'. Such campaigns encompassed not only the demand for the vote, but also property and educational rights for women, access to the professions and temperance (anti-alcohol). The possibility that women might continue to organise and vote as a bloc, perhaps even creating 'women's parties', was therefore taken seriously in some countries. Indeed there were some attempts in the inter-war years to create women's parties, but they failed (Anderson and Zinsser 1990: 212). More realistic and, as it turned out, more justified, was the expectation that women would tend to support parties of the Right and Centre-Right, and, given their greater tendency to profess and practise religion, parties with specifically Christian orienta- tions. That, for example, was the reason why in 1919 Pope Benedict XV pronounced in favour of voting rights for women (Anderson and Zinsser 1990: 366).

Attempts to examine whether particular types of voter are more likely to make particular types of electoral choices, and to explain why this might be, have focused on the salience of factors which have mostly arisen out of historical and economic circumstances. Social divisions (cleavages) are reflected in the range of parties amongst which the voter can choose. Electoral choice was thought to be determined largely by aspects of any individual's social status, such as their socio-economic class, a characteristic which has, however, posed problems for women, see Box 3. 1. Nevertheless it was recognised that, in particular, the impact of religious belief and practice on political choices might result in voting differences between men and women, and that, to a perhaps lesser degree, gender in itself might be a factor influencing choices. In 1975 it could, however, still be said that 'the political behaviour of women remains an

---

Box 3.1 Socio-economic Status

Pollsters, market researchers and other social statisticians usually assign socio-economic status to any person on the basis either of income or of current or (for the retired) former occupation. Women living in a family have traditionally been assigned to a socio-economic status group from the occupation or income of the 'head of the household'. For example the large opinion poll company Ipsos Mori includes on its website a statement that the '*social-class* or *socio-economic classification* of the respondent [is] normally based on the occupation of *the head of the household* in which the respondent lives' (consulted 8 January 2007). In France, as in the UK until 2001, the national statistics office identifies the senior male person as the head of the household. In 1967 Mattei Dogan justified this traditional practice: 'The wage of the working wife usually constitutes an additional salary which does not change the family's social position . . . Widows quite often live in very difficult material conditions; yet from the psychosocial point of view they remain attached to the socioeconomic milieu in which their late husband belonged' (quoted in Goot and Reid 1975: 129). While such attitudes now seem very old-fashioned, the prac- tices continue and it is notable how few surveys, in reporting their find- ings, indicate the basis upon which individuals have been assigned to any given socio-economic category.

incidental concern of many [studies] . . . women are of interest only in so far as they resemble, or fail to resemble, men' (Goot and Reid 1975: 123)

In the post-war years, it was often asserted that 'women are more conservatively inclined than men' (quoted in Goot and Reid 1975: 125). Certainly in 1955 Maurice Duverger's pioneering study of *The Political Role of Women* took the clear view that women as a whole were more likely to vote for parties of the Right than parties of the Left. This observation was substantiated in numerous studies of the 'political gender gap' – that is in broad terms the difference between the proportion of women voters voting for a particular political orientation and the proportion of male voters doing so: in France in the 1951 General Election, 57.5 per cent of male voters voted for candidates from the parties of the Left against only 46.8 per cent of female voters – a difference of more than 10 percentage points. Over 20 years later in 1973, the proportions were still 50 per cent for male voters and 41 per cent for female voters (Mossuz-Lavau and Sineau 1983: 27). In West Germany between 1953 and the 1970s the gap between the proportion of women voters who voted for the Centre-Right CDU and its allies and the proportion of women voters who voted for the mainstream Left SPD 'was never less than 11% and . . . amounted to 25% in 1957' (Kolinsky 1989: 201). In the United Kingdom throughout the 1950s, the gender gap in favour of the Centre Right, as calculated by Norris (see Box 3.2 below) 'ranged from 11 to 17 points' and in the 1970 General Election it was still 11 points (Norris 1997a: 134). A similar situation was found in Australia when the political preferences of men and women were first examined in 1967: 'The male/female variable mattered at every split in Aitkin's study of the 1967 data. In every sub-group, such as manual workers, union members, churchgoers, income, age, home-owners, husbands and wives and so on, men were more likely than women to identify with the ALP [the mainstream left Australian Labour Party]' (Curtin 1997).

In the United States, the gender gap was not dissimilar, even though the structures of party politics differ from those in Europe (see Burrell in Lovenduski and Norris 1993). If the Republican Party is taken to represent a more right-wing stance, then in the 1950s the situation was analogous to that in Europe, since women 'were found to be 3 to 5 per cent more likely than men to be Republican voters' (Evans 1981: 40). In the mid to late 1970s women were still 'about 5% more Republican than men' (Box-Steffensmeier et al. 2004: 517).

However, what was true in first three post-war decades (see Figure 3.2) seems no longer to be so in the first decade of the twenty-first century, and the 'modern' gender gap (see Box 3.2) reverses the equation.

Box 3.2   The Gender Gap

The term 'the gender gap' is used with different meanings and different degrees of precision in various studies. At its simplest it often means the gap in percentage points between the proportions of eligible men and eligible women who undertake an action such as voting or choosing a particular party or candidate. Thus if, as in France in 1973, 50 per cent of male voters and 41 per cent of female voters vote for parties of the Left there may be said to be a nine point gender gap in the left-wing vote. This is also the formula used by Box-Steffensmeier et al. (Box-Steffensmeier et al. 2004: 518).

Kolinsky, however, uses the term to compare the choices made by one sex. In the 1957 election in West Germany, she refers to a gender gap of 25 per cent (Kolinsky 1989: 201). This is the rounded difference in percentage points between women voting CDU (53.5 per cent) and women voting SPD (28.9 per cent). The gender gap in the right-wing vote (male voters 44.6 per cent, female voters 53.5 per cent) was 8.9 percentage points.

Norris calculates the gender gap in the United Kingdom so as to compare both men and women and voting preference as:

Women (% Conservative – % Labour) – Men (% Conservative – % Labour)

Thus for 2005, confirming the move by women towards the Left (figures from *The Observer*, 8 May 2005), the gender gap can be calculated at –6 as follows:

Women (32% Conservative – 38% Labour = – 6) – Men (34% Conservative – 34% Labour = 0) = – 6.

A still-more complicated formula is sometimes used in the United States:

(% Women Democrat vote -% Women Republican vote) – (% Men Democrat vote – % Men Republican vote)/2

Such formulae can be adapted to any system where there is a choice between two major parties or groupings. A positive gap (Inglehart and Norris refer to this as 'the traditional gender gap') indicates that women are voting more to the right than men, a negative one (referred to by Inglehart and Norris as 'the modern gender gap') that they are voting more to the left.

'Gender realignment' (Inglehart and Norris 2003: 85) has taken place. In their extensive survey, Inglehart and Norris found that in every country where women were more conservative at the beginning of the 1980s that tendency had weakened by the mid-1990s (for some examples see Figure 3.2). In the United States throughout the 1980s and 1990s, a higher

Figure 3.2   The gender gap in six EU countries in the 1970s and 1990s: percentage supporting (1970s) or voting for (1990s) parties of the Left

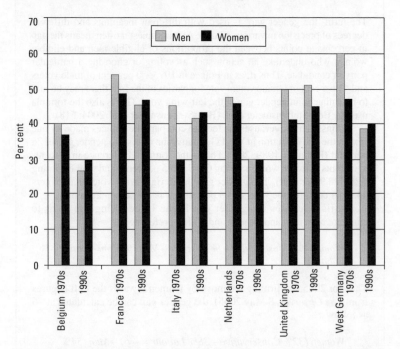

Source: Data from from Inglehart and Norris 2003: 77; Buffotot and Hanley 1998: 11; Norris 1996c: 339.

proportion of women than men expressed partisan preferences for the Democrats (Box-Steffensmeier et al. 2004) and voted for them – the average gap between 1980 and 2004 was 7.7 percentage points, peaking at 11 percentage points in 1996 and falling back to the average in 2004 (Carroll 2004).

The trajectory of gender cleavages outside the United States has been less clear-cut. In the United Kingdom in 1987 patterns of voting by men and women were identical; the traditional gender gap had apparently disappeared. Similarly, the previous year, in France, men and women had voted for the Left in identical proportions (Mossuz-Lavau 1997: 36). But neither in France nor in the United Kingdom was there an accelerating, or even a steady leftward trend. If the overall picture was one of a slightly higher vote for the Left by women, there were exceptions in 1992 in the UK when 44 per cent of women voters and 41 per cent of men voters voted for the Conservatives (Stephenson 1998: 70) and in 1993 in France

(Mossuz-Lavau 1997: 38). In the UK, although women as well as men contributed to the substantial swing to Labour in 1997 – indeed the swing was two percentage points higher amongst women voters than men – in general they remained slightly more likely than men to vote Conservative. The difference was very small compared with the substantial lead enjoyed by Labour overall. In 2001 women overall preferred Labour to the Conservatives (Campbell 2002: 24). In 2005, 38 per cent of women voters voted for the Labour Party and 32 per cent for the Conservative Party. Male voters voted for both parties in equal proportions (34 per cent each) (*The Observer*, 8 May 2005).

One key feature of the gender gap is that it is not necessarily uniform across all age ranges. In the UK, Pippa Norris has identified a 'gender-generation gap': 'older women have usually been the most conservative' (Norris 1997: 134). In 1978, Mossuz-Lavau and Sineau found notably less support for parties of the Left amongst women over 65 than amongst either younger women or men over 65. In 1997 in the UK, only amongst those over 65 did a higher proportion of women vote Conservative than Labour (Campbell 2002: 24). This 'gender-generation' gap can affect perceptions of the overall gap. If, as is the case, women's greater longevity means that older women form a higher proportion of all women than older men do of all men, and they tend to be more conservative, that affects the aggregated average conservatism attributed to all women. However, the traditional gender-generation gap also seems to be disappearing. Inglehart and Norris found that in 'post-industrial societies' (those of the 20 most affluent countries in the world) the 'traditional' gender gap in political preferences was strongest amongst those born before 1937, whilst amongst those born after 1957 a 'modern' gap had opened up. If it is assumed that, whilst political preferences and values may change for a number of reasons, simply growing older is not necessarily one of them, then 'as younger voters gradually replace [the current] older generations the shift toward left-leaning values among women should become stronger in affluent nations' (Inglehart and Norris 2003: 99–100). As one example, by 2001 the preference for Labour in the UK had extended to women in all age ranges (Campbell 2002: 24).

The generalised Left–Right dichotomy can also obscure other important differences between male and female voting behaviour. Female voters in general seem to eschew extremes: this has been observed in Germany, Austria and Italy, for example (Achin and Lévêque 2006: 26), while in France the extreme right National Front has been much more strongly supported by male than female voters. The gap between the proportions of men and of women voting for the National Front candidate, Jean-Marie Le

Pen, in the first round of the presidential election of 1995 was 6 percentage points (18/12) (Mossuz-Lavau 1997: 37), in 2002 4.3 (19.2/14.9) (Belloubet-Frier 1997: 55, fn 26) and in the 2004 regional elections the gap had widened to 9 points (Achin and Lévêque 2006: 26).

Explaining Voting Behaviour

A number of explanations can be advanced for these developments. These depend to some degree on whether the changes in women's voting behaviour are conceptualised as convergence – that men and women are becoming more similar in their voting behaviour – or as divergence – men and women continue to differ in their behaviour, but in new ways. Moreover, these trends have to be seen in the context of general political de-alignment. Whilst political analysts argue that the old cleavages retain some salience, it is also clear that in many affluent countries there is a general trend towards political de-alignment (Hague and Harrop 2004: 156–8). At the end of the twentieth century and the beginning of the twenty-first, partisan identification and party loyalty seem to have become less stable, and new cleavages, around post-material issues, sensations of insecurity and reactions to globalisation have become evident. Changes in the voting patterns of women are a major component in a shifting landscape, but not the only one.

The convergence thesis emphasises the move away from the differences that resulted in women being more likely to vote for right-wing parties than men were. A number of theories have been suggested for why this was previously so. In the United States it is suggested that in the 1950s it could be explained because the categories of women who were most likely to turn out to vote were comprised of the types of people who were most likely to favour the Republican Party (Evans 1981: 40). In Europe the explanations advanced also tended to be structural, linking the undertaking of paid employment, religious practice, social attitudes and voting preference. It would, however, be simplistic to assume straightforward causal relationships. All these characteristics may be expressions of a fundamental set of values and choices adopted more or less consciously and willingly. Nevertheless there are clear correlations which some post-war commentators (for example Lipset, quoted in Inglehart and Norris 2003: 89) saw as key explanations for women's greater support for conservative and Christian Democratic parties. At a period when higher proportions of women than men were not highly educated or in paid employment, in France those not in paid employment were found to be likely to have more conservative attitudes, both socially and politically, which also predisposed them to vote for the Right (Mossuz-Lavau and Sineau 1983). Moreover in the late 1970s, Mossuz-Lavau and Sineau's extensive survey found that women who were not in paid employment were more likely than either men or women in employment to go to church at least once a month, while, compared with similar men, women in paid employment were also more likely to engage in religious practices at least occasionally (Mossuz-Lavau and Sineau 1983: 63). Similarly in Australia Simms found, on the basis of surveys in 1974, that there was a strong relationship between support for conservative political parties and belief in 'traditional' sex-role stereotypes, for example that 'the father should be the master of the house' (Simms 1981: 103). Such stereotypical beliefs were, however, held by a higher proportion of women without higher education or who were full-time home-makers.

Even those women who were in paid employment at this period were less likely than men to be members of trade unions (26 per cent compared with 41 per cent of men in France in the 1970s; Mossuz-Lavau and Sineau 1983: 44) and consequently less likely to be involved with the trade union movement which tended to encourage left-wing identification amongst union members.

The impacts of these attitudes and experiences can still be seen in the generation gender gap. In the late 1970s, Mossuz-Lavau and Sineau found that differing life expectancies between social classes, and between men and women, meant that a much higher proportion of over 65 year old women than men had low educational attainment, low incomes, and lived alone. And it seemed to be these women who preferred the conservative Right (Mossuz-Lavau and Sineau 1983: 212–18).

From the point of view of convergence theorists, there are thus two key factors explaining developments in voting behaviour over several decades. These are, first, the changes in women's lifestyle and economic position that result from increased levels of paid employment outside the home, and, second, the increased secularisation of modern society which has diminished the impact of religious belief and practice. In both these respects, women's situation has become much more similar to that of men than was previously the case and their voting behaviour is steadily reflecting this.

It is equally possible to discern a trend that is not convergence but divergence in voting patterns and political choices. This process is perhaps most marked in the USA, but not confined to it. Thus Inglehart and Norris show that in Western Europe the political preferences of men and women in the middle age cohorts run together, while amongst the younger groups women diverge leftward (Inglehart and Norris 2003: 84). The key arguments advanced to explain this include, first, a structural or rational choice argument (see Inglehart and Norris 2003: 88 and Campbell 2004) which suggests that women's experience of, and roles within, home, family, work environment and state and social support still differ from those of men. It has been suggested that being a parent of a son or a daughter may also cause different male and female experiences to weigh, if vicariously, in a 'rational' voter's preferences (see Box 3.3).

Box 3.3   Daughters and Left-Wing Voters

In 2005 two economists, Andrew Oswald and Nattavudh Powdthavee, followed up work that shows that having children affects people's economic preferences, and looked at the effect of having children on voting preferences. They used data from the British Household Panel Survey, which conducts annual interview surveys of a panel of households involving over 10,000 individuals, and from the similar German Socio-economic Panel. They started from the proposition that at a subconscious level people are influenced by two factors: pay discrimination exists against women, so their pay tends to be lower than men's, and women tend to derive more benefit than men from public goods such as community safety, health and education. Consequently women's economic welfare is less affected by high taxation than men's (because progressive taxation means that proportionately less is paid on lower incomes) and enhanced more than men's by the provision of public services. This means that 'women are intrinsically more left-wing than men' (Oswald and Powdthavee 2005a: 3). They concluded that in both the United Kingdom and Germany men tended to become more sympathetic to female priorities and hence more left-wing when they had daughters. Conversely, the mothers of sons moved towards more right-wing (lower taxes, fewer public services) attitudes. These propositions were sustained by an economic model, drawing on evolutionary theory to suggest that fathers will attach some weight to the preferences of their daughters. Comprehensive statistical analysis of the data confirmed empirically that 'having daughters makes people more left-wing (or, strictly speaking, more likely to vote for the Labour or Liberal Democrat parties). Having sons, by contrast, makes them more right-wing. The effect seems large and not merely statistically significant' (Oswald and Powdthavee 2005: 17–18). Similarly for Germany, using data covering 1985–1999, they found that '[f]or every daughter that a German man has, he is approximately 2.5% probability points more likely to vote for the Left [SPD rather than CDU/CSU]' (Oswald and Powdthavee 2005b). They admit that their model describes a 'stylized world', although their framework does correctly predict what their statistical analysis confirmed. Whether it fully explains it is less clear.

These differences will lead to different voting choices. Susan Carroll has suggested that this difference in choice is most marked amongst affluent and highly educated women and equally amongst the poorest women, who are usually single: 'these two groups of women share economic independence from men' (Carroll 1988: 256). The implication is that the growing structural independence from men amongst certain groups of women, and in particular younger women, allows them to express their own specific interests. Women whose increasing autonomy means that they weigh up political choices on their own account, rather than in the light of how policies may affect their menfolk, may sometimes make the same choices as men and sometimes not (Box-Steffensmeier et al. 2004: 526–7).

Nevertheless there is accumulating evidence that women's issue priorities, which form one of the bases on which they make electoral choices, differ in aggregate from men's. Box-Steffensmeier's detailed analysis suggests that a poor economic record (rising inflation) did not deflect women's preference for the Democrats in the United States in the 1980s because it was outweighed by the party's position on welfare (healthcare and education) (Box-Steffensmeier et al. 2004: 526). Similarly research in both Sweden and the UK found that social policy and healthcare are prioritised by female voters, while men attach more importance to taxation and the economy (Campbell 2004: 45). That there are generation differences – at the time of the UK election in 2001, younger women tended to prioritise education while older women were more concerned about healthcare – serves to reinforce a structural rational choice theory which explains differences on the basis that women vote for parties whose policies advance their own welfare.

Research in the United States has now suggested that the development of the gender gap there has been the result of changes in men's partisan preferences, whilst women's preferences have largely stayed steady. The hypothesis is that men are more likely to hold conservative and restrictive views on social welfare spending and, as debates about the role of government in welfare spending (and related taxation levels) became more prominent, men attached greater importance to those issues and shifted their votes to the party that expressed their preferences (Kaufmann and Petrocik 1999: 882–3).

Rational choice theories of voting behaviour are predicated upon the view that, as individuals, men and women are essentially similar, and as social structures allow women to behave like men and exercise choice autonomously, they will do so. Both men and women will make choices that maximise their welfare. Differences arise only in their objective assessments of what contributes most to their welfare. Another approach to voting behaviour, however, proceeds from the argument that men and women are fundamentally different, and their voting behaviour may be based on cultural factors that arise from these differences. The question is summed up by Rosie Campbell: it is 'whether men and women *systematically* organise their political views and choices in the same way' (Campbell 2004: 28, emphasis added). For instance, studies of political values show that the greatest differences between men and women emerge over issues of the use of force and violence, peace and war, and environmental policy (Norris 2003: 156; Campbell 2004: 32; and for the United States see also Kaufmann and Petrocik 1999: 876 and Cook and Wilcox 2006: 124). Likewise, their support for welfare spending, health-care and education may be related to a female 'ethic of care' (Gilligan 1982). In one formulation, a specifically female moral reasoning privileges an empathetic approach to specific needs. In another the gendered division of labour places women in caring roles so that they prioritise related issues (Tronto 1993: 176–7). In either case women are likely to value the activity of caring and evaluate society by how well it performs its caring responsibilities (Lister 2003: 102–3; and see Chapter 6). Women are therefore more likely than men to prefer parties which seem to prioritise care for individuals and for the environment.

A linked but not identical argument suggests that the spread of specifically feminist values, claiming proper enforcement and enhancement of women's rights, has formed part of a general rise in post-materialist values. Maybe feminists have developed new values which then shape their issue preferences and cause them to prefer left-leaning parties. Increased support for such parties can thus be explained by the rise in feminist consciousness (Conover 2006). If this viewpoint is to be used to support explanations of the 'modern' gender gap, it is necessary to show that if the attitudes and values of women, especially younger women, have been changing (Norris 2003: 164), then those of men have not, or at least not at so fast a rate. Cook and Wilcox (2006) found that men as well as women might hold feminist values that were distinctive and different from those of non-feminists. Inglehart and Norris found that slightly more women than men in post-industrial societies profess feminist values, although attitudes have been evolving in parallel across the generations, and the gap has not widened markedly. A detailed study in the UK, however, found that women born after the Second World War 'were significantly more feminist than men of the same generations and this had a significant effect on vote choice' (Campbell 2004: 42). Moreover, there is a 'chicken and egg' aspect to the argument. It is not clear which comes first – support for leftward-leaning politics or feminist sympathies (Norris 2003: 163; Cook and Wilcox 2006: 125).

Conclusion

Whatever the reasons for the evolution of the gender gap, it is certainly no longer the case that women clearly display a greater tendency than men to vote for more right-wing parties. In the United States the gender gap now takes the form of a preference amongst women for the Democrats which is sufficiently clear and persistent to be described as a 'pervasive feature of the political landscape' (Box-Steffensmeier et al. 2004: 527). A similar trend can be discerned, if less starkly, in parts of Western Europe, though not in post-Communist countries (Norris 2003: 164). Predictions about the likely development and shape of gender differences in partisanship and voting must depend upon underlying assumptions about the nature of male and female experience of society. They may also need increasingly to draw upon more disaggregated analysis. Age, ethnicity, occupational status and marital status are all likely to contribute to any woman's choices in different ways. As we have seen, some of the behavioural phenomena sometimes interpreted as deriving from gender turn out on closer examination to derive from higher proportions of women in particular social categories. Moreover, the history of female voting behaviour since universal enfranchisement suggests that there is nothing fixed or immutable about the nature of these differences. If the individual is not gender-neutral, and society constructs masculine and feminine individuals as different, then it is likely that individual perception, interest and choice will differ. But, as Anne Phillips argues, the characteristic of being masculine or feminine, 'of sexual/bodily identity . . . is not the only or defining characteristic of a person, for what will seem to be the most essential feature will change . . . with the issue at stake' (Phillips 1991: 58). Political preferences and voting behaviour arise from the interaction of gender with socio-economic structures (and changes), and with governmental and political strategies and actions (Box-Steffensmeier et al. 2004: 527). As voting patterns become more fluid, and parties increasingly develop as 'catch-all' parties, seeking to attract voters by attending to as many of their priorities and interests as possible, the parties have responded by attempting to shape their strategies to appeal specifically to both masculine and feminine genders. This can involve the adaptation of policy programmes, and also of the style of politics, to proposals and modes that might be expected to have particular appeal to women. This presupposes first, that women do have preferences which differ from those of men, and second that any adaptation will not alienate many men, a risk the parties might not wish to take. A key part of such adaptation may in the case of some parties be a move towards increasing the proportion of women amongst their parliamentary representatives. The current position is discussed in the next chapter while other strategies for change are discussed further in Chapter 5.

4
The Representation of Women

Over a period of roughly a century and a half, women in developed industrial countries have increasingly taken their place as citizens and as political beings. They have done so in a framework of representative democracy and, since the demise of the Soviet bloc, almost without exception within capitalist liberal democracies. The nature of democracy remains, however, a complex question, raising many issues to which there are not necessarily agreed answers. But these questions and the range of possible answers have important implications for women. In the hope that considering how familiar concepts work in relation to the position of women may cast additional light on them (see p. 3) this chapter explores the nature of representation, the proportions of women amongst the representatives and the reasons for those proportions. With rather few exceptions, women are disproportionately under-represented in the institutions of representative democracy and this chapter discusses why that is so and why it may be a cause for concern, while the following chapter considers the strategies adopted to change the current position.

The Nature of Representation

Communities need mechanisms which enable conflicts to be resolved without recourse to violence, and co-operation between individuals to occur in ways which promote the survival and welfare of all those individuals. Normally political authority is bestowed upon a person or persons within the community so that they can determine between conflicting claims or ensure the execution of actions that promote the common good. Their legitimacy always depends on consent or at least acquiescence, but that may derive from any one of a number of sources: for example, from violently enforced acceptance, as in dictatorship and tyranny; from acknowledgement of hereditary rights accruing to particular people, as in an undemocratic monarchy; from a belief in a God-ordained order of affairs, as in a theocracy; or from the sense that all participate, and are hence implicated, in society's decision-making, as in a democracy.

The dominant form of modern democracy in the modern world is representative democracy. Representative liberal democracy and its institutions as they have evolved have been criticised as restrictive, stifling and patriarchal and for failing to deliver what women want and need. One solution proposed was to increase democratic participation especially at local levels, or in spheres of life – such as workplaces – that liberal democracy tends to relegate to the private, and hence non-political, arena. As Anne Phillips cogently points out, however, this model of democracy both presumes that everyone, including women, has ample time for political activity, and places a considerable emphasis on the workplace (see Chapter 2) but '[men] and women have a different relationship to work and a different relationship to time and no version of democracy that rests its case on increased participation at work can be neutral between men and women' (Phillips 1991: 45).

In representative democracy all citizens are held to be involved in deliberation, debate and decision-making, but indirectly, through their representatives. For some theorists of democracy the key point remains the process of deliberation, but for others the context of modern democracy is essentially a competitive one. Society is taken to be composed of individuals whose social and economic interests are inevitably in conflict or competition. The business of government is to deal with conflict and competition in ways which satisfy the largest possible number of people (Held 1996: 179; Mansbridge 1998: 144). The people may be envisaged primarily as individuals, in which case democracy can be conceptualised as a competitive elitist mechanism, or primarily as belonging to groups, in which case a pluralist model will apply (Held 1996: 197 and 217). In both formulations, voters seek to further their interests by voting for the representative who will pursue them most vigorously, while politicians further their own interests by competing for votes, usually through parties which seek to aggregate and promote interests in such a way as to ensure that they attract the largest possible number of votes (see Young 2000: 19).

These approaches to modern democracy raise complex questions about what representation means. What do representatives actually represent, and how should they do so? Clearly any representative stands for a collection of individuals. But on what basis should individuals be grouped in order to go about choosing their representative? It is possible to envisage a range of common characteristics which all those represented by a particular person might share (Squires 1999: 202). People might theoretically be grouped by age, for example, so that all those aged, say, 18–19 could choose a representative. Equally, ethnic origin might be the key characteristic, as in Slovenia where the parliament has seats reserved for Slovenian citizens of Hungarian and Italian origin (Geddes 2003: 185). They might share the interests that derive from an occupation or vocation (as for the Irish Senate Seanad Éireann) or – as in the United Kingdom until 1948, when the seats for members of parliament to represent university graduates were abolished (Eleanor Rathbone, one of the earliest British women MPs, was elected in 1929 as member for the Combined British Universities) – an educational level.

In practice in most modern states representation has been based either upon place of residence – geographic representation of constituencies – or upon political orientation – ideological representation of beliefs (Squires 1999: 202), or a combination of the two. Constituency members represent the people who happen to live in the territory of their constituency. Members elected by a proportional representation system on a national or regional party list (as are half the members of the lower house of the German parliament) may have a geographic attachment, for instance to a region, but primarily represent those who broadly share their political orientation. But even representatives whose role is to represent those of similar political loyalty may find considerable diversity amongst their supporters. Hence the 'constituents' of any MP, whether chosen on a geographic or political basis, may, for example, be old or young, employers or employees, of varied ethnic origins, and so on, with all the associated and varied political and economic needs, concerns, desires and aspirations.

How such diverse groups are to be represented then comes into question. For analytical clarity it is possible to distinguish four models of representation (see Box 4.1) but in practice elements of all four tend to become intermingled. As Joni Lovenduski argues, it is 'the multi-dimensional nature of representation' which complicates discussions of how women should be represented even if there are 'some common basic concerns with the quality of political representation' (Lovenduski 2005: 14 and 16).

Overarching the models of representation described in Box 4.1 is a more general dichotomy of representation: it can be either substantive or descriptive. The concept of *substantive representation* covers representatives *acting* to ensure that the key interests of any individual or group find a voice. In Anglo-American pluralist democracies it is often assumed that what needs to be represented are not so much the interests of individuals but rather of groups in society. In contrast, republican political thinkers

---

Box 4.1   Models of Representation

- **Trustee** Voters should pick a good person who will know best and trust them to determine their own course of action 'Your representative owes you, not his industry only, but his judgment; and he betrays, instead of serving, you, if he sacrifices it to your opinion' (Edmund Burke, 1774).
- **Delegate** The representative 'acts as a conduit conveying the views of others' (Heywood 1994: 207). He or she is given instructions and required to carry them out.
- **Mandate** This definition of representation developed after the emergence of political parties. Voters are held to vote primarily for the party to which an individual belongs, rather than for the individual. Hence the party is given a mandate to carry out the policies of its manifesto. The representative subscribes to the manifesto and is required to put through the general programme and to deal with issues that arise in light of the party's overall stance.
- **Resemblance** This model requires that the representative should be drawn from, share the characteristics and further the interests of the group represented (e.g. their class, gender, ethnic origin) so that the voters can be confident that their life experiences will be valued and taken into account. This raises the question of what aspect of a person's identity is most crucial to a person's life experiences – being black or being female? Being a graduate? Being a worker?

---

and traditions (found in France for example) are more likely to argue that all individuals have an overriding shared interest in the common good, to place 'a determined emphasis on universal as opposed to particular concerns' (Phillips 1991: 49) and to reject any advocacy of group interests. In both cases, however, the point is that there should be within the political institutions a responsiveness to the political needs and concerns of all citizens: what representatives *do* is what matters; what they are is irrelevant.

Descriptive representation, on the other hand, is closely linked to the resemblance model of representation. In other words, what representatives *are* is seen as crucial, because only those who actually belong to the groups they represent can truly know what their key interests are and be trusted to pursue them. However, despite the existence of a few political institutions that do use social characteristics as a basis for representation (as General de Gaulle unsuccessfully proposed for the French Senate in 1969, and as is nowadays found in the Irish Senate), no one is seriously proposing that for national elections every elector should be assigned to a constituency consisting of similar people, and required to return one of that group as their representative (Mansbridge 2000: 107). The concept of descriptive representation is a rather wider one. It is deemed to exist where representative assemblies, in their composition, broadly reflect the overall composition of society. Judith Squires calls this 'microcosmic representation': 'a group [the assembly] includes the same proportion of each relevant sub-group as the population from which it is drawn' (Squires 1999: 203). This, it is argued, both ensures that the key interests of all members of society are represented, and makes this fact clearly visible.

Representing Women: Why and What?

'Should the mechanisms of representative democracy aim to represent women as women, and if so, what would the representatives be representing – women's ideas, interests or identities?' (Squires 1999: 194). Even when women's rights to participate in the choice of representatives and to serve as representatives and in governmental posts have been asserted, the level of representation not of, but by, women remains controversial. It is possible to take the view that the extent of women's presence in representative bodies is in fact not an issue. In particular there are two interlinked arguments, drawn essentially from the republican approach to democratic representation and the trustee model of the representative. What is represented in the assembly, it is argued, is each of the individual citizens who make up society. Each citizen is equal before the law and the state, and has entirely equal rights. The political system does and should recognise no distinctions – whether social, religious, cultural or sexual – between mentally competent adult citizens (Mossuz-Lavau 1998: 66). Each may well in fact have slightly different interests and concerns, deriving from their particular circumstances, personality and individuality, but it is the role of each representative in particular and the assembly in general to use rational, logical good judgement to arbitrate in conflicts and find the outcomes that will be to the maximum benefit of the whole of society. From this point of view what is required of a representative is intelligent rationality, honest integrity and a clear view of what a good society would be like – and those mental attributes know no distinction of persons. Those who take this approach are not necessarily complacent about the low levels of female presence in the assemblies. They may well deplore and combat these levels in so far as they derive from continued inequalities or active discrimination against women, or even simply from the choices made by many women that they practically cannot, or do not wish to, take up a role as a representative. Moreover they recognise that small numbers may have a symbolic importance: whether rightly or wrongly they convey an impression that women are kept out in ways in which men are not. Anne Phillips notes that one of the arguments in favour of strategies to increase the presence of women is a 'role model' argument. If more women undertake visible and leading roles in politics, as in any other profession, this will encourage others and challenge unfounded assumptions about what women can or should do (Phillips 1998: 228).

So the 'equality' approach may, however paradoxically, be combined with serious attempts to remove obstacles to female participation in representative assemblies (Mossuz-Lavau 1998: 69). But there is always a fear that recognising any distinction between individuals might mean recognising an impossible multiplicity of social or cultural distinctions, which would render representation virtually unworkable and fragment society into differentiated and conflictual factions (Badinter 1996: 19). In the last analysis, 'the characteristics of those elected may diverge in any number of ways from the characteristics of those who elected them, and this is not always seen as a matter of democratic consequence' (Phillips 1998: 225). While low proportions of women may be deplored, representation is still held in principle to function as satisfactorily for women as for men, and women should have no cause to complain that their voices are not heard. Any individual woman has as much ability as any individual man to vote against a representative whom she feels is not working in the interests of all of society. What matters is what the representatives do and how they are held to account. The republican universalist viewpoint thus assumes that interests and ideas should be represented, but sexual and other innate differences (race, for example) should not.

The opposing viewpoint, generally supported by feminists, argues that ideas and interests cannot be represented if the gender identities that are embodied in sexual difference do not also come into the picture. From this point of view there are negative arguments which counter the universalists' approach, and positive ones which argue for the necessity of representation of gender identities. The main negative argument is that the allegedly abstract, neuter individual is in fact a man (Held 1996: 74). Equal universal rights simply assimilate women to the masculine model (Agacinski 2000: 104). The appeal to logic and rationality is an appeal to characteristics which are profoundly masculine: as Carol Gilligan, arguing for women's 'different voice', emphasises, women in general seem to place much less store by 'rights' which are the key property of the abstract universal individual, and much more by relationships, which are impossible in the abstract (Gilligan 1982: 130, 164 and 170–1).

A second negative argument maintains that it is too idealistic to suppose that representatives will act as trustees for an elevated vision of the general good of society. Modern society is an essentially pluralist one and if the 'tyranny of the majority' is to be limited and constrained then the social and economic interests of major groups need to be specifically represented by those who share the interests because they share the characteristics that produce them. Underlying this is the assumption that delegate or mandate models of representation are not entirely feasible in modern democracy. Events occur and contexts change, and male representatives, even if they have been elected on a programme that women support, cannot be trusted always to remember and correctly interpret the interests of women when their manifesto seems outdated (Phillips 1998: 236). Using this argument to support specific measures to improve the proportions of women involves the assumption that women, taken together, have distinctive interests: that men cannot represent these, and that women can and will. This is the 'agency' argument: that only women can act for women (Sawer, Tremblay and Trimble 2006: 19).

There are also more positive arguments in favour of a descriptive pluralist model of representation which would take gender identity into account. One is that justice requires that so substantial a section of society should not be so largely absent from political roles. Moreover, the system will not be legitimate if that is the case (Darcy, Welch, and Clark 1994: 15–18). Feminists argue that not only are there quite specific forms of discrimination which keep women out, but also that there is a structural discrimination arising from an unjust sexual division of labour within society which underpins these forms. The universalist model of representation fails adequately to recognise or compensate for this. These are the 'justice' and the 'symbolic' arguments – that women have a right to participate fully in public life and that their absence from representative institutions both damages the legitimacy of those institutions and depresses the status and aspirations of women as a whole. However, these arguments deal essentially with the problem that the universalist approach has in fact produced a visibly 'unbalanced' outcome. They do not tackle the problem of exactly what is or should be represented (Phillips 1998: 232–3; Sawer, Tremblay, and Trimble 2006: 19; Squires 1999: 205).

A second positive argument in favour of increasing the proportion of women representatives is that they will introduce new and beneficial elements into political behaviour and policy-making. First, they may

---

Box 4.2   Needs, Concerns, Interests, Ideas and Identity

In discussion of what is to be represented a number of concepts are utilised, sometimes almost interchangeably, sometimes with sharp distinction made between them.

Women's *needs* can be taken to be women's requirements for the entitlements and environment that allow them to survive and act as agents (Einhorn 2006: 179). These may give rise to 'invisible' problems, which affect women's lives and which only they can identify, and be expressed in 'the survival strategies that women have created in response to their powerlessness' (Diamond and Hartsock 1998: 198). Needs stake political 'claims in . . . obviously moral terms' (Phillips 1999: 72).

Women's *concerns* can be taken to be those issues upon which decisions need to be taken within society that women perceive as particularly important or relevant to their lives and activities. These are often taken to be different from the concerns of men, because of the sexual division of labour that means that women's lives differ from men's. Many of these concerns were traditionally repressed or silenced and have been voiced only as feminist ideas have inspired new thinking or practices (Phillips 1995: 70). Many relate not to the activity of production, but to reproduction (Diamond and Hartsock 1998: 198). The specificity of women's concerns have been forcefully articulated by 'radical and eco-feminists who have taken strong positions on women in relation to peace, the environment, violence and pornography' (Stokes 2005: 235, fn 10)

Women's *interests* can be defined as the social, political and economic responses and solutions which will be conducive to their welfare and advancement. Some discussions of interests have tended to assume that it must be 'transparently obvious to any intelligent observer' (Phillips 1995:

→

---

improve the practice and style of politics. It will be to the advantage of society if competition for office is widened. Secondly, they will in some areas have deeper expertise and knowledge than do most men, which will benefit policy-making (Darcy, Welch, and Clark 1994: 15–18). Thirdly, they may improve political practice. During the debate that preceded the introduction in France of constitutional and legal measures aimed at roughly equal proportions of male and female representation (see Chapter 5), Janine Mossuz-Lavau argued vehemently that the presence of a higher proportion of women in the French National Assembly would transform the misogynistic male chauvinist atmosphere of the assembly, and quoted a number of female politicians in support of the view that policy would become more practical, more grounded, maybe even less militarily assertive (Mossuz-Lavau 1998: 7–9, 79, 93–4). It may, however, require the presence of a 'critical mass' of women to achieve

➔
69) what material responses and solutions would most advance the welfare of any particular group. So what matters is that the advocate for any set of interests should be articulate, competent, forceful and energetic. Politics consists of the competitive regulation of conflicts between responses within a largely zero-sum environment. Others deny that such a rational, calculating, competitive concept can or should form the basis for stable, humane and acceptable politics (Diamond and Hartsock 1998: 196).

Ideas in this context are the organised and rationalised expressions of a vision, an image or an aspiration. When ideas about social, political and economic goals and solutions come together to offer a picture of how life should be that seeks to be both more or less complete, and above all persuasive, the outcome is an ideology. Modern politics and representation have very largely been based on political parties which embody specific visions of the nature of a good society, and in particular of how resources – of power or wealth – ought to be distributed or redistributed within it (Phillips 1995: 1).

Identity derives from the characteristics with which one is born, or which one acquires as a consequence of life experiences. People normally have an identity attributed to them by society which finds it convenient for both official and unofficial purposes to count and categorise individuals. But people may also choose to participate in group identities; group identification involves self-categorization as a member of a particular group, while group consciousness goes further, including ideas about what it means to be a member of a particular social group. It 'involves identification with a group and a political awareness or ideology regarding the group's relative position in society along with a commitment to collective action aimed at realising the group's interests' (Miller et al. 1981: 495).

this (see Chapter 6). Anne Phillips takes this argument a step further, and sees the argument for increasing the proportion of females as part of a wider 'project for increasing and enhancing democracy' with the hope that women might bring a more consultative, and participatory consultative style to the practice of politics (Phillips 1995: 189). These arguments can be categorised as 'deliberative democracy' arguments (Sawer, Tremblay and Trimble 2006: 19).

In all these arguments the notions of needs, concerns, interests, ideas and identity are strongly intertwined (see Box 4.2). Women, even if they are not necessarily conscious of it, can be conceptualised as constituting an interest group in the broad sense of a collection of people who are in a socially specific position with special interests in certain areas, most notably those arising from the social division of labour within the family and equally from the ways in which these are reinforced through public policy and legal and economic arrangements (Sapiro 1998: 164–6). However, their interests are cross-cut by others – such as those of ethnicity, class and even marital status. While this formulation of interests underpins the argument for specific interest representation outlined above, it does so rather weakly, not really explaining why women might be so different from any other group, and thus becoming open to the criticism that acknowledging any one particular claim lays the system open to an unsustainable proliferation of claims for representation from all sorts of different interests.

On the whole, however, representation in modern democracies has been based on the notion that interests can be aggregated and an arbitration between them achieved on the basis of ideas; in other words, that there is a function for ideology. The inequalities of social class, which are held to result in objective conflicts of interest between the classes, have formed the basis for the most salient political cleavage in the politics of most developed countries. Feminists, however, often argue that parties on both sides of the class divide have failed to recognise the exclusion of women (Phillips 1995: 176; Squires 1999: 221–2).

The alternative notion, which involves a shift from concern with the representation of interests 'to a rather different language of perspectives or approaches or concerns' (Phillips 1995, p. 176; and see Box 4.2), is more controversial. The argument is that gender is a structure that imposes a particular position on women and makes women – all women – different from men. Gender politics acknowledges that women will do things differently; that 'they adopt a care rather than a justice perspective and a maternalist rather than a universal conception of citizenship' and that 'one cannot delegate the task of representing identities in the way one can delegate the task of representing interests' (Squires 1999: 225). The argument from gender identity deals with the problem of proliferation since (apart perhaps from age) there is no other division which allocates very nearly everybody instantly to one category or the other. But it can be criticised for essentialism, that is, for assuming that all members of the group are like each other and that they necessarily (whether they realise it or not) share the same values and interests (Mansbridge 2000: 108; Young 2000: 87–8). One counterargument, while rejecting this formulation of identity, none the less recognises that specific social groups do exist because their members share the experience of social structures that render them underprivileged or oppressed by comparison with others. This does not, Iris Marion Young argues, constitute their 'identity as individual people' (Young 2000: 99) and the demands of such groups are usually claims for 'fairness, equal opportunity and political inclusion'

Table 4.1 Female membership of legislative assemblies by selected country (and European Parliament) in percentages

Country	Lower or single house					Upper house		
	Date of most recent election	Total number of seats	Percentage of women	Percentage on 1 January 1997	Percentage point change since 1997	Date of most recent election*	Total number of seats	Percentage of women
Sweden	09 2006	349	47.3	40.4	6.9			
Norway	09 2005	169	37.9	39.4	-1.5			
Denmark	02 2005	179	36.9	33.0	3.9			
Netherlands	11 2006	150	36.7	31.3	5.4	06 2003	75	29.3
Spain	03 2004	350	36.0	24.6	11.4	03 2004	259	23.2
Belgium	05 2003	150	34.7	12.0	22.7	05 2003	71	38.0
New Zealand	09 2005	121	32.2	29.2	3			
Germany	09 2005	614	31.6	26.2	5.4	n.a.	69	21.7
European Parliament	2004/2007	785	30.3	27.9	2.4			
Australia	10 2004	150	24.7	15.5	9.2	10 2004	76	35.5
Canada	01 2006	308	20.8	18.0	2.8	n.a.	100	35.0
Poland	09 2005	460	20.4	13.0	7.4	09 2005	100	13.0
United Kingdom	05 2005	646	19.7	9.5	10.2	n.a.	751	18.9
Italy	04 2006	616	17.3	11.1	6.2	04 2006	322	13.7
United States of America	11 2006	435	16.2	11.7	4.5	11 2006	100	16.0
Czech Republic	06 2006	200	15.5	15.0	0.5	10 2006	81	14.8
France	06 2002	574	12.2	6.4	5.8	09 2004	331	16.9
Hungary	04 2006	386	10.4	11.4	-1			

Source: Data from Inter-Parliamentary Union consulted 11 January 2007. Data updated to 30 November 2006 except for European Parliament where data updated to 1 January 2007 following EU enlargement.

* n.a. = not applicable

(Young 2000: 107). Since she rejects the notion of an essential identity she cannot argue for identity to be represented. She does however argue that not merely interests but an overarching perspective – a way of looking at things derived from the similar structural relations of the people in the group – can and should be represented, and particular efforts need to be made to ensure that the perspectives of marginalised groups are. And this is almost always (though theoretically not exclusively) likely to be best done by those who share the structural relationships that generate the group's perspectives. Anne Phillips argues along the same lines. If it were clear exactly what women's interests were, then all that would matter would be their substantive representation, and that the representatives could be called to account. But women's interests are not clearly present on the political agenda and there may be much work to do to sort out exactly what they are. In those circumstances what Young calls perspective is important and 'it will be far more difficult to separate out what is to be represented from who is to do the representation' (Phillips 1998: 235; see also Mansbridge 2000: 100).

These debates about representation may seem somewhat abstract, but in one form or another they underlie the discussions about the current proportions of women in representative assemblies and strategies for increasing them. It is to the current levels (set out in Table 4.1), which are in many cases widely acknowledged to be unacceptable for the reasons discussed above, and to what may have caused these proportions that this chapter now turns.

Levels of Female Representation

In most developed countries with, in recent years, the conspicuous exception of the Scandinavian countries, the balance of men and women in the representative assemblies has been very far from mirroring that in society. Only in Scandinavia did women, who typically make up over half the population of any country, hold, on average in 2005, more than 20 per cent of legislative seats (see Table 4.2).

Moreover, these broad averages conceal quite wide variations between individual countries (see Table 4.1). That table also shows that over the course of the past decade or so the proportion of women members of parliament has tended to increase, though in most cases by fewer than ten percentage points.

In general, but not invariably, the right to become a member of parliament was acquired by women at or about the same time as the right to

Table 4.2   Regional averages for female membership of legislative assemblies in percentages

	Single house or lower house	*Upper house*	*Both houses combined*
Nordic Countries	40.0	n.a.	40.0
Americas	18.3	18.3	18.3
Europe – OSCE members excluding Nordic countries	17.0	16.4	16.9

Source: Data from Inter-Parliamentary Union at http://www.ipu.org/wmn-e/world.htm consulted 9 January 2006. Data updated 30 November 2005.
    n.a. = not applicable.

vote. In New Zealand, however, where the right to vote was acquired in 1893, the right to become a member did not follow until 1919. Female membership of national parliaments has not on, the whole, presented a picture of steady progress. In New Zealand, for example, the first female member was not elected until 1933. Elizabeth McCombs was then aged 66, and had stood unsuccessfully as a Labour Party candidate in two previous elections. In 1933, she was elected to the seat which had become vacant because of the death of her husband. She died in 1935 (http://www.dnzb.govt.nz/dnzb/; accessed 13 January 2006). The first woman elected to a national representative assembly in the developed world was Jeannette Rankin, elected as Republican Congresswoman for Montana in 1916, ahead of the constitutional amendment which secured votes for women in all states of the USA. In the United Kingdom Constance Markiewicz was elected to the House of Commons in 1918 as Sinn Fein candidate for a Dublin constituency. She never took her seat in London but after Irish independence was elected to the Dail in 1923. Nancy Astor was the first and, from 1919 to 1921, the only woman to sit in the House of Commons. She was elected in a by-election in the constituency her husband had previously held. He had become ineligible to hold a House of Commons seat on succeeding his father in the House of Lords. In contrast in Germany in 1919, 37 out of 423 members of the 1919 constituent National Assembly were women.

A detailed analysis of female representation in the parliaments of the 15 western European members of the EU since the 1940s shows that only in Scandinavia have the proportions of women shown a steadily rising trend. This analysis also shows, however, that in a number of the countries which had previously had very small proportions there was a marked acceleration in the 1970s and 1980s (Mateo Diaz 2005: 39–48).

Women in Local Government

Representational democracy occurs at local as well as national level. Many of the considerations discussed above apply to local representation, and in many countries local government forms an early stage of a career ladder for representational politicians, who will move from local to national assemblies. This seems to be as true for women as for men. Equally, in France, for example, women who have come to positions of executive power through co-option may seek electoral legitimation through candidacy at local level (See the experience of Elizabeth Guigou recounted in Guigou, Favier and Martin Roland 2000). However, there may also be differences in local government which can affect women's position within it.

First, women in a number of countries have a longer history of public activity at local than at national level. In both the United Kingdom and the USA women could vote and stand for election in local or state legislature elections well before they achieved that right in national elections. By 1900, 1,000 women held elected positions in UK local government (Anderson and Zinsser 1990: 684), while in the USA the first woman mayor was elected in 1886. Second, there is some evidence to suggest that women may be more interested in local than in national political issues (Lovenduski, Norris and Campbell 2004: 65), although this will to some extent depend on how such issues are categorised. Education, for instance, about which women tend to be more activist than men, according to a survey in the USA (Schlozman et al. 1995: 280), is a subnational issue in federal states and the UK but not in France or Italy. Third, local government can seem to offer possibilities for policy change which will ensure specific and observable results (Dolan, Deckman and Swers 2006: 188–9). A survey of Australian women local government representatives found that the main reason why women entered local politics was their dissatisfaction with the way that local government was being conducted as it affected them or their local community (UNESCAP 2001: 21).

The upshot has been that women are in general better represented at local than at national level though as at national level they are dispropor-

Table 4.3   Women in local government, 2005

	Women in state legislatures or equivalent	Women in local assemblies	Women as mayors or council leaders
Australia[1]	23.6	28.3	15
Belgium	31	29	7.6
Canada	20.3	21.7[2]	14.5[2]
Czech Republic	n.a	22.7	15.6
France	n.a	33	10.9
Germany	33	23.8	5.1
Hungary	n.a	17	14
Italy	n.a	16	7
Netherlands	n.a	23.5	19.4
Norway	n.a	33.5	16.8
Poland	n.a	13	5
Spain	37	23.5	12.4
Sweden	n.a	41.6	20
UK	35.5[3]	27	n.k
USA	23.5	28[4]	17.3[5]

Notes:
n.a = not applicable
n.k = not known
[1] 2000.
[2] 2006
[3] 2006: Scotland, Wales, Northern Ireland, Greater London
[4] 2001: city councils only
[5] 2006: proportion for cities with population over 30,000

Sources: Data from Centre for American Women and Politics 2006b; Council of European Municipalities and Regions 2005; European Union 2006; Federation of Canadian Municipalities 2005; Trimble and Arscott 2003; UNESCAP 2001.

tionately absent from leading posts (see Table 4.3). Sub-national government has in some cases provided an interesting test bed for changes in electoral systems. The changes in the electoral system for some local bodies in France under the parity laws provide one example, and the new national assemblies in Wales and Scotland another; and the proportions of women have been markedly affected (see Box 3.2). But even in local democracy the position is broadly one of under-representation. The next section of this chapter turns to the complex and controversial causes of the levels of representation described above.

Causes of Under-representation

Explanations for the levels of the representation of women can be divided into three categories: social structural or socio-economic, political or politico-structural and cultural or ideological (Mateo Diaz 2005: 52; Paxton and Kunovitch 2003: 88). Analysts differ over which factors should be included under each heading. Factors from all these categories interact in different combinations within each national system. Statistical analyses paint a rather 'broad-brush' picture, especially when they include data from a very wide range of countries. Moreover, multivariate regression analysis, which is the statistical technique utilised, does not necessarily tell the whole story even though it provides a reliable and robust identification of the factors significantly associated with higher proportions of female representatives, which offers useful pointers to those concerned to shape strategies for increasing the proportions. Every female representative is present in the assembly as a consequence of two sets of interlocking decisions: 'supply' decisions – her decision to undertake political activity, to associate herself with a political organisation, to offer her candidacy and undertake the necessary campaigning to achieve election – and 'demand' decisions – the decisions of a political organisation to endorse her activity, and to select her as a candidate and the decisions of sufficient members of the electorate to vote for her or for the list on which she appears depending on the electoral system in use. These are complex and individual decisions. As Mateo Diaz points out, there may be a circular 'chicken and egg' element. It is by no means obvious (Mateo Diaz 2005: 50) whether a low proportion of women representatives helps to explain certain social and cultural features within the polity concerned which influence those decisions, or whether it is those features that influence the proportions. For the discussion below, the features that appear to influence the decisions have been categorised as socio-economic, structural and cultural/ ideological.

Socio-economic factors affecting the proportion of
women representatives

The wide variation evident from Table 4.1 is the more striking because in many key social and economic respects the countries are not so very dissimilar. The supply of women available and willing to become political representatives may be linked to the levels of female education, since educated women are more likely to be competent and confident in putting themselves forward. It may also be that the extent to which women work outside the home affects the supply of women representatives, if, as Mossuz-Lavau and Sineau found for France (Mossuz-Lavau and Sineau 1983: 41), participation in the labour force results in greater political activity. However, as the variation between rather similar countries might suggest, broad statistical analyses have failed to find a significant relationship between the proportion of women in the assembly and either women's participation in the labour force or women's educational attainment in that country (Paxton and Kunovitch 2003: 89).

A more refined hypothesis suggests that political elites and particularly members of parliament tend to be drawn disproportionately from amongst highly educated, gainfully employed, professional people (Kenworthy and Malami 1999: 240). The proportion of such women within the general population determines the size of this 'social eligibility pool' from which female representatives are likely to be drawn (Sanbonmatsu 2002: 794). A study of the 20 most affluent countries of the world did indeed find that 'women's share in national legislatures is . . . likely to be boosted by increased numbers of women in professional jobs' (Kenworthy and Malami 1999: 261). It is arguable that political representation can be seen as a professional job like any other. As and when women are increasingly accepted in many previously male-dominated positions – as judges, journalists, professors or managing directors, for instance – so they make their way increasingly into political posts. The obstacles they face in any of these spheres may not be so very different.

Socio-economic equality and empowerment for women is almost invariably a necessary condition if relatively high proportions of female representation are to be achieved, but it is not sufficient. There are intriguing variations. As Mateo Diaz points out, in both Belgium and Portugal women were markedly more strongly present as representatives than in France and the United Kingdom, although inequalities in income, labour force participation and presence in professional jobs were certainly no less (Mateo Diaz 2005: 82). In the decades since second-wave feminism (see Chapter 7) emerged, socio-economic progress and political progress for women have generally advanced alongside each other in developed countries, but it is not possible to say that either causes the other, and both are affected by other factors. In particular 'when both high levels of [economic] development and a PR [proportional representation] electoral system exist simultaneously, significant levels of [female] representation are achieved, if either of these elements is missing the expected levels of representation are more modest.' (Matland and Montgomery 2003: 31). This chapter now considers the structural features of political systems that interact with socio-economic characteristics.

Structural Factors Affecting the Proportion of Women Representatives

Socio-economic factors influence the supply of women able and willing to take on positions as representatives. But their ability actually to do so is structured by the nature of the political system. The nature of the political regime, of the electoral system, and of the party system – the orientation and balance of the political parties – and the presence of formal or informal quotas for women may all be relevant.

One hypothesis might be that the longer men and women have enjoyed voting rights, the higher the proportion of female representatives will be. Mateo Diaz examined this statistically for fifteen West European countries and found that in general 'the earlier men and women obtained the right to vote and to stand for election, the better their balance in Parliaments is' (Mateo Diaz 2005: 67). However, knowing the date at which women achieved the vote in any country does not make it possible to predict with any accuracy what their current proportion of membership will be.

Moreover, liberal democracy does not automatically have a beneficial effect on the proportions of men and women in parliaments. As a result of Marxist-Leninist formal commitment to sex equality, assemblies in countries with Marxist-Leninist regimes have usually had a relatively high proportion of women members (Kenworthy and Malami 1999: 239; Paxton 1997: Table 1). Paxton found that in 1988 they had about 17 to 18 per cent more women in their assemblies than comparable non-Marxist countries (Paxton 1997: 452). Assemblies of the type found in Marxist regimes are largely token and symbolic. All power rests with the party, and the legislature has no scope for independent action. In such circumstances perhaps Helga Nowotny's aphorism 'where power is, women are not' (Nowotny 1981: 147) can be reversed: maybe where power is not, women are. Moreover, the Communist party controlled the selection of candidates (including sufficient women to accord with its ideological rhetoric) and voters were presented with minimal or no choice. In Hungary in the mid-1980s, the author was told that the introduction of choice between two candidates (both, of course, vetted by the party) in local elections was likely substantially to reduce the number of women elected. This was born out by the impact of the fall of the Communist regimes. Those regimes had produced high levels of educational achievement by women and female labour force participation, as well as habits of rather high levels of female representation. But in the new regimes '[m]en negotiated the rules of the democratic game and men filled the new halls of power. Women's share in national parliaments plummeted from a[n] . . . average of around 30 per cent to less than 10 per cent, in some countries below 5 per cent' (Montgomery 2003: 1).

Within liberal democratic regimes, the nature of the electoral system may be important. Electoral systems vary greatly, from the geographically based one-member constituency, to the ideas-based national list proportional system. Female candidates in one-member constituencies are highly visible to the media and to voters and, since they do not fit the established pattern, may be deemed riskier (Paxton 1997: 445). Moreover, many such constituencies are 'safe seats', returning the same candidate over a succession of elections. The (usually male) incumbent will normally only be replaced when he retires, or if there is a sharp swing to the rival party. Opportunities for new representatives, including women, are limited in such a system.

Proportional representation (PR) systems all involve multi-member constituencies, but may vary in design. Germany and Italy, for example, have mixed systems involving an element of both. Some countries have rather small electoral districts with rather few members, so that, as in plurality systems, women are quite visible as candidates, while in larger lists, as for example in the Netherlands where there is a single national list system, individuals are less prominent. In general, at national level PR systems seem to be conducive to higher proportions of female representatives (Paxton 1997: 454). A study of the 20 most affluent countries showed that an electoral system which ensured at least five seats for each electoral district, so that women could more readily be included as part of a clearly mixed list, was significantly likely to be more conducive to the election of women (Kenworthy and Malami 1999: 256). Other features of PR systems which affect the levels of female representation include the influence that electors have over the order of precedence within the lists. Where lists are 'closed lists', with the order that determines who actually takes up the seats the party wins decided by the party, women can more easily be imposed. Where voters can influence the order, as in Norway, there is some evidence that women may be placed lower (Matland and Montgomery 2003: 29). Moreover, not all PR systems are equally proportional: some have minimum thresholds – five per cent of the total vote in Germany, for example – which parties must surmount in order to be represented. Matland and Montgomery suggest that higher thresholds, by reducing the number of parties and thus increasing the size of each party's cohort, may improve the chances of women. In general, then, PR does favour the representation of women, but a good deal depends on the details of the PR system.

The balance and strength of the political parties within any political system is another factor which may influence the proportion of women within the representative assembly. Left Wing parties tend both to be less reticent about overturning established patterns of behaviour and more committed to an ideology of gender equality. The proportions of seats in the assembly held by Left Wing parties may therefore affect the proportion of women members. France provides a specific example of this effect: the number of women in the National Assembly declined from an initial high point (albeit a very modest one at 42, some seven per cent, half of whom were Communists) in 1946 to levels of under two per cent (eight to eleven members) in the 1960s as the proportion of Communist members declined. In the twenty most affluent nations, the share of seats held by Left Wing parties in 1998 was significantly related to the proportion of women members (Kenworthy and Malami 1999: Table 3). Mateo Diaz looked at the presence of ministers from Leftist parties in the governments of 15 West European countries and found that in most cases, if the government was predominantly drawn from Left Wing or Centre parties, the proportion of women representatives increased significantly. This was, she found, particularly apparent in the early 1960s and the 1970s. There is good evidence that Leftist parties tend to promote the presence of women in representative assemblies (Mateo Diaz 2005: 76).

Another structural feature that differs between parties is the mechanisms used to select the candidates whom the party will present for election. First, they may either be centralised at national level, so that the national executives (or their equivalents) of the parties choose the candidates, or they may be devolved to local or constituency-level party bodies (Norris and Lovenduski 1995: 199–203). Second, they may vary in the extent to which party members can actually participate in the selection process, whether at local or national level (Matland and Montgomery 2003: 32). Third, they may depend heavily on informal processes, especially the patronage of leaders or powerful elites, at either local or national level, within the party, so that personal relationships and loyalty matter, or they may be subject to procedures which are not only well-defined, but also well-observed and transparent (Norris 1996a; Norris and Lovenduski 1995: 204). Clear procedures are likely to benefit women, both because they may well be outside the patronage network, and because the fact that procedures have to be constructed and approved may lead to debates about the dearth of women which may pressure parties into action to remedy it (Matland and Montgomery 2003: 33).

Consideration of the structural frameworks of political activity thus helps to illuminate the position of women as representatives. Structures can be changed and the presence of women in assemblies may be promoted by specific measures to encourage it. These can range from very formal and binding quotas to informal measures and understandings within a particular party. They are discussed in the next chapter, but first it is important to consider the cultural settings within which these factors operate.

Cultural and Ideological Factors Affecting the Proportion of Women Representatives

An examination of both socio-economic and structural factors helps to provide a 'big-picture' overview of levels of female representation. Armed with certain facts and figures about any polity we can with some degree of reliability predict the likely pattern of female representation. The factors discussed above may allow us to 'account for nearly two thirds of the variation in women's legislative seats around the world' (Kenworthy and Malami 1999: 259). But they fully illuminate neither the issues that lie behind any individual's decision to undertake a political career, nor the multiple decisions of parties, selectors and voters that propel a woman into parliament. As Fox and Lawless point out, for example, the 'eligibility pool' argument about increased representation is predicated on the notion that women who are professionally similar to men will make the same choices as men do about whether to stand for office (Fox and Lawless 2006: 88). This assumption is not necessarily well founded. Usually a woman's arrival in an assembly can be seen as the result of a three-stage process (Matland and Montgomery 2003: 20). First she must progress from being eligible (as most adult women are to a greater or lesser extent) to actually putting herself forward as a potential candidate. Then she must progress from aspiring to become an elected representative to being a candidate. And thirdly, she must achieve election. At each of these stages a mixture of motivations, and barriers, will be present.

From eligibility to aspiration

At the first stage, the confidence and status engendered by a certain level of education and professional experience will help, as the statistical analyses have shown. At the second stage, adherence to a political party with an encouraging stance and supportive candidate selection mechanisms assists. Both then and at the third stage, an electoral system which makes the choice of female candidates not seem too risky a strategy may facilitate choices. But at every point the decisions, both of the potential representative and of the other decision-makers upon whose choices her progress depends, are conditioned by more intangible factors, linked to cultural and ideological habits and assumptions (Duerst-Lahti 1998: 22–3; Norris and Lovenduski 1995: 21–2).

In order to move from eligibility to aspiration, a woman must be motivated to be active in this sphere, must believe that this is an appropriate thing for her to do, and must believe that she could potentially be successful. Motivation depends upon a potential candidate knowing and caring about politics. Women however tend to be less knowledgeable about and interested in politics than men. In the United States there has been since 1960 a persistent gap of around 12 percentage points between the proportions of men and women who claim to follow governmental and public affairs most of the time (Dolan, Deckman and Swers 2006: 139). Equally, analysis of the British Election Survey for the 1992 election showed that men and women who were matched for their similarity in a large range of other characteristics showed 'striking and significant differences' in their scores for political knowledge (Frazer and Macdonald 2003: 73). I am not arguing that women participate less in social and political life broadly defined (see Chapter 7). Indeed, they claimed to do so slightly more than men. But they were less knowledgeable about, and possibly less engaged in, formal political activity. Surveys elsewhere have found similar results (Matland and Montgomery 2003: 22).

That fewer women than men ever nurture political ambitions (eight per cent of women against eighteen per cent of men in one survey in the United States; Duerst-Lahti 1998: 22) is likely to be related to beliefs about whether doing so is an appropriate thing for a woman. The impact of beliefs and attitudes is complex. First women themselves may believe that politics is not appropriate for them, for either positive reasons – that they ought rather to be doing something else – or negative ones – that they are not temperamentally suited to such activity. Second, men may hold such beliefs, and, because they do, may consciously or unconsciously discriminate against women. Where men are dominant they may block possibilities for women.

An Australian respondent to the Inter-Parliamentary Union survey of women politicians in 1998 commented on the widely held views that it is 'women's role to be wives and mothers [which] are still strong in Australia. This creates psychological and emotional barriers to women participating in formal politics' (Inter-Parliamentary Union 2000: 25). The prevalence of such values can be gauged, for example by the extent

Table 4.4 Hours and minutes spent on domestic work per day in 10 European countries[1] and proportions of women in parliament[2]

	Women	Men	Women's share of the daily domestic work (%)	Percentage of members of parliament who are women
Sweden	3.42	2.29	59.89	42.7
Norway	3.47	2.22	60.98	36.4
Finland	3.56	2.16	62.24	36.5
Germany	4.11	2.21	65.03	30.9
Belgium	4.32	2.38	64.48	28.2
United Kingdom	4.15	2.18	65.56	18.4
France	4.30	2.22	65.95	10.9
Estonia	5.02	2.48	66.93	17.8
Hungary	4.57	2.39	65.66	8.3

Notes:
[1] Countries surveyed at various times between December 1998 and September 2001
[2] Proportion (percentage) of women in the single or lower House of Parliament on 30 January 2001

Source: Calculated from data in Eurostat (2005: 5) and Inter-Parliamentary Union (2006).

to which domestic tasks are, or rather are not, shared within households. Mateo Diaz, considering fifteen West European Countries, found that in countries where Eurobarometer surveys suggested household tasks were more equally shared, there was some likelihood of a higher proportion of female representatives (Mateo Diaz 2005: 63). The data on time allocation collated at Table 4.4 points in the same direction. Stereotypical approaches to gender roles have been increasingly challenged, as observed by the British Conservative Party woman MP who noted that in her party 'There was an older generation than us who didn't approve of us being political . . . when we came along and were stridently political, this was a shock to them' (quoted in Norris and Lovenduski 1995: 118). Nevertheless, the notion that a woman should be primarily oriented towards the private sphere and family concerns remains very deep-rooted. A belief that women should stay at home and care for their families is, in America for example, correlated with lack of support for the idea that women should become political leaders (Wilcox, Stark, and Thomas 2003: 47).

Closely linked to this are essentialist notions that the characteristics required to be a good politician are not characteristics which women possess. Both women and men may doubt women's suitability for political roles. Women may be felt to be less rational and less robust than men. Moreover, the influence of gender assumptions within society may lead women to be daunted by the possibility of social disapproval if they take on the vigorous, indeed combative, activism which seems to be required of a political aspirant. It is those aspects of personality which are regarded as particularly required by politicians and leaders which are most in contrast with those by which society causes women to define their own identities. The result may be a painful and discouraging tension (Dolan 2005: 48; Stevens 1986: 131). Githens puts it succinctly: 'Male behaviour is considered inappropriate for a woman and female behaviour typified as caring, compassionate, sensitive and non-aggressive is inappropriate for a politician' (Githens 2003: 43).

Positivist political scientists have attempted to measure the impact of these factors in two ways: first, on the basis that certain religious denominations support traditional approaches to gender roles, they have asked whether high levels of adherence to Roman Catholicism correlates with lower proportions of female representatives. This has been found to be so, both worldwide and amongst the 20 most affluent nations (Kenworthy and Malami 1999: 254; Paxton 1997). A second way of measuring the impact of stereotypes and assumptions is to look at responses to the World Values Survey question about whether on the whole men make better political leaders than women do (see Figure 4.1). There are marked differences between countries in the response to this question. In the second half of the 1990s, more than three-quarters of men and women in the Western European countries where this question was asked rejected the idea that men make better political leaders, while in East European countries a majority of men (sometimes a very substantial majority – 67 per cent in Poland, for example) held this view and in many of them so did a majority of women (Wilcox, Stark, and Thomas 2003: 45–6). Such views seem, unsurprisingly, to be quite strongly correlated with the proportions of women representatives (Paxton and Kunovitch 2003: 102).

Such views can change, as they have done markedly in the United States over the past three decades. In the early 1970s, 29 per cent of respondents to the National Election Study believed that woman's place was in the home. In 2000, only nine per cent did so (Dolan 2005: 42). In 1974, 47 per cent of respondents to the US General Social Survey thought most men were better suited emotionally to politics, but by 1998 the proportion was only about 23 per cent while the proportion of respondents who agreed that women should take care of running their homes and leave running the country to men more than halved from 36 to 15 per cent between 1974 and 1998 (Dolan 2005: 42–3). Across a range of advanced countries, the views of the older age cohorts on whether they agree that men make better political leaders than women differ from those of the younger ones (see Figure 4.1). In general, Norris and Inglehart found substantial differences between older and younger generations in post-industrial societies, although younger women differ much more from older women than younger men do from older men (Norris and Inglehart 2005: 261). However, the link between changing attitudes and the sex balance in representative assemblies is far from direct and imme-diate. Changes in attitudes may remove one barrier; specific strategies and actions are required to effect changes in the composition of political life.

Thirdly, in order to move from eligibility to aspiration, a woman must want to do it, and think that it is important (Norris and Lovenduski 1995: 116 and 166–82). Positive motivations for moving from eligibility to aspiration are usually moral or ideological – 'a vision for the community, country or society . . . coupled with a powerful sense of social justice' (Inter-Parliamentary Union 2000: 73). Interviews with politicians confirm this: 'I wanted to change society into one of more justice and equality. I therefore entered the party that came closest to my aims. I learned that if you want to change something, you need power' said a female politician from Western Europe in 1998. A counterpart from Eastern Europe had not dissimilar motivations: 'I was politically moti-vated early in my life because of the injustices done to my people during the Communist regime. My parents, who were dissidents, were a source of special inspiration for me. At the time of political transition, I saw the opportunity to contribute to building a free and democratic State.' Feminist motives may also be a driver, as they were for the West European woman politician who said, 'the main incentive for my activi-ties was that there were too few women active and in power and that, where equality was concerned, there was a big gap between theory and practice' (Inter-Parliamentary Union 2000: 73–5).

Fourthly, a woman aspirant must believe that it is worth doing; that she has the characteristics that could potentially result in success. A key element in this is the confidence that comes from membership of the pool of people who have the qualifications generally regarded as conferring a likelihood of success. In many countries members of representative assemblies are highly educated. In some, such as the United States, expe-rience in senior corporate positions or as a lawyer or in a similar profes-sional position is regarded as almost indispensable. So in the United

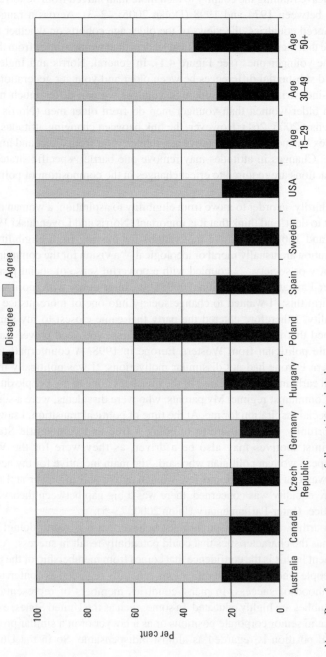

Figure 4.1   Attitudes towards women leaders by country and age cohort. 'On the whole men make better political leaders than women do'

Note: Bars for age groups are averages of all countries included.

Source: Calculated from World Values Survey question D059. Data from surveys between 1997 and 2000

States one explanation for the paucity of female representatives often advanced is that there are simply too few high-level women in the positions that act as 'feeders' to a political career (Fox and Lawless 2004: 264–5). In other countries a long record of service to the party or in a trade union may be equally or more important. However, in politics as in business, women may tend to judge their credentials more harshly than men do, and so with equal qualifications and experience may rule themselves out when a man would not (Alban-Metcalfe and West 1991: 168; Thomas 2005: 12). Fox and Lawless (see Box 4.3) found that 'women, even in the top tier of professional accomplishment, tend not to consider themselves qualified to run for political office' (Fox and Lawless 2004: 274). Amongst the respondents to their survey only 26 per cent of the women who even considered running thought of themselves as 'very qualified' for elective office whereas 36 per cent of the men did (Fox and Lawless 2004: 274).

Box 4.3   To Run or Not to Run?

Elections are a very public process. It is not difficult to identify those who have run for office as a representative. But there are large numbers of people in society who share many or all of the same attributes as the candidates but who, consciously or unconsciously, have decided not to stand. It may be important to know the factors that lead to this decision. However, identifying people who might have done something but did not poses particular problems.

Two American researchers, Richard L. Fox and Jennifer L. Lawless, found an innovative way of tackling the problem in their Citizen Political Ambition Study (Fox and Lawless 2004), identifying and contacting members of the four professions from which the highest proportions of representatives and elected officials in the United States are drawn. These were lawyers, senior business people, teachers and educational administrators at all levels (primary to tertiary), and political activists. Slightly more men than women responded (1,969 versus 1,796), and the response rate of the business people was lower than that of the other categories. In general, however, the sample was wide enough to be representative.

Fifty-nine per cent of the men and 43 per cent of the women said running for office had at least 'crossed their mind'. However, only 216 men and 105 women stood for election. The proportion of men surveyed who actually held office was nearly twice as high as that of women (seven against four per cent) but this was because even those women who had considered running were less likely than men actually to do so. Nevertheless, if they did they were just as likely as the men to be successful.

If women are less confident than men in their competence, then encouragement may be another crucial factor in their decision and ability to become a candidate (Duerst-Lahti 1998: 23). Fox and Lawless found that in the United States there were marked and substantial differences between men and women in the encouragement that they received from party leaders and political activists. Forty-three per cent of the men who had considered running for office received such encouragement, but only thirty-two per cent of the women did (Fox and Lawless 2004: 273). Where such encouragement is forthcoming, it may be crucial. 'I joined the Socialist Party without knowing anyone and without being from a socialist background. Subsequently, it was the women in the party who encouraged me to get more deeply involved and to register on a list for the elections to the cantonal Parliament' (Inter-Parliamentary Union 2000: 75).

Family support is also very important. Even in advanced and modern societies, women take prime responsibility for household and childcare tasks (see Table 4.4). Amongst the elites surveyed by Fox and Lawless in the United States, women were seven times more likely than men to be responsible for more of the household tasks and for childcare. Single women are often assumed to have fewer such obligations, but they may (like United Kingdom MP Ann Widdecombe, or the Central European MP who told the IPU that she cared on a daily basis for her 86 year old mother) have responsibilities for elderly parents. If she is to move from eligibility to aspiration, a woman needs to be sure that these responsibilities can be covered – if successful in achieving election she cannot resign from them as she would from her previous job. It has long been suggested that one of the difficulties which deter women from contemplating candidacy is the 'triple shift'. In many political cultures, selection as a candidate requires one to demonstrate professional achievement and a history of political activism. To this 'double shift' a woman will have to add a 'third shift' of work fulfilling household responsibilities. As a Central European female politician told the IPU survey, after her election 'My husband had to do all those tasks that fell to me as a housewife before' (Inter-Parliamentary Union 2000: 151). Eighty per cent of the female members of parliament surveyed worldwide by the IPU were receiving help from partners, parents or children.

From aspiration to candidacy to election

The next step is the move from aspiration to candidacy. Whatever the structure for candidate selection (see p. 84), 'in liberal democracies parties are the main gatekeepers' (Norris and Lovenduski 1995: 198) except in the United States where in 'most states parties have lost their gatekeeping role' (Norris and Lovenduski 1995: 22). The 'party gate-keepers', the 'selectorate', has traditionally been perceived as the great-est obstacle to progress in increasing the proportion of women representatives. Matland argues that the gatekeepers are subject to both external and internal pressures, stemming from their perceptions of the acceptability of a female candidate to the electorate, from their percep-tions of what their rival parties are doing and from their own cultural and ideological assumptions about women's competence and roles (Matland and Montgomery 2003: 24). As Pippa Norris points out, the least risky option, which gatekeepers are likely to choose, will normally be to pick a candidate who closely resembles previous representatives. The fact that people with these characteristics (usually male, middle-aged profession-als) most often obtain nomination encourages those who are like that and can discourage those who are not. Unless the pressures and incentives are changed, the usual outcome is the reproduction of the status quo (Norris 2004).

However, in Western Europe and the English-speaking world, the advance of feminist ideas means that parties on the whole find them-selves obliged at least to speak a language of equal opportunity. This has not on the whole been true in the former Communist countries. In the transition to democracy, women found themselves without either an appropriate discourse or useful resources to press for the adoption of female candidates. The language of sex equality had been co-opted by the previous regimes and therefore could not readily be utilised after their collapse (see Chapter 7). Moreover, women's reaction to the nature of the previous regimes had not been to organise in opposition to it but to retreat into private life, which meant both that they were burdened by heavy domestic responsibilities, and that they had little experience of political organisation which had been monopolised by the Communist parties. '[W]omen may not have felt that they had the time, resources or popular support to become active in electoral politics' (Matland and Montgomery 2003: 39) and new parties were by and large organised in their absence and under no pressures, internal or external, to include them.

Even where the pressures on the parties may have been greater, getting past the gatekeepers has often proved very difficult indeed. For example, until relatively recently in the United States women candidates were likely either to be discouraged or adopted only in hopeless seats safely held by the other party (Carroll 1994). However, more recent evidence does suggest that growing awareness of the gender gap in voting and increased influence of women in the parties has resulted in women aspirants in the United States receiving as much support as men do (Dolan, Deckman, and Swers 2006: 156; Ondercin and Welch 2005: 67).

This is not necessarily the case elsewhere. Joni Lovenduski's research in 2001 and 2002 on women who wished to be candidates illustrated 'widespread discrimination against women and institutional sexism in the main British political parties' (Lovenduski 2005: 65). She documented assumptions that women were not suited to politics, or not appealing to electors. 'If you go into an industrial area, your members will say to you "a woman will never manage in this industrial area" . . . and if you go into a rural area they will say a woman will never do in a rural area' (Liberal Democrat woman quoted in Lovenduski 2005: 71). Conservative women reported questions about responsibilities to children and husbands, and Lovenduski observed that 'constituencies expected to get two people, the candidate and his wife . . . By presenting their women partners, male candidates affirmed their commitment to . . . traditional gender relations. When women presented their male spouses, they challenged such traditions' (Lovenduski 2005: 70). In all three parties, she concluded, there was institutional sexism, in the sense that women were not judged on the same basis as men. Even where the party had clear procedures intended to avoid patronage (see p. 84) there were loopholes which allowed for 'the overt expression of selector preferences for white male candidates' (Lovenduski 2005: 76). She also found a tendency, in the parties that were formally committed to progressive policies on sex equality, to include 'token women' on their candidate shortlists whom there was no intention of adopting.

One of the greatest obstacles to an increased proportion of female candidates, and hence of representatives is the small number of seats that change hands at any election. Every assembly normally contains a large number of members who have served in the previous assembly. In the lower houses of 25 established democracies between 1979 and 1994, an average of 22 per cent of members were replaced at each election, with turnover in majoritarian systems 'dramatically lower' than under PR (Studlar and Matland 2004: 93 and 107). Parties are naturally reluctant to cause members who may have made a career out of service to the party to lose their jobs. In PR systems this can mean that newcomers, especially women, are placed in the lower, unelectable, places in a party list. In Belgium, for example, in the 1999 general election, the law required at least one-third of the candidates in each list from each sex. But women occupied only about 15 per cent of the top places and only 21 per cent of the successful candidates were women (Mateo Diaz 2005: 91). Even in the progressive Social Democrat party in Sweden, it took effort by women to ensure that all the female candidates were not relegated to the bottom of the list but 'zipped' with the men (see Box 5.1; personal information). In first-past-the-post systems, the electorate may of course vote for an opposing candidate, and especially where there is a 'landslide' result, this can produce substantial change (as in the UK in 1997). But such circumstances are rare and turnover rates low. In the United States, for example, in elections both for the House of Representatives and the Senate, 85 per cent or more of sitting members (incumbents) who stand again are successful. Hence opportunities for newcomers, and even more for female newcomers, are often very limited indeed. In the absence of special measures the nature of the membership of any assembly is likely to change very slowly indeed.

In order to progress from candidacy to election, women need successful campaigns and victory. Success in electoral campaigns can depend on a number of factors. In the United States campaigning is expensive and to be successful a candidate needs to raise substantial funds. One of the perceptions that have held back female candidacies has been a conventional view that women were less able than men to raise funds. However, Burrell argues that since 1988 US 'women's fund-raising prowess equals men's' (Burrell 2004: 39).

Success may also depend on favourable representation in the media. Research in the United States has suggested that media coverage of races for the Senate differs as between men and women candidates: women candidates for the Senate tend to be portrayed in the press as less likely to succeed than male candidates. Further down the hierarchy of elected office, the amount of media coverage was more balanced but women's policy positions were afforded less attention than were men's, while there was much more comment on their physical appearance. Television viewers were also more likely to have favourable impressions of men than of women (Dolan, Deckman and Swers 2006: 167–72; Ondercin and Welch 2005). Studies of the 1992 and 1997 election campaigns in the UK found that women politicians were largely absent from both TV and press coverage of the elections (Stephenson 1998: 11–12). Perhaps surprisingly, however, media coverage did not seem to affect women's chances of victory.

Once adopted for open, rather than 'hopeless', seats, female candidates are as likely as male ones to win. Extensive research undertaken in Western Europe and in the English-speaking world to ascertain whether the perception that the electorate is reluctant to vote for female candidates is justified has found no evidence to support this. In general voters are influenced by the party label, not the gender of the candidate. This is particularly true in PR multi-member systems where the voter may have no influence on the exact composition of party representation, but seems also to be true in single-member constituencies (Matland and Montgomery 2003: 25).

In and out: the 'revolving door phenomenon'

The tendency of representatives, once elected, to keep on being selected and winning – the incumbency effect – has certainly slowed down the pace of change, particularly in the absence of rules designed to disrupt it (see Chapter 5). Nevertheless there tends to be a sense that change will come, even if slowly, as incumbent women stay in position and are joined by newcomers. In the United States state legislatures, where women overall constituted, in 2003, some 22 per cent of the membership, Rosenthal found women representatives have come to be even more likely than their male counterparts to adopt increasingly professional outlooks to politics as a full-time career, which leads onwards from employment by a party or party-related body to election perhaps first at local and then at national level, with the expectation that this may be a working life-long activity (Rosenthal 2005: 210).

However, there is some evidence to suggest that this is not necessarily so for women everywhere. Studying the women in the French National Assembly between 1997 and 2002, Manda Green identified a 'revolving door syndrome': 'French women leave politics much more quickly than men . . . This not only holds down the numbers of women in politics but, crucially, it reduces their chances of capitalising on their experience. It is all the more insidious because it remains invisible: attention is fixed on the entrance, not the exit' (Green 2004: 4). She ascribes this tendency to rapid departure to both institutional and cultural factors. She notes that parties have tended to select women in marginal constituencies: a land-slide victory for a party which has done this extensively will bring in a number of women, but any swing against their party next time around, as very often occurs, will mean they are not re-elected (Green 2004: 335). And some are discouraged by the overtly masculinist 'willy-jousting' that contributed to British MP Tess Kingham's decision not to stand for a second term in 2001 (see Childs 2004: 65; Kingham 2001; Boothroyd 2002: 437). Women members may feel isolated and disenchanted for personal or policy reasons, or unwilling to go along with a system in which they cannot reconcile the requirements and stance of the party leadership with their own principles. British politicians Mo Mowlam and

Clare Short may be examples. Women may leave in disgust, or they may simply feel that, set against the pressures of an MP's life, the rewards and the scope for action which it offers are inadequate. Even in the Swedish parliament, where the proportion of women has become notably high, in '1998 . . . a lot of young women did not run for the next election because they preferred to pursue academic studies or wanted to do something else. Before, it [work as a parliamentarian] was a life-long commitment' (interview with Swedish male MP quoted by Mateo Diaz 2005: 145). The existence of a 'revolving door' tends to strengthen arguments that women are incapable, and to diminish the number of role models and mentors. Retention of female representatives is an aspect of representation by women that has been inadequately considered by both academic research and party strategists.

Conclusion

The arguments for increasing the representation of women are complex and controversial but can broadly be categorised as stemming from considerations of justice, of symbolism and legitimacy, of the need to improve deliberation within democracy and of the need for women to act to protect their interests. Additionally there is a utilitarian argument that parties which support increased representation for women may increase their pool of available talent and also be electorally advantaged (Sawer, Tremblay, and Trimble 2006: 19). Socio-economic, cultural and ideological factors all combine to affect levels of women's representation. It seems to be the case that socio-economic and ideological factors may assist in increasing the proportion of women in representative assemblies. The electoral system that determines how votes are translated into seats also influences outcomes, and certain types of system may make the implementation of strategies for change easier (Squires and Wickham-Jones 2001), as we shall see in the next chapter. However, the main obstacles to increasing the proportions of female representatives in the post-industrial world are selection, and the rather slow rate of turnover in assemblies, while retention is also an issue. The next chapter turns to party strategies in response both to the voting gender gap described in Chapter 3 and to the issues of representation raised in this chapter.

5

Strategies for Increasing Representation by Women

There is widespread acceptance that the current arrangements for representation by women are inadequate. Parties are aware that female voters make up a crucial portion of their electorate, and female choices can either benefit or disadvantage them. Ensuring that women's voices are heard within the party structures that form the main channels for organising electoral choice in liberal democracies is one part of the response. Improving the proportion of female representatives is another. Pressure on parties and regimes to 'do something about it' comes both from external sources – from benchmarking against others, from a 'contagion' effect which makes it hard for any party to stand out against what others are doing – and from internal sources – from women, and some men, associated with the party. The socio-economic context shapes the environment within which any strategy operates. Similar strategies may have very different outcomes. But pressures for action are mounting as many in society, especially women, and in particular in the parties, realise that if nothing changes it could take one or two centuries for women to achieve roughly proportionate representation (Norris 2004: Chapter 8). This chapter considers, first, responses within the party system to the voting behaviour discussed in Chapter 3, and secondly, strategies adopted to deal with the issues around the representation of women discussed in Chapter 4.

Party Responses to Voting Behaviour

Women's parties

Over a century and a half, parties have proved to be essential mechanisms for the expression of political choice in liberal democracies, whose functions, amongst others, include the aggregation of interests – the conversion of 'a multitude of specific demands into more manageable packages of proposals' – the setting and implementation of collective goals for society and being 'objects of . . . emotional attachment (or antagonism) exerting a powerful influence upon the behaviour and opinions of their supporters' (Hague and Harrop 2004: Chapter 11). The desire to see these functions performed in the service of women's interests has occasionally led to attempts at women's parties. Stokes suggests they tend to arise in response to specific circumstances of major change or conflict, and perhaps most readily where there is an established tradition of separate political organisations for women (Stokes 2005: 130).

An example of the emergence of a women's party from very particular circumstances was the non-sectarian Northern Ireland Women's Coalition (NIWC) founded in 1996. When it failed in its initial efforts to persuade the established parties to increase the proportion of women amongst the candidates for election to the all-party talks on peace, it constituted itself as a party with the aim of supporting efforts for peace and furthering women's rights. It was able to take advantage of the rules which, in the hope of furthering cross-community acceptance of the outcome of the peace process, allowed for representation on the basis of relatively few votes, and participated in the talks that led to the 1998 Good Friday agreement (Fearon 2002). In 1998, the NIWC achieved two per cent of the vote for the devolved Northern Ireland Assembly and held two seats until 2003, when its vote dropped to 0.8 per cent (BBC 2003; Elections 2003). It never intended to become a permanent political party (Fearon 2002), the peace process appears to be holding, and the NIWC was always under-resourced. Its activity has largely ceased.

Feminist movements (see Chapter 7) prompted the emergence of women's parties in some countries. In the United States at the beginning of the twentieth century, a National Woman's Party grew out of the suffrage movement to campaign for equal rights for women, but it was never more than a small pressure group. There were similar attempts in Europe, for example in post-war Denmark (Henig and Henig 2001: 44) and in Norway (Skjeie 1993: 232). In Iceland, the second-wave feminism of the 1970s resulted in the presence of women's lists in municipal elections from 1982, and the foundation of a Women's Alliance to present a women's list in the general election in 1983. This achieved members in the national parliament. However, it did not contest the 1999 election independently, instead joining a combined list with other progressive parties. In 2000 it merged with them to form a Social Democratic Alliance. Undeterred, in Sweden in 2005, Gudrun Schyman, former leader of the post-Communist Left party, founded a Feminist Initiative women's party to challenge the ruling Social Democrats (*The Economist*, 14 April 2005).

Communist regimes accorded a particular place to women's organisations. The tenets of Marxism-Leninism stated that with the resolution of
the class conflict the 'woman question' would also be resolved and
insisted upon formal equality between men and women. The outcome
was frequently quotas for women in various assemblies, though not, for
example, in the politburo or the party where decisions were actually
taken. There were also strong party-linked structures for women. There
was thus a tradition of women's political organisation. This has had an
ambiguous impact. Whilst on the one hand, as to some extent in Russia
and in Bulgaria, this had made women accustomed to organisation and
'skilful and knowledgeable in the public arena' (Kostadinova 2003: 318),
on the other hand they achieved their positions without competition, and,
as in Lithuania, the association of women's organisations with the Soviet
regime 'left behind a cultural stigma against women's political participation' (Krupavičius and Matonytė 2003: 102). Nevertheless the tradition
of women's organisations underpinned attempts to organise women's
parties in post-Communist countries. In Russia a grouping of women's
organisations formed the women's party 'Women of Russia' in 1993,
which was to some extent based on the successor organisation to the
Soviet Women's Committee. Women of Russia took more than five per
cent of the vote in 1993 and returned 23 members of parliament between
1993 and 1995, but has since been unable to break through the proportional representation hurdle that requires a party to achieve at least five
per cent of the vote before it can be represented (Moser 2003: 159) and
did not participate in the 2003 election, when its former leader Ekaterina
Lakhova ran on the list of the United Russia Party. Similar women's party
initiatives have appeared in other post-Communist countries such as
Lithuania, Ukraine and Bulgaria.

The record of women's parties is not encouraging (Matland 2003:
328). They have generally proved short-lived. Women's Parties have
appeared and disappeared in Australia (Sawer 2002: 11) – one was
founded in 1995 and refounded in 2002 but had disappeared by 2005.
Outside Iceland and Russia they have not won national seats. It can be
argued that their impact has been to achieve somewhat higher representation for women through encouraging the established parties to put up
female candidates and through causing them to place women's issues on
the agenda. For example since 1999, despite the demise of the Women's
Alliance, approximately one-third of the members of the Icelandic
Parliament have been women. Although in both Russia and Lithuania
women's parties were a response to imperviousness to women's demands
by other parties (Matland 2003: 341, fn 5), it is arguable that activists

might often have achieved more by working within broader-based parties. The fate of women's parties could even encourage other parties to draw the conclusion that there is little demand for the representation of women and to downgrade women's issues accordingly.

Party structures for women

Broadly based political parties seek to construct a political programme that accommodates the interests generated by a range of cross-cutting cleavages and to organise the delivery of the vote in support of a manifesto or programme. Once women could vote, then parties needed to ensure the support of the female vote. In some parties this resulted in the incorporation of women, to a greater or lesser extent, into the existing party structures. In the United States, the two main political parties moved very promptly after the enfranchisement of women to adopt a rule requiring their national committees to consist of equal numbers of men and women – the Democrats in 1920 and the Republicans in 1924 (Freeman 2000: 111–12). A reconstitution of the Republican National Committee in 1952 ended the parity rule, but the minimum female membership remains at one-third (Baer 2003: 128). However, Freeman notes that decisions are taken by the committee chairmen or the committee executive, where women are few: equal representation has not meant equal influence (Freeman 2000: 119 and 121). The party convention at which the presidential candidate is selected remains a far more crucial part of the life of the party, however, and at these the proportion of female delegates never exceeded 18 per cent until in 1972 the Democrats began a process of reform which has since the 1980s resulted in parity (Baer 2003: 131–3). In the Republican Party most of the time 'there seems to be an informal "glass ceiling" for women at about one-third of the delegates' (Baer 2003: 132). In Australia, the Australian Labour Party responded to poor electoral performance by requiring that women must constitute a minimum of 25 per cent of delegates to the party National Conference (Simms 1993: 19).

Other parties set up specific women's sections or women's offices. Socialist parties tended to favour this mechanism, for example in the Netherlands Socialist women organised separately from 1905 (Leijenaar 1993: 209), while the Labour Party in the United Kingdom set up a women's department in 1919. However, the women's sections were not integrated into party decision-making, and although there were reserved seats for women on the National Executive Committee (NEC), these were filled by nominees of the male-dominated trade unions (Lovenduski

2005: 61). In the 1990s the rules were changed to ensure a 40 per cent quota for women on the NEC.

Such women's sections were perceived as ways of educating women and encouraging them into party loyalty and support. They did not on the whole offer women a route to candidacy for seats, nor to leadership positions, and have indeed been interpreted as a way of corralling women in coffee morning and envelope-stuffing roles so that their participation in the party is not essentially political but 'a[n] . . . extension of women's social networks and voluntary labour in the community' (Lovenduski and Norris, 1993b: 40). The UK Conservative party has a women's section but, despite the (exceptional) emergence of Margaret Thatcher as party leader in the 1970s, women have been very much more active at local level than in the national policy forums; in 2005 the Board – the main decision-making body – of the party had two female members out of seventeen. In Germany women have been organised into separate sections in the three main parties (CDU, SPD, FDP), and there has been a marked 'deficit of women's influence' (Kolinsky 1993: 128).

Against this Leijenaar argues that in the Netherlands, for example, as issues of women's equality have more recently become more salient, the women's sections have been able to put pressure on the parties from a more radical stance. Similarly in Germany, in the Socialist Party from 1973 the women's section transformed itself and became an active pressure group for women's equality. In the United Kingdom, women's action groups (the Labour Women's Action Group and the Labour Women's Network) and the work of the Labour Party women's officer, were very influential during the late 1980s and the 1990s in the moves to improve the representation of women (Lovenduski 2005: 112–14)

The integration of women into party machinery has thus been one response of the political parties to women's voting behaviour. Such strategies often interact with moves to introduce procedures or rules to encourage or ensure a reasonably balanced representation of both sexes in a country's democratic institutions (see Box 5.1). The next section turns to strategies for improving the descriptive representation of women.

Strategies for Increasing Female Representation

Two types of strategy can be identified. Parties may use one or both. First, attempts may be made to influence the supply of candidates. Schemes that encourage, support, train, mentor and finance female aspirants or candidates are 'supply-side' schemes. 'Demand-side' strategies concentrate on forcing open opportunities for women. Strategies can be categorised (Childs, Lovenduski and Campbell 2005: 23; Lovenduski and Norris 1993: 8–11) as:

- Rhetorical strategies, involving increased attention to women's issues and claims and declarations of commitment to increased representation for women. These strategies may produce increased effort on the supply side, with encouragement of female aspirants, and may lead on to more active strategies, but their disadvantage is that the women may be heavily dependent on patronage and risk being seen as 'tokens' (Norris 2004).
- Positive action or equality promotion, which can include the provision of training, mentoring and financial support to female aspirants and the setting of indicative targets for the representation of women within party structures and on lists of candidates. Such strategies affect both demand and supply.
- Equality guarantees, involving quotas. This may be described as 'positive discrimination' despite the ambivalent and potentially deleterious meanings of the phrase (Bacchi 2004: 132–3). Such measures open up the demand for female candidates. At their simplest, quotas involve a requirement that a fixed minimum proportion of places must be occupied either by women or by persons of each sex. Such strategies affect demand.
- 'Parity' (see Box 5.3 below) is sometimes distinguished from quotas and seen as a fourth type of strategy.

Rhetorical strategies are now common to almost all political parties in liberal democracies. There are a very few exceptions, generally associated with far-right standpoints. The small *Staatkundig Gereformeerde Partij* (SGP – Reformed Political Party) in the Netherlands, a conservative Christian Party which in 2006 had two members in the lower house of the Dutch parliament, where it has been continuously represented since 1922, refuses to allow women to be full members of the party or stand as its candidates. This is probably the only such case in western countries and has resulted in the withdrawal of state funding (about €1 million) for the party. Statements like that of the United Kingdom Independence Party Member of the European Parliament, who opined (in jest, he later alleged) in July 2004 that women should focus on cooking and cleaning (*The Observer*, 25 July 2004), are rare in the extreme.

The next step beyond rhetorical strategies are measures which can be categorised as positive action. These may embrace both supply- and demand-side strategies. A first step may involve tightening up procedures to decrease the possible influence of prejudice and stereotypes. Centralisation of candidate selection procedures gives party leaders scope to insist upon women-friendly systems. This is the approach attempted by the British Conservative Party, when in 2002 they developed, with the help of an academic psychologist, a candidate assessment process based upon the skills required in an MP. Assessed against such 'objective' criteria, women fared as well as men and the party leadership hoped that this would increase the proportion of women on the central approved candidates list and convince the party membership that women were included on their merits (*The Guardian*, 3 February 2003; *The Times Higher Education Supplement*, 23 May 2003). Only 19 Conservative women were returned in 2005, however, and further improved selection procedures became a key demand of Women2Win, a campaigning group for increased women's representation set up in the party that year. Following his election as the party leader, David Cameron announced he would set up a 'priority list' of candidates equally balanced between the sexes (*The Times*, 18 January 2006) aimed at increasing the number of female candidates in winnable seats. However, the party's constitution does not allow for quotas or the imposition of candidates on individual constituencies, and local resistance was expected to continue.

Encouragement, financial support, mentoring and training are a further stage in equality promotion strategies. Women within the Democratic Party in the United States in 1985 and later in the Australian and British Labour Parties set up EMILY (Early Money Is Like Yeast) organisations to finance and resource women candidates, and, in the United States, to pump-prime fund-raising from other sources (Lovenduski 2005: 115; Sawer 2002: 11). The importance of individual fund-raising by candidates in the USA has resulted in a growing number of Political Action Committees (fund-raising groups) supporting the candidacies of women of varying persuasions (Dolan, Deckman and Swers 2006: 175). In the late 1980s in the UK, the Labour Women's network within the Labour Party, amongst other activities, trained aspirant women candidates (Lovenduski 2005: 113). Parties of the Right, for example in both the UK and Australia, have usually preferred to concentrate on supply side strategies such as training and mentoring. On the demand side, internal quotas or targets for the proportion of women have increasingly been adopted, in particular by parties of the Left.

Discrimination, quotas and a preference for women

Strategies of affirmative action or positive discrimination are justified and promoted on the basis that only strict and 'hard' provisions enshrined either in internal party statutes or in national legislation will overcome the gender imbalance embedded in representative institutions. They have been conceptualised using two different types of discourse – a discourse of quotas and a discourse of parity. In practical terms the results and outcomes of the application of both concepts are very similar, but the way in which their rationale is presented is different.

The aim of quotas is to compensate for a long history during which certain voices have not been adequately heard within governing institutions. Given the entrenchment within western society since the nineteenth century of principles of merit and non-discrimination it requires, as Carol Bacchi points out 'a significant re-thinking of social arrangements to take to heart . . . [the] insight that the background social rules of our society privilege certain groups' (Bacchi 2004: 143) and so reforms which challenge these privileges are thought of as 'special temporary privileges' even if the changes they are intended to effect are meant to be permanent. Once historical disadvantage has been overcome, once the presence of 'ordinary' women as much as 'ordinary' men is taken to be normal and accepted in all areas of society, and any structural barriers that impeded this have been removed, then quotas, it is supposed, will cease to be necessary.

> I do not want a world in which women have to speak continuously as women – or men are left to speak as men. Those who have been previously subordinated, marginalized or silenced need the security of a guaranteed voice . . . [b]ut . . . the proposed changes look forward to a future when such procedures become redundant . . . the notion of the citizen could begin to assume its full meaning and people could participate as equals in deciding their common goals. (Phillips 1991: 7)

The most common type of quota is one internal to a party, mandated by the party for its own structures and nominations of candidates. The adoption of quotas began in Norway in the 1970s, and the late 1980s and early 1990s saw an increasing range of parties turning to this policy (see Box 5.1). Miki Caul found that those parties which make use of quotas are, firstly, those which already had more women amongst the party leadership; secondly, those with leftist values since they were likely both to

Box 5.1　Quotas for Candidacies for Election to the Lower House of the Legislature

Australia: electoral system is majoritarian (Alternative Vote) with two major parties present in 2007. One, the Australian Labour Party (ALP), introduced a party quota of not less than 35 per cent of each sex in 1994, and increased that to 40 per cent in 2002.

Belgium: electoral system is proportional representation by party list with eight major parties present in 2007. A national law introduced in 1994 required quotas of not less than 25 per cent of each sex in each list. In 2002 a further law required equal proportions, and equal distribution through the list.

Canada: electoral system is majoritarian ('first-past-the-post') with four major parties present in 2007. Two, the New Democratic Party (NDP) and the Liberal Party (LPC), have party targets. NDP's target, adopted 1985, is for half its federal election candidates to be women. The LPC target, adopted 1993, is 25 per cent.

Czech Republic: electoral system is proportional representation by party list with five major parties present in 2007. One, the Social Democrats (CSSD), has a party quota of 25 per cent women.

France: electoral system is majoritarian (two ballots) with six major parties in 2007. Following constitutional change in 1999, a law passed in 2000 requires all parties to present equal proportions of candidates of each sex on pain of financial penalty (see Box 5.4).

Germany: electoral system is the additional member system, with five major parties present. Four have quotas or targets for the party lists from which half the seats are filled. Two parties – the Democratic Socialists (PDS) since its creation in 1990, and Bündnis 90/die Grünen (Alliance 90/the Greens) since 1986 – have a quota of equal representation of both sexes. The Social Democrats (SPD) introduced a 40 per cent quota for women in 1988. In 1996 the Christian Democrats introduced a target (not a quota) of not less than one-third women on the party list.

Hungary: electoral system is the additional member system with four major parties present in 2007. One, the Socialist Party (MSzP), has a quota for the party lists, but not constituencies, of not less than 20 per cent women.

Italy: electoral system is the additional member system (75 per cent from constituency seats, 25 per cent party lists) with some eleven parties present in 2007. Six of these parties have quotas for their party lists. The Greens (founded 1990) and the Italian Communist Party (PdCI) have a requirement of equal proportions, while the Communist Refoundation

→

have more women amongst the leadership and to be receptive to their demands; and thirdly, parties which found themselves in competition within their party system with not dissimilar parties which had already adopted quotas. In other words, she identified a 'contagion' effect (Caul 2001: 1225). But, on the basis of studies of innovation in other fields, she

→

Party (PRC, founded 1991) and, since 1991, the Democrats of the Left (DS) specify not less than 40 per cent of each sex as do the Democratic Socialists (SDI), a component of the governing coalition, while a further coalition partner, Democrazia è libertà, has a 30 per cent quota.

Netherlands: electoral system is proportional representation (national list) with seven parties present in parliament in 2007. One of these, the Labour Party (PvdA), has since 1987 had a quota which now requires equal representation, while the Green Left (GL) has since 1990 had a (now largely ignored) target of equality.

Norway: electoral system is proportional representation (nineteen constituency lists) with seven parties present in 2007. One (the Liberal Party) has since 1975 had a 40 per cent quota for women, the other four – the Socialist Left Party (SV) since 1975, the Norwegian Labour Party (DNA) since 1983, the Centre Party (SP) since 1989 and the Christian People's Party (KrF) since 1993 – all require not less than 40 per cent of each sex in their lists.

Poland: electoral system is proportional representation (36 constituency lists) with six major parties present in 2007. Only one of these has a quota, the Democratic Left Alliance (SLD) having since 2001 had a 30 per cent quota for candidate lists.

Spain: electoral system is proportional representation (52 provincial lists) with seven major parties present in 2007. A law of 2006 when implemented will require all parties to present not less than 40 per cent of each sex. Currently one party, the Socialists (PSOE), has a 40 per cent quota.

Sweden: electoral system is proportional representation (30 constituency lists) with seven parties present in 2007. Three of the parties, the Left Party (V) and the Green Party of Sweden (MP) (both since 1987) and the Swedish Social Democratic Labour Party (SAP), since 1993, require at least half of the party's candidates to be women, with the SAP implementing a zip list (see Box 5.2).

United Kingdom: electoral system is majoritarian ('first-past-the-post'), with three major parties present. None has a quota, but see Box 5.2 for all-women shortlists for the Labour Party.

United States: electoral system is majoritarian ('first-past-the-post'), with two parties present. Neither has a quota.

Sources: Compiled from Caul (2001), http://www.quotaproject.org, Matland and Montgomery (2003), CIA World Factbook and personal information.

hypothesises that Western European parties which had not already adopted quotas by the mid-1990s are now unlikely to do so. Parties in Eastern Europe have lagged behind.

Party quotas are in one sense 'voluntary', or in Mateo Diaz's terminology 'soft', in that they are upheld only by the internal regulations of

Box 5.2   Zipping and Twinning

In proportional representation party list electoral systems, the order in which the candidates appear on the list determines the order in which they are taken into the assembly. Thus in a notional district with 100 seats up for election a party list would comprise 100 candidates. If that list secured 20 per cent of votes cast, the first 20 candidates on the list would join the assembly. However, a list which respected a quota but placed all the female candidates in the lowest places would be highly unlikely to achieve increased female representation. For such lists to be effective in increasing the proportion of women in the assembly it is necessary

- for the number of seats to be filled to be sufficient to allow even a relatively moderate share of the vote to result in several candidates being successful. One of the reasons why the brief experience of PR in France between 1986 and 1988 produced little change in the sex balance of the National Assembly was that the districts were small (typically with 3–5 members for each) and most lists were headed by men, frequently the incumbents whom the parties were concerned to protect (Sineau 2001: 126).
- for women to be allocated positions that are high enough on the list to ensure they are successful.

For this reason some quota systems have been designed to ensure that women are well placed, either by alternating them with men (in a so-called 'zip' list) or at least by insisting that a minimum number are found amongst those likely to be successful. For example, in Belgium for the 2003 elections, electoral law provided that both men and women must   →

the party. And these regulations may themselves be far from binding, as in the case of the Netherlands Green Left where in 1990 the party regulations set a target, but the active policy to achieve it has since been quietly abandoned (personal information). Nevertheless, if they are accepted as binding and enforced they may in fact be 'far-reaching in scope and imposed as a strong party regulation' (Mateo Diaz 2005: 27). When the party holds a substantial proportion of the parliamentary seats, this can have important effects upon the sex balance within the parliament, as was the case in the United Kingdom in 1997. They are, however, only as effective as the energy and rigour with which compliance with them can be enforced. Quotas for candidacies, whether imposed by party policy or national legislation, are not too difficult to implement where the electoral system involves party lists at district or national level, but will

→

figure amongst the top three candidates in each list, and at elections there-after the top two must be a man and a woman.

Where first-past-the-post systems operate, one technique that has proved successful was constituency 'twinning'. This was applied by the Labour Party to the first elections for the new legislative assemblies for Scotland and Wales. The Scottish and Welsh systems are a version of the additional member system. Members (73 in Scotland, 40 in Wales) are returned for individual constituencies and the assembly numbers are made up on a proportional basis (56 members from 8 regional lists in Scotland, 20 from 5 lists in Wales). The Labour Party was persuaded that while all-women shortlists were then illegal, twinning would not be. The constituen-cies were divided into pairs that were both reasonably close to each other and expected to be more or less equally likely (or not) to be winnable. Candidates – one man and one woman – were selected jointly by the two constituencies. The effect was substantial. Labour took the majority of the constituency seats (53 out of 73 in Scotland and 27 out of 40 in Wales) and achieved a proportion of 50 per cent women amongst Labour MSPs and 54 per cent women amongst Labour Assembly Members in Wales. In conse-quence the Scottish parliament from 1999 to 2003 had 37 per cent women members, and the Welsh Assembly 40 per cent.

Twinning arrangements were possible because the assemblies were new: there were no incumbency problems. However, they had been envis-aged only as 'one-off' measures. In the 2003 elections the Labour Party in Scotland relied on incumbency and on a commitment to quotas in selec-tion and managed to maintain the number of Labour women MSPs while in Wales it also utilised the Sex Discrimination Electoral Candidates Act and used all-women shortlists in six constituencies, increasing its female membership from 15 to 19 (Childs, Lovenduski, and Campbell 2005).

not necessarily result in the return to the assembly of more women with-out additional measures (see Box 5.2).

In first-past-the-post systems, finding ways of combining national quotas with a degree of constituency autonomy has taxed the parties. Tactics include all-women shortlists and 'twinning' of constituencies (see Boxes 5.1 and 5.2). Whilst the impact of party quotas can be substan-tial, as in the regional assemblies of Scotland and Wales, and the 'conta-gion effect' may help to promote their adoption, they have the disadvantage of being limited in scope and most prevalent in parties which may already be relatively women-friendly. For this reason some countries (see Box 5.1) have imposed them by statutory measures.

Legislation has in some countries also been necessary for another reason. Quotas, whether voluntary (soft) or statutory (hard), have needed to tackle the tension between the singling out of one sex for 'special' treatment and the existence of legislative or constitutional provisions that provide for equal treatment of men and women and no discrimination between them. Women have in general, and with good reason, welcomed such provisions. Problems arise, however, when strict numerical limits are imposed for access to certain positions which, in the interests of including members of one sex, automatically result in the exclusion of the other. This was the situation that was challenged in litigation in the United Kingdom (see Box 5.3). Equally such considerations resulted in the annulment of the 1994 Italian electoral legislation imposing zip lists for the 25 per cent of the lower house seats that were filled by a PR system. Such conflicts could only be resolved by further legislation. In some countries equal treatment provisions are incorporated within the constitution and, if practices which recognise sex differences are to be legal, constitutional amendments may be needed. Mateo Diaz (Mateo Diaz 2005: 24–5) subdivides legislation on quotas into four types:

- law making it possible for parties to adopt quotas by setting aside the normal prohibitions on discrimination between men and women to enable men to be excluded from certain positions in order to ensure that the quota is reached. The United Kingdom Sex Discrimination (Electoral Candidates) Act of 2002, the 1999 amendment of the French constitution and the 2003 amendment of the Italian constitution are laws of this type.
- law which imposes quotas for candidates for certain types of election. Such a law was, for example, passed in Belgium in 1994 and in France in 2000.
- law such as that introduced in Finland in 1995 which requires quotas for all 'indirectly elected public bodies' (such as municipal executive boards) (Holli and Kantola 2005: 77) but not the legislative assembly.
- law which reserves a certain number of seats in parliament for certain groups. Both Belgium and Slovenia, for example, have such provisions for linguistic or ethnic groups. There are no OECD countries which have laws reserving seats for women. Those countries which do, such as Morocco, Pakistan and Tanzania, normally reserve between ten and twenty per cent of seats. Rwanda, which reserves thirty per cent, and achieves more than that, tops the worldwide ranking for the proportion of women in parliament.

Box 5.3   Voluntary Quotas in the United Kingdom Labour Party

The Labour Party:

In the 1980s (see Lovenduski and Randall 1993: 136–41):

- was the focus of feminist pressure, especially from an active feminist pressure group within the party, the Labour Women's Action Committee;
- was forced by electoral defeat in 1983 to adopt a modernising agenda;
- was aware that women were tending to vote for parties of the Left;
- was aware that the post-1979 requirement that all MPs face re-selection before election was not dislodging incumbents and opening up possibilities for women;
- introduced quotas for internal party positions and after 1987 required that in any seat for which there was one or more female applicants, the shortlist must include a woman;

In the 1990s (see Childs 2004: 34–6):

- saw the Labour Women's Network campaigning for more women in elected office;
- was supported by an EMILY's list founded by wealthy Labour supporter Barbara Follett and providing training and financial support to female candidates;
- adopted a policy that all-women shortlists would operate in half the winnable seats, and in half the Labour-held seats in which vacancies occurred;
- was overruled by an Industrial Tribunal (Jepson and Dyas-Elliott *vs.* the Labour Party and Others 1996). The selection of candidates was held to be a procedure leading potentially to employment and hence subject to anti-discrimination law preventing the exclusion of men; but
- saw a major increase in the number of women members in 1997, mostly selected before 1996 from all-women shortlists in targeted winnable seats or vacancies following retirement (Childs 2004: 36);

In the 2000s:

- saw the number of its female MPs reduce slightly in 2001;
- saw the Labour government achieve the passage of the 2002 Sex Discrimination (Electoral Candidates) Act exempting electoral shortlists from the sex discrimination legislation until 2015;
- reverted to all-women shortlists in 30 seats – half those where retirements were anticipated, and all those where retirements were announced after 2002 (Childs, Lovenduski and Campbell 2005: 38);
- saw the proportion of female Labour members improve in 2005;
- lost one seat (Blaenau Gwent in South Wales) where the imposition of an all-woman shortlist resulted in a local man who had expected to become the candidate successfully standing as an independent, and lost it again to an independent at the by-election following his death in 2006.

Parity

The second conceptualisation of affirmative strategies to tackle sex imbalance in representative assemblies is the notion of parity. This notion is defined as the right of men and women to an equal position and equal treatment in all spheres of life, and in particular the equal representation of women and men in decision-making positions. While it is virtually indistinguishable (Mateo Diaz 2005: 23), its proponents take the view that it is both conceptually and philosophically different from a quota, and an advance upon it. 'It goes a step further than quotas as it is based on the idea that women are not a minority: they represent more than half of the humanity – (a quantitative dimension) – and one of its two components – a qualitative dimension' (Lobby 2006). Parity is seen as an absolute principle, in contrast to the pragmatic piecemeal solution of quotas and is strongly linked to the view that true democracy requires the equal presence of both sexes in 'the representation and administration of nations' (Allwood and Wadia 2000: 193; Mossuz-Lavau 1998: 36). Such an approach expresses an essentialist position, for it rests on the premise that the one indelible difference between members of the human race is the sexual difference, and that this difference is so crucial that it should be reflected in the structures of democracy, indeed of the whole of society. Sexual difference, it is argued, is fundamental and produces a clear-cut division into two groups. 'Humanity is dual, and cannot be legitimately represented without its double face' (Vogel-Polsky 1994, cited in Mateo Diaz 2005: 22). The concept of parity provides, therefore, an argument against the universalist position that all people are the same and no account should be taken of difference, and in particular against the view that if account is taken of sexual difference, then age, or ethnic difference or other characteristics should also be recognised, since it asserts that all other social categories are made up of the two sexes and sex is the sole personal characteristic to be mentioned on an individual's birth certificate and identity papers (Allwood and Wadia 2000: 210). However, since the parity argument rests upon the universality of the dual nature of humankind, it does not assume that its achievement will change politics (see Chapter 8). Female representatives will represent the interests of the nation, not the gendered concerns of feminine issues (Sawer 2002: 8).

The concept developed during the late 1980s. In a report of 1989, following a 1988 resolution, the Council of Europe first employed the concept of parity and linked it to democracy (Allwood and Wadia 2000: 3). It received a clear boost after it appeared as a key element in the Platform Action of the United Nations 4th International Conference on

Figure 5.1   Proportion of women in single or lower houses of parliament: France and Europe

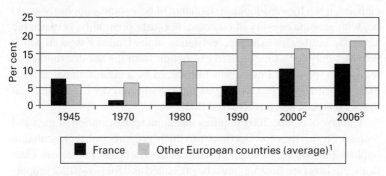

Notes:
1   1945–1990: average of Sweden, Denmark, Norway, Netherlands, West Germany, Spain, UK, Ireland, Italy, France; 2000–2006: average of Organisation for Security and Cooperation in Europe Countries.
2   15 December 2000.
3   February 2006.
Source: Data for 1945–90 from Henig and Henig 2001: 105. Data for 2000–6 from Inter-Parliamentary Union at http://www.ipu.org/wmn-e/world.htm.

Women in Beijing in 1995. The concept took root particularly strongly in France, because of these discussions; because during the 1980s and 1990s the proportions of women in the French parliament were amongst the lowest in the European Union (see Figure 5.1); and because of the rejection of quotas as they have been understood elsewhere. The Constitutional Council ruling in 1982 (see Box 5.4) against their incorporation in electoral legislation prompted feminist campaigners, seeking to move forward, to take up the argument that quotas were an alien concept imported from English-speaking feminism – to which French feminists were broadly hostile (Ezekiel 2002: 346) – that humiliated women by confining them to a numerically unequal position, since the quota proportion was likely to be treated as a maximum, not a minimum (Mossuz-Lavau 1998: 32). Only the true equality represented by parity – with its double implication of both duality and equality – was acceptable. What the initial defeat of the quota proposals had done was paradoxically to shift the debate to demands for, effectively, a much stronger fifty per cent quota (Baudino 2005: 95).

A further distinction between quotas and parity is that quotas are normally advanced as a temporary expedient, in place to remedy a historical disadvantage, and required only until such inequities have been compensated for and eradicated. Parity, on the other hand, is intended as permanent. Rather than a backward-looking attempt to remedy past deficiencies, it is a forward-looking statement of how society ought always to be, with genuine equality of outcome, not just opportunity, between the sexes. So unlike, for example, legislation in the United Kingdom which provides only for a time-limited exemption from the sex discrimination legislation, parity in France was introduced by a constitutional amendment which should last as long as the constitution does. The practical impact has been less positive (see Box 5.4).

The law of 6 June 2002 requires the equal representation of men and women on the lists for elections to which proportional representation applies. For one-ballot elections such as the European Parliament elections, zip lists (see Box 5.2) must be presented and for two-ballot proportional elections they must be equally represented in each group of six. For general elections (on a single-member constituency basis), parties which do not present equal numbers of men and women as their candidates will be penalised by being refused a proportion of the state subsidies to which they would otherwise have been entitled over the life of the parliament.

In the municipal elections of March 2001 in the communes to which the law applied, the number of female town councillors more than doubled from 21.9 per cent to 47.5 per cent. However, in simultaneous elections in the *départements* (counties) to which the law does not apply, only 20 per cent of the candidates and less than 10 per cent of the councillors subsequently in office were women (Bird 2003; Dauphin and Praud 2002). The more stringent requirements of the law when it applied to list systems also had an impact on the 2004 regional council elections. The representation of women leapt from 27.5 to 47.6 per cent (Opello 2006: 145). In contrast, the electoral system ensured that the results of the general election of 2002 were not spectacular: 71 women were elected (12.3 per cent) (Bird 2004). Financial penalties, calculated with reference to the proportion by which a party's female candidates fell short of 50 per cent, were applied. The majority mainstream Right *Union pour un mouvement populaire* (UMP) suffered the largest penalty (€4.2 million). The Socialist Party, which lost €1.65 million (*Le Monde*, 2 March 2006), found itself obliged to reduce its headquarters staff by four posts to accommodate its losses (*Le Nouvel Observateur*, 25–31 July 2002).

By late 2006 the Socialists and the UMP had picked their prospective candidates for 2007. The Socialists had nominated nearly 50 per cent women, the UMP had set itself a target of 30 per cent and

Box 5.4   Parity in France: A Chronology

1970s	Socialist Party imposes internal quotas (ten per cent in 1974, fifteen per cent in 1977 and twenty per cent in 1979) for its party decision-making bodies and for candidacies for those elections using a party list (Allwood and Wadia 2000: 59).
1980	Centre-Right Minister for the Condition of Women proposes bill requiring at least twenty per cent of either sex as local election candidates. The bill is passed by the National Assembly but falls with the 1981 general election.
1981	Successful Socialist party manifesto includes pledge of a women's quota.
1982	A bill reforming the electoral system for local elections incorporates Gisèle Halimi's amendment that no more than 75 per cent of candidates may be of the same sex (Baudino 2005: 88).
1982	The Constitutional Council (ruling 82-146 DC of 18 November 1982) rules against bill on the grounds that it infringed the principles of the 1958 Constitution and the 1789 Declaration of the Rights of Man and the Citizen (which is incorporated in the Constitution) which prevent any division of electors or candidates into categories.
1986	General Election uses a proportional electoral system with constituencies of three to five members. Proportion of women in National Assembly rises from 5.7 to 5.8 per cent.
1988	General Election reverts to single-member constituency dual ballot system. Proportion of women remains at 5.8 per cent.
1992	Publication of *Au pouvoir, citoyennes* (Women citizens, seize power!) by three feminist campaigners. A campaigning and lobbying network quickly springs up.
1994	Six of the lists for the European Parliament election are equally balanced between men and women.
1995	At the presidential election, only Arlette Laguiller of the extreme left Workers' Struggle Party (*Lutte Ouvrière*) (one of the two female candidates) fails to make any reference to how to increase the representation of women, and only the extreme right National Front candidate, Jean-Marie Le Pen, opposes such measures.
1996	71 per cent of respondents in a public opinion poll are in favour of parity (Allwood and Wadia 2000: 200).
1999	Following Socialist victory in 1997 and intense debate amongst politicians, feminists and intellectuals (see Allwood and Wadia 2000: 194–200; Amar 1996; Dauphin and Praud 2002), the provision in Article 3 of the Constitution that 'the law favours the equal access of men and women to elected mandates and positions' is enacted.
2000	Law of 6 June 2000 provides an implementation mechanism.
2001	Local elections – first elections under parity law.
2002	First general election under parity law.

reached this, explaining they could not reach 50 per cent because 'we have too many incumbents. It's difficult to tell men who haven't done badly that they must give up' (UMP official quoted in *Le Monde*, 20 September 2006).

Electoral system change

Quota and parity structures work differently in different electoral systems which (see Chapter 4) themselves have different effects on the chances of women. Systems which contain some element of proportionality seem in general to favour women; during the 1970s, 1980s and 1990s, when the proportions of women representatives grew in all Western European and English-speaking countries, the growth on average, at least until a ceiling was reached, was stronger under such systems (Siaroff 2000; Studlar 2002: 2). While the details of the ways in which they operate, and the political culture in which they are embedded, account for substantial variation within systems which do include some proportionality, it is clear that single-member constituencies consistently act as a barrier to female candidates. Electoral systems do change: transition from Communism produced new systems in several ex-Communist countries and Poland had no fewer than four changes to electoral law between 1989 and 2001 (Benoit and Hayden 2004: 397). Italy and France both experimented with new systems in the 1980s and 1990s.

Electoral system change ought therefore to be a possible strategy for increasing female representation. In New Zealand, which changed from 'Westminster-style' single-member constituencies to a German-style mixed-member system in 1993, the principal motivation for the change was disquiet at the discrepancies between votes cast for the leading parties and seats obtained by them. But one effect was to increase the already relatively high proportion of female members (from 21.2 per cent in 1992 to 29.2 per cent in 1996 and 30.8 per cent in 1999) (Studlar 2002: 6). The design of completely new systems may present particular opportunities, as in Scotland and Wales (see Box 5.2) where the adoption of the additional member system was at least in part motivated by a wish to facilitate female representation. In practice change in established electoral systems is almost always driven by 'office-seeking' – that is, essentially partisan advantage – and not policy change considerations (Benoit and Hayden 2004: 397). Such change may, as in France and Italy, have little initial impact and is thus seldom a feasible strategy for increasing female representation.

Conclusion

Long-term social change and the orientation of social and political culture can have an indirect effect upon the level of the political representation of women in any country. Modernising changes in attitude, most apparent in the younger generation in post-industrial societies, at least have the effect of removing cultural barriers to female participation in politics (Inglehart and Norris 2003: 146). There may be a virtuous circle at work here. As social and political culture changes, so female representation may increase. And as female representation increases, so measures to promote the necessary changes can be formulated, advocated and introduced.

Similarly the proportion of female participation in the workforce may support increased female representation, but the relationship is far from direct. High levels of female participation do not necessarily translate into high levels of representation if, for example, that participation is part-time, or poorly supported by the nature of the welfare state (see Chapter 2) or concentrated in lower-level, not top professional, employment (Childs, Lovenduski and Campbell 2005: 94; Squires and Wickham-Jones 2001: 20–1).

If the increases in the proportion of female representation are to be achieved at anything other than glacial speed, then specific political measures are required. However, the range of possible strategies open to any individual party or indeed political regime is limited by the dominant ideology and discourse within which it operates. Carol Bacchi argues that affirmative action – including strategies to increase female representation – is predominantly construed as preferential treatment, an interpretation which fails to challenge prevailing social values. This is the interpretation which results from a universalist emphasis upon norms of equality. On the other hand affirmative action may equally be construed as social justice. This is a 'sub-dominant' (Bacchi 2004: 129) interpretation which tends to rely upon notions of difference, but also to advocate substantial structural change.

Strategies to increase female representation range from the 'soft' and largely rhetorical – which if they bring change at all are likely to do so only very slowly (Childs, Lovenduski, and Campbell 2005: 94) – to the 'hard', with legal and financial sanctions attached. Drude Dahlerup (Dahlerup and Freidenvall 2005: 29–30) distinguishes between incremental strategies which depend largely on equality promotion measures and fast-track strategies involving quotas. These require a shift from a concept of equality involving equality of opportunity to one requiring equality of outcome, and will, if well implemented, 'force parties to scrutinize and change their male-dominated gender profile' (p. 42). The notion of reserved seats has not proved acceptable in the western world although zip lists within very large multi-member districts would come close to achieving the same result. But in no western country has that been fully imposed. Whilst marked change has occurred in some places, for example in 1997 in the United Kingdom, the final result was still not spectacular and since it was strongly based in the political fortunes of one party, is vulnerable. The evidence suggests that, at a minimum, successful strategies (Childs, Lovenduski, and Campbell 2005: 98–9; Squires and Wickham-Jones 2001) need to:

- encourage and support women in participation, and provide finance (as required), training and mentoring for them;
- ensure that women are not discriminated against in candidate selection;
- ensure that women are not discriminated against at the point of election (for example by relegation to the lowest places in PR electoral lists);
- ensure that women are not marginalised in the decision-making process;
- ensure that the structures and operations of political institutions do not deter women, for example by eliminating sexual harassment and promoting humane working hours.

Each of these propositions poses challenges to dominant ideas and values and to the vested interests of incumbents and existing power structures. They are much harder to implement than a rhetorical strategy of 'let it happen', with effective sanctions required at every point from the local constituency to the national level. But the preponderance of the evidence suggests that without effective strategies change will occur very slowly, if at all. The speed and nature of such change is one of the dominant issues concerning women in politics today.

6
Women and Positions of Power

The previous chapter discussed the position of women in representative and legislative bodies. This chapter now turns to the position of women in executive bodies and in decision- and policy-making roles. In other words, it turns from considering the average behaviour of women as a group to considering women's political behaviour as exceptional individuals (Walby 1997: 139). Many of the considerations detailed in Chapter 4 in relation to women's candidacies for electoral office apply as much to the access of women to executive as to representative roles. However, this chapter is concerned in particular with women in leadership positions. Until the second half of the twentieth century, women were almost completely absent from political elites in western countries. The two rare exceptions were, first, those who acquired a monarchical position by inheritance or (even more rarely) marriage, such as the reigning queens of England (Mary, Elizabeth, Anne and Victoria) and the empresses Maria Theresa in Austria and Catherine the Great in Russia and second, those (scarcely acknowledged) who acquired political influence as the result of private relationships, whether as mistress or wife (for example Mme de Maintenon at the court of Louis XIV between 1675 and 1715) or as the hostess of a political salon (for example Georgiana, Duchess of Devonshire, in London in the mid-eighteenth century). The first type of power has almost disappeared, as royal prerogatives have passed to governments, whilst, as Mary Wollstonecraft pointed out over two hundred years ago, the second is liable to be pernicious. '[I]f women are not permitted to enjoy legitimate rights, they will render both men and themselves vicious to obtain illicit privileges' (Wollstonecraft 1975: 89).

It remains the case, however, that marriage to or connexion with a politically successful or wealthy man can in certain, rather unusual, cases still be perceived as a source of political influence. Eva Peron in Argentina in the late 1940s and early 1950s is perhaps the most distinctive example of a woman who wielded political power without holding a formal position (Randall 1982: 120). The presence in 2006 in *Forbes*

Magazine's annual list of the one hundred most powerful women of the world of the wives of the president of the USA and of the king of Jordan, neither of whom holds a formal political position, suggests that at least the perception that power may accrue from a private relationship has not wholly disappeared (see www.forbes.com/lists).

The exact locus of power within any society is a matter for debate. However, there is broad agreement that within developed industrial societies political (and economic) power is concentrated in the hands of a relatively small group of people. These people can in almost all cases be identified by the positions that they hold. It is their formal positions within institutions that gives them scope and legitimacy to impose their decisions. Effectively the members of the elite are those who, for the time being, are the rulers, distinguished from all the others who are ruled (Drew et al. 2000: 4). The discussion which follows concentrates upon positions of political power, but the importance of economic power should not be forgotten. *Forbes Magazine*'s hundred most powerful women has a large proportion of business women with women who have been prominent in the political sphere making up just over a quarter of the total. Following Randall (Randall 1987: 115), we can categorise the political elite as comprising heads of government and ministers and the senior personnel of political parties, trade unions and major interest organisations, civil services, local government services, the judiciary and the media.

Elites are by definition exclusive, since those who rule in any one society can never be numerous. As W. S. Gilbert pointed out, if everybody were somebody then nobody would be anybody. This small 'political class' was, until a rather recent period, substantially recruited on the basis of social background. The experiences, wealth and social know-how acquired through family, education and other contacts ensured that access to ruling positions could be achieved. 'The supposition was that members of the elite were characterised by the ability to rule effectively, knew how to gain access to necessary resources and could correctly calculate avenues to success' (Drew et al. 2000: 5). However, although such elites were in consequence somewhat exclusive there was always sufficient social mobility to ensure that some 'outsiders' gained access to the elite. Moreover, as liberal democracy developed in western societies it was, theorists argued, maintained by a system of competition between the elite leaderships of groups and parties representing varied social interests (Parry 1969: 61 and 147). Nevertheless, the presence of women in the posts that constitute elite positions is very limited indeed (see Table 6.1). Circulation and mobility into the elites seems to have applied to men and to have had very little impact upon women.

Table 6.1 Female heads of state (HoS) and prime ministers (PM) since 1945 (Australia, Canada, European Union 25, Iceland, New Zealand, Norway, Switzerland, Turkey, USA, former Yugoslavia)

	Name	Type: country	Dates in office
HoS	Wilhelmina (1880–1962)	Monarch: Netherlands	1890–1948
HoS	Charlotte (1896–1985)	Monarch: Luxembourg	1919–1964
HoS	Juliana (1909–2004)	Monarch: Netherlands	1948–1980
HoS	Elizabeth II (1926)	Monarch: United Kingdom/Canada/Australia/ New Zealand	1952–
HoS	Margrethe II (1940)	Monarch: Denmark	1972–
PM	Margaret Thatcher	Great Britain	1979–1990
PM	Maria da Lourdes Pintasilgo	Portugal	1979–1980
HoS	Beatrix (1938)	Monarch: Netherlands	1980–
HoS	Vigdís Finnbogadóttir (1930)	President: Iceland	1980–1996
PM	Gro Harlem Brundtland	Norway	1981, 1986–1989, 1990–1996
PM	Milka Planinc	Yugoslavia: Federal Prime Minister	1982–1986
HoS	Agatha Barbara (1923–2002)	President: Malta	1982–1987
PM	Kazimiera Danuta Prunskiena	Lithuania	1990–91
HoS	Sabine Bergmann-Pohl (1946)	Interim President: German Democratic Republic	April–October 1990
HoS	Mary Robinson (1944)	President: Republic of Ireland	1990–1997
PM	Edith Cresson	France	1991–1992

Table 6.1 continued

	Name	Type: country	Dates in office
PM	Hanna Suchocka	Poland	1992–1993
PM	Kim Campbell	Canada	1993
PM	Tansu Çiller	Turkey	1993–1995
PM	Jenny Shipley	New Zealand	1997–1999
HoS	Mary McAleese (1951)	President: Republic of Ireland	1997–
PM	Helen Clark	New Zealand	1999–
HoS	Ruth Dreifuss (1940–)	President: Confederation of Switzerland	1999–2000
HoS	Vaira Vike-Freiberga (1937)	President: Latvia	1999–
PM	Irena Degutienė	Lithuania: Acting PM	May and October 1999
HoS	Tarja Kaarina Halonen (1943)	President: Finland	2000–
PM	Anneli Tuulikki Jäätteenmäki	Finland	17 April–18 June 2003
HoS	Radmila Sekerinska	Macedonia: Acting PM	May–June & November–December 2004
PM	Angela Merkel	Germany: Federal Chancellor	November 2005–

Sources: Data from http://womenshistory.about.com/od/rulers20th/a/women_heads.htm and http://www.terra.es/personal2/monolith/00women3.htm; accessed 12 April 2006.

Access to Top Positions

In all organisations, discretion, individual judgement, prejudice and possibilities for patronage, and co-option exist. As we saw in relation to candidate selection in Chapter 4, access to powerful posts can be achieved and controlled in various ways. There are five main ways in which such access can occur for women. Adapting the classification suggested by Apfelbaum and Hadley (Apfelbaum and Hadley 1986: 200), we can say that they are through:

- charisma
- inheritance
- achievement of professional eminence
- selection
- merit.

Charisma – the quality of individual personality which produces personal magnetism – was identified by Max Weber as one of the potential sources of power and leadership (Bendix 1994: 300). Charismatic leadership, according to Weber, is based neither on traditional beliefs and hierarchies, nor on rational principles, but depends on recognition by followers that the leader possesses some form of inspiration not available to other people. Apfelbaum and Hadley cite Joan of Arc as the most conspicuous case of such a female leader. This recognition in turn results in an emotional connection between the leader and the followers, which can be cultivated. For example, the range and careful symbolism of portraits of Queen Elizabeth I (ruled 1558–1603) – the British National Portrait Gallery has 57 in its collection alone – indicate, unusually for a woman, the importance attached to the charismatic elements of her position. In the structures of modern democratic society pure charisma is never a basis for power, but it can be an important element in sustaining a power base. Charisma, which, because of its emotional underpinnings, can result in both intense loyalty and considerable loathing, has certainly been an important element in the power attained by many of the most prominent female leaders, most notably Golda Meir and Indira Ghandi (see Box 6.1) and Margaret Thatcher.

Inheritance as a basis for political power and leadership may seem anachronistic in modern democracies and confined largely to hereditary monarchs (see Table 6.1) but has in fact played a part in the attainment of powerful positions by a number of women as a number of female elected representatives, especially in the early years, followed on from their

---

Box 6.1   Pioneers: the First Three Female Prime Ministers Worldwide

1   **Sirimavo Bandaranaike, Sri Lanka**
     Prime Minister, 1960–1965, 1970–1977, 1994–2000.
2   **Indira Gandhi, India**
     Prime Minister, 1966–1977, 1980–1984.
3   **Golda Meir, Israel**
     Prime Minister, 1969–1974.

---

husbands. No fewer that 47 of the women who have served in the United States Congress, 8 in the Senate and 39 in the House of Representatives (including four of the women in the House of Representatives in 2005) were originally elected or appointed to fill vacancies created by the death of their husbands (Center for American Women and Politics 2005) and the first three women who sat in the British House of Commons all replaced husbands who had either died or become ineligible. This was also true of the first two female prime ministers worldwide (see Box 6.1); in the specific conditions of South-East Asian politics, dynasty – involving charisma and inheritance – may play an important role. Aung San Suu Kyi, Nobel Peace Prize winner and imprisoned leader of the opposition in Burma, is the daughter of Aung San who was briefly prime minister of Burma in the period leading to independence. Those who follow the 'widow's track' to office may in fact develop substantial political careers, which can be more distinguished than those of their husbands (Dolan, Deckman and Swers 2006: 243).

Professional eminence is often based upon technical expertise and forms a basis for the attainment of leadership positions in technical and academic fields. Politics is not a notably technical profession, and relatively few women have reached senior political decision-making positions in this way. Nevertheless it has been an element in the appointment of a number of ministers, especially in countries where ministerial positions are not completely linked to long party-political careers. For example, one of the most popular French politicians of the 1970s, 1980s and 1990s, Simone Veil, twice a minister (1974–9 and 1993–5) has never been a member of the French parliament, and owed her position in part to her eminent professional career as a judge, while American secretary of state Condoleezza Rice made her career as an academic. Her academic distinction boosted her credibility as a political adviser and subsequently a member of the administration.

Particularly at the most senior levels, however, selection – that is choice on the part of a limited number of existing members of the elite – is perhaps the most crucial factor. There is, even in open and democratic political structures, a great deal of scope for personal discretion and patronage. Procedures for appointments to senior posts vary and the outcomes, for example in the composition of the senior civil service, vary very considerably (see Figure 6.1). For senior leadership and decision-making posts in civil services and similar bureaucratic organisations, there are generally institutionalised procedures. For posts as ministers, patronage is undoubtedly crucial.

Key factors include, first, institutional culture: a study in Denmark (Højgaard 2002) concluded, for example, that the relatively high proportion of women in government (43% in 1998) was not matched by equivalent proportions at the top of the civil service (15%) or businesses (5%). A principal reason suggested was that public services are subject to pressures for bureaucratization and to rules requiring equal treatment, while in Denmark politics are subject to pressures from an ideologically egalitarian culture. The same observation has been made of New Zealand (Olsson and Pringle 2004) and is borne out by Figure 6.1 which shows the high proportions of women in the public service in Australia and Canada, both of which have a strong commitment to equal opportunities policies and diversity in their public services and monitor the outcomes carefully. These pressures do not operate in business.

In institutions where either rules or ideology or both are less entrenched, women may not fare well. Many studies have illuminated the 'general domination of masculinity in bureaucratic life' (Halford and Leonard 2001: 63; Davies 1999) and the way this inflects choice. As Elizabeth Brimelow remarked of the British civil service a quarter of a century ago, selecting a person for promotion requires 'a certain effort of the imagination. You have to see the officer in the higher grade' (Brimelow 1981: 329). If there are few if any women already at the higher level that may be particularly difficult. If the image of leadership that predominates in any organisation portrays leaders as visionary and heroic – and that is very widely the case – then women are disadvantaged. They do not figure in the dramatis personae of the myths of the great leader 'with "fit" being more important than equity at senior levels for a whole raft of organizational cultural reasons' (Still 2006: 186).

Some women attempting to claim leadership positions in politics have done so in ways that deliberately challenge some aspects of the 'great leader' stereotype. French presidential elections are unusual in that they

Figure 6.1   Proportion of senior civil service posts occupied by women

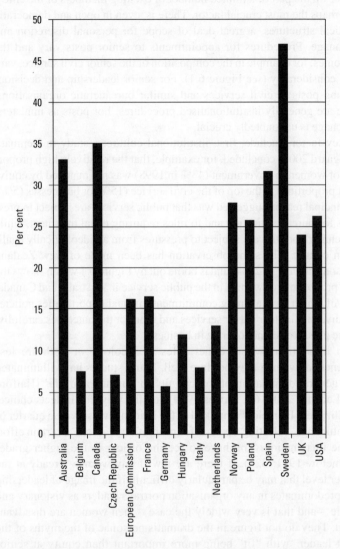

Note: First and second levels below the minister as at September–December 2005 except for Australia (Senior Executive Service as at June 2005), Canada (Federal Public Service of Canada Executive Group 2003–4), European Commission (Grades A*14–16, 2005) and USA (Senior Executive Service in 2003).

Sources: Data for Australia from APSC (2004–5); for Canada from PSHRMA (2003–4); for EU Countries and Norway from EU (2006); for the USA from USOPM (2004: 73).

allow candidates to bring issues to the attention of all citizens, who constitute a single constituency. This affords a valuable opportunity for communication on the part of those who cannot realistically expect to succeed. Candidates with a message emerge from outside the dominant party structures. Whilst all took rather small shares of the vote, three of the four female candidates in the 2002 elections used their marginality as an argument in the campaign and made it clear that their experience allowed them to represent a plurality of identities (Footitt 2002: 229). They also sought to reach their voters through less conventional modes of communication. The fourth female candidate was Arlette Laguiller, the veteran campaigner for the Trotskyite Left Party *Lutte Ouvrière* (Workers' Struggle), whose popularity may owe something to her gender as well as to her perseverance (she has been a candidate in every presidential election since 1974) but whose campaigns are firmly based on the theme of anti-capitalist class struggle.

The importance of stereotypes and expectations makes the pioneering appointments of women to leading positions particularly important. Once a model exists it becomes more possible for a woman to fit into a particular role. This explains the significance of US President Bill Clinton's appointments of Janet Reno as Attorney General and Madeleine Albright as Secretary of State. These two tough, competent and determined women facilitated the ability of elites, media and the general public to 'fit' women into leading positions (Clift and Brazaitis 2000: 21). President George W. Bush's appointment of Dr Condoleezza Rice as national security advisor in 2001 and secretary of state in 2005 seemed to follow on more naturally, and press discussion of the possibility of one (or even two) female candidates as front runners for the presidency in 2008 became more serious, more realistic and less flippant.

A second factor is status and attribution of competence. 'There may be truth in the contention that women have to prove clearly that they are successful whereas the men are assumed to be successful until they definitely demonstrate that they are failures' (civil servant quoted in Fogarty, Allen and Walters 1981: 44; see also Glen and Sarkees 2001: 123). Status characteristics theory suggests 'attributes differentiating group members become the basis of ability expectations, even when the attributes bear no obvious relation to the task on which the group is working'. Those who are high in the status hierarchy have their performance assessed more favourably. So men benefit compared to women on the basis of their gender, and white women compared to black women on the basis of their ethnicity. 'Women are evaluated as being less effective leaders, and in many situations they are held to higher performance standards than are men' (Lucas 2003: 464).

A third factor is background and experience: the Danish study (Højgaard 2002) showed that top female politicians came from higher status social backgrounds and had occupied higher status posts in their previous careers than top male politicians, as had top female civil servants who also had higher educational qualifications than their male counterparts. In other words, access conditions to leadership posts were harder for women than men. In many countries the holding of an elective position is a prerequisite for appointment to the political executive, which limits the opportunities to the (often small) category of women who have achieved election.

Patronage and context constitute a fourth factor: the political members of the executive are themselves usually appointed directly by the president (in the United States) or the prime minister, even if such choices may be affected by multiple complex constraints. For example, appointment as a minister may only be open to those who already have a substantial record in elected positions, or may (less frequently) be based upon more technocratic considerations. The formation of a coalition government is usually accompanied by negotiations between the parties involved about the distribution of portfolios. Gender balance may be a consideration in some cases. The paucity of other women in Mrs Thatcher's cabinets was much remarked upon. Gender balance as a gesture can backfire, however, as was the case when Alain Juppé, prime minister of France, appointed 12 women (29 per cent) to his government in 1995, only to sack eight of them six months later. In France a high proportion of the women who have served as ministers in the 1980s and 1990s (many of them with brilliant careers in the highly selective French educational system behind them) had been 'spotted' by the president or the prime minister. Apfelbaum and Hadley, on the basis of a number of interviews with such women, argue that, for as long as they are backed by their appointer, they enjoy the advantage that their decisions are unchallenged since they are legitimated by the higher authority (Apfelbaum and Hadley 1986). But, as Mariette Sineau argues, their lack of a solid political or electoral power base puts them in an ultimately precarious position (Sineau 1997: 53) for which specific technical competence is only a partial compensation (Sineau 2001: 174).

Merit as a basis for the attainment of a leadership position brings into question difficult considerations about the ways in which the criteria against which merit is judged may be determined. Many systems of selection, especially those with a strong procedural basis, are formally based upon notions of merit. '[N]aive causal explanations for success and failure in achievement situations are different for men than for women. A man's successful achievement on a task is generally attributed to ability, whereas a woman's success on the same task is explained by luck or effort. However, failure on a task by men is attributed to bad luck and failure by women to low ability' (Kruse and Wintermantel 1986: 186). Moreover, bureaucratic processes (see below) are double-edged for women. Those who adopt a non-masculine style may measure up poorly against hard, abstract, assertive criteria, whilst those 'who are cynics, disinterested or do not have a "caring" style' may equally be disadvantaged by their failure to conform to a 'romanticised' image of the caring, sharing, teamworking female leader (Still 2006: 187).

Another way in which leading political positions are in some cases obtained is also based upon the notion of the competitive and comparative assessment of merit. Whilst selection by procedure or patronage is the norm for most leading positions, a number of political positions differ from that norm because they are filled by an electoral process. This is the case for the selection of United States presidential candidates through primary elections (see Box 6.2). Leaders of political parties or of trade unions may be designated by some form of voting by the membership. It was in-party electoral systems that brought both Margaret Thatcher and Angela Merkel to the leadership of their parties. While both already had governmental experience, neither was at the time notably prominent within their party. It can be suggested that both of them, as well as the first female prime minister of New Zealand, Jenny Shipley, conform to a pattern of women coming to political leadership within political contexts which, for their parties at the time, were markedly difficult. Equally Kim Campbell, Canadian prime minister in 1993, was elected to the leadership of the Conservative Party and consequently became prime minister at a point when the party's reputation had been damaged by scandals while '[i]n Australia too, there have only ever been two women state premiers (Joan Kirner in Victoria and Carmen Lawrence in Western Australia). Both were appointed mid-term and after their party had been exposed to humiliating scandals. As a result, both faced the prospect of unwinnable elections which they duly lost' (Ryan and Haslam 2005).

For women who succeed, through the mechanisms described above, in attaining elite political decision-making positions, there are important factors which shape the ways in which they are able to operate as a member of the elite, and it is to those that this chapter now turns.

Box 6.2   Women in United States Presidential Elections

Running for president

- In the 19th century two women ran for president on the Equal Rights Party ticket: Victoria Woodhull in 1872 and Belva Lockwood in 1884 and 1888.
- In 1964 Senator Margaret Chase Smith had her name placed in nomination for president at the Republican national convention.
- In 1972, Representative Shirley Chisholm ran for the Democrats presidential nomination in the Democrats primaries.
- In 2000 Elizabeth Dole, who had served as US Secretary of Labour, US Secretary of Transportation, Federal Trade Commissioner and president of the American Red Cross, ran for the Republican presidential nomination. After failing to attract sufficient early support, she withdrew from the race.
- In 2004 Ambassador Carol Moseley Braun sought the Democrats presidential nomination. She had been the first African American woman to be a Democrat senator. She withdrew from the race before the first binding primaries.
- In January 2007 Senator Hillary Rodham Clinton announced that she was a candidate for the Democrats' presidential nomination. She had been First Lady from 1993 to January 2001 and Democrat senator for New York state since January 2001.

Running for vice president

- In 1972 Frances (Sissy) Farenthold finished second in the balloting for the Democrats' Vice Presidential nomination.
- In 1984 Representative Geraldine A. Ferraro became the first woman ever to run on a major party's national ticket as Walter F. Mondale's Vice Presidential running mate.

Source: Center for American Women and Politics (2005b).

Conditions for the Exercise of Decision-making Power

Studies of women in top decision-making positions have concentrated upon women in managerial positions in industry and commerce. The considerations which apply to these positions, however, also apply to women in policy-related decision-making positions, in public services and political parties. Decision-making power is exercised under certain conditions, and several crucial factors – context, time, style and the attribution of responsibilities – are explored below.

Context: The bureaucratic nature of elite institutions

An institution is usually defined as a combination of structures, procedures and routines within which individuals operate. Institutions thus
shape both what people do and how they think about what they do. They
set the boundaries for what action is possible, and equally for what individuals can envisage as possible (Marchbank 2005: 17). In western societies the institutions which incorporate elite decision-making positions
are all, to some degree, bureaucratic. A century ago Robert Michels
(Michels 1958: 353 and 333–6) demonstrated how organisations which
specifically repudiate bureaucratic forms (in his case a socialist political
party) may nevertheless end up rigid, routinised and hierarchical. In
describing institutions – governments, civil services, political parties,
trade unions, large companies – as bureaucratic, I am focusing on the
aspects which Max Weber isolated as being characteristic of bureaucracy
(Bendix 1994: 424–30). These are that they are based on principles of
settled procedure, of rational decision-making, of technical competence,
of recruitment and careers based upon specified and transparent criteria,
of even-handedness in decision-making (so that like cases always
produce identical outcomes) and of internal hierarchy and obedience,
with adherence to the norms of the institution overriding personal attachment and loyalty. Weber was specifying an abstract template – an ideal
type – by which the existence of a bureaucracy could be detected. The
development of the bureaucratic form, which embodies a rational-legal
concept of authority, can be seen as a key characteristic of the emergence
of a modern form of social organisation.

The development of bureaucratic forms has indeed been an important
feature of the structuring of democratic societies. They provide an efficient way of managing large organisations. They allow for transparency,
predictability and the reduction of decisions based on personal whim or
bias. Organisations can be held to account for their decisions, by their
members, their shareholders, or by the general population through their
representatives in democratic bodies. Moreover, when principles of hierarchy and obedience have been internalised within them, political and
business leaders can be reasonably confident that their instructions will
be carried out.

There are two perspectives on the impact of bureaucratization on the
position of women and their ability to exercise power. The first, liberal,
perspective emphasises the premium placed by modern bureaucratic
organisations on equality. Bureaucratic arrangements require indiffer-
ence between – that is, equal treatment of – all individuals, through the

use of rational, abstract objective criteria. Provided that the criteria are correctly applied, any differences between the average position of men and women within an organisation will be an outcome of their merit and their choices, not a shortcoming of the organisation. In so far as short-comings persist they will result from a legacy of outdated unjustified prejudices, which forward-looking organisations will seek to eradicate. Those who emphasise the need for equality and for dealing with each individual on her or his merits may not see this as incompatible with arguments for diversity; much depends upon the way in which the 'objective' criteria are framed. If companies believe the 'research from America, Britain and Scandinavia' which shows 'a strong correlation between shareholder returns and the proportion of women in higher executive echelons' (*The Economist*, 23 July 2005), they will ensure that their appointment criteria reflect this.

An alternative strand of argument looks at bureaucracy from the point of view not of equality but of gender difference, and suggests that bureaucratic structures are unfriendly towards women. Ferguson's influential and radical theoretical work in the early 1980s argued that feminist analysis should link 'the feminist critique of male dominance to a larger set of criticisms of all power relations, including those manifested in administrative hierarchies' (Ferguson 1984: 122). The issues arise from two key premises about the underlying principles and ideologies which bureaucratic structures are taken to embody. The first is that the underlying principles of bureaucratic organisations are rationality (Ross-Smith and Kornberger 2004: 282), abstract evaluation of problems and solutions and 'a morality of rights and rules' (Gilligan 1982: 73). The second premise is that this is not how most women think or operate. '[C]ulturally feminine characteristics do not fit the Weberian model of bureaucratic organisation.' Gilligan states that her psychological studies of women's responses to situations have shown empirically that they tend to concentrate on the morality of interdependence and issues of relationships, which bureaucratic procedures cannot handle.

This leaves open the theoretical dilemma of whether bureaucracies are so inherently gendered as masculine-dominated structures that women cannot – and possibly would not want to – have an appropriate place within them, or whether public (if not private) sector organisations are characterised by 'a complex mix of administrative, professional and gender discourses' within which 'possibilities may exist for individual women actively to modify, challenge or resist conforming to the dominant, traditional gender-power relations' (Halford and Leonard 2001: 84–5; see also Maddock and Parkin 1993; Newman 1996: 28).

The work of Camilla Stivers (Stivers 1993) suggests that public administrations may be particularly marked by traditional gendered culture. She argues that in public administrations, 'commonsense notions . . . are deeply dependent on traditions which privilege men and the pursuits considered suitable for them' (p. 7). She suggests (p. 10) that 'As long as we go on viewing the enterprise of administration as genderless, women will continue to face their current Hobson's choice, which is either to adopt a masculine administrative identity or accept marginalisation in the bureaucratic hierarchy.' Moreover, the 'new public management' approaches, with their emphasis on merit, may have changed managerial cultures, but women will need to demonstrate that they can, in a competitive environment, perform just like the men. In Australia, some women have chosen to tackle these dilemmas by entering the administrative hierarchy on its current terms but doing so with an explicitly feminist approach (Chappell 2002; Eisenstein 1996; Yeatman 1990). Eisenstein (1996) coined the term 'femocrat' (see Box 9.3) to denominate 'a powerful woman within government administration with an ideological and political commitment to feminism.'

There are thus two possible approaches to the impact of bureaucratisation: one is the equality approach which advocates a more perfectly rational-legal structure to allow women to achieve top positions without hindrance from prejudice. In response, equality policy (see Chapter 9) places a strong emphasis on procedural equity and probity. However, since modern contexts, for example technical innovation and globalisations are undermining the 'bureaucratic pattern of an orderly progression' (Kanter 1993: 305), this approach may be of limited value. The difference approach, however, suggests that only a wholesale rejection of the bureaucratic model will allow individuals to relate to power in effective and humane ways.

Leadership time

Lyon and Woodward suggest that society imposes a particular, gendered, model of 'leadership time' upon top professionals and politicians. Time can be envisaged as comprising two types: a 'masculine' public linear type that involves both one type of activity at any one point, and a rational and carefully organised deployment made possible only by a level of support that enables the manager to demonstrate freedom from private obligations, and a 'feminine', cyclical, multi-tasking and repetitive type. The 'Western and masculine time-frame . . . virtually presupposes a private social support system traditionally provided by female family

Table 6.2   'Leadership time' – average hours of work in employment across 27 industrialised countries

Category	Male	Female
Overall average	40	36
Business leaders	55.85	55.18
Political leaders	65.10	66.15

Source: Data from Woodward and Lyon 2000: 93. Data collected 1993–1995.

members' (Lyon and Woodward 2004: 91). However, they argue, on the basis of the very extensive 'gendering elites' survey carried out in 27 countries in the mid-1990s, that 'the leadership time of a politician is different from that of a business leader' (Lyon and Woodward 2004: 91). The 'myth of the heroic leader', to which both the men and women in the gendering elites survey appeared to subscribe, requires the leader to operate within the 'masculine' model, and to be reliably consistently available to undertake leadership duties (Woodward and Lyon 2000: 98). This requirement is particularly demanding for politicians, since they need to be available not only (and especially if they are ministers) to their officials, but also to their political and/or legislative organisation, to their constituents or those they represent, and for representational, media and networking opportunities. Many of these requirements (for example, constituency duties) necessarily occur during the 'private' time of their interlocutors. This may help to explain the longer hours worked on average by elite politicians (see Table 6.2). Despite this, the survey found that they did not regard it as particularly onerous. British prime minister Margaret Thatcher notoriously prided herself on her stamina and her ability to manage with rather few hours of sleep a night. Woodward and Lyon suggest that both men and women are socialised into accepting the demanding nature of 'leadership time', not least since very heavy workloads serve as an indicator of status.

Nevertheless, leadership time poses problems especially for those who cannot rely on the 'affective' support of family members. Paid-for support tends (like all employment) to operate on an essentially 'linear' basis. Moreover, female politicians can be caught in a 'double bind': it will not assist their image or their career if they can be accused of neglecting their children (Woodward and Lyon 2000). Female ministers like British minister Margaret Beckett with a spouse occupied full-time in supporting her are rare indeed (Diem-Wille and Ziegler 2000: 171)

Box 6.3   A Minister and Her Child

Frédérique Bredin, minister for youth and sports in the French cabinet in 1992, recalls, in her memoirs of the period, an occasion when she was attending a very formal meeting chaired by the prime minister about an urgent and controversial matter. A note was brought in to her, but in the face of the prime minister's obvious disapproval of the interruption she did not dare open and read it. At the conclusion of the meeting, at eight o'clock that evening, she phoned her office to let them know the outcome. Her secretary enquired anxiously whether she had received the message. Her son's head teacher had phoned to say no one had collected the little boy and the teacher had taken him home with her, since the only alternative would have been to take him to the police station. It later transpired that the au pair girl, who should have picked him up, had been suddenly stricken with homesickness and departed with no warning or word to anyone.

Mme Bredin, feeling desperately guilty, rushed to collect her four year old from his head teacher, who clearly did not think much of a mother who could forget her child. But, she remarks, 'only when the initial emotion had subsided did it occur to me – no one, not the head teacher, not my secretary, not even I myself – had thought to phone my husband' (Bredin 1997: 29, translation by author).

and there is no cultural expectation that male spouses will provide support, as French minister Frédérique Bredin once discovered (see Box 6.3).

The demands of leadership time weigh equally upon men and women, but have tended to act as a particular disincentive to women. Whether women's choices about employment in senior positions are genuine free choices expressing personal and rational preferences (Hakim 2004) or heavily constrained by gendered structural and social pressures remains a matter of controversy. Empirically, however, situations like that found in the European Commission – a champion of equal opportunities legislation, see Chapter 9 – where there is a marked dearth of women in decision-making positions, are not uncommon. Women who might be suitable for the positions are not coming forward so that in 2005 only just over 15 per cent of all candidates for the most senior posts were women and there were no female candidates at all for 15 senior level posts. There is agreement that the long hours and late meetings culture of the Commission plays a significant deterrent role (Levy and Stevens 2006; *European Voice*, 20 April 2006).

Styles of leadership

The debate in relation to women in management tends to revolve around management style and priorities. Again, there is in this area a version of the equality/difference debate.

One approach to women as leaders has been characterised as the 'women do lead differently' approach (Stanford, Oates and Flores 1995: 10). It is asserted that women in general possess particular skills in communication, interpersonal relationships and negotiation and conflict resolution (Collins and Singh 2006: 14). 'Some theorists also attribute to women leaders the rare ability to create easily a strong *esprit de corps*' (Stanford, Oates and Flores 1995: 10). These, as compared with what are taken to be the male qualities of self assertion, independence, control, and competition, are characteristics which may be valued in subordinates but not, when displayed by women, as leadership qualities (Alimo-Metcalfe 1995: 8). Essentialists assume that differences are innate. Others argue that women and men are socialised by family, social and media pressures and by differences in their experiences into differing reactions and styles.

A second approach to leadership by women finds little or no difference in leadership styles. A number of studies have suggested that variations amongst men and amongst women may be as great as those between them. For example women who become leaders may, to a greater extent than those who do not, exhibit behaviours (thinking strategically and taking risks) that are also notable amongst men who are leaders (Collins and Singh 2006: 15; Oshagbemi and Gill 2003). Two leading American journalists, exploring the likelihood of a female president of the United States, suggested that the first female president was likely to have 'the body of a woman but the character traits of a man'. Amongst the leading American women politicians they interviewed they found a general view that the actions of British prime minister Margaret Thatcher during the Falklands war had made a marked difference to the perception of women leaders: she 'did a great thing for women leaders' – it can no longer be said that women leaders cannot be tough (Clift and Brazaitis 2000: 21). Finally, a third approach is to dismiss the debate as irrelevant. What matters is effectiveness, not style. This approach is borne out by the results of the 'gendering elites' study, where there was found to be no statistical difference between men and women leaders in their perceptions of the extent to which they were able actually to exercise power (Vianello 2000: 144).

Media and public image

Leading decision-makers exercise their responsibilities under fierce scrutiny from the media. For this reason the manipulation and control of public image has become a concern of all leaders. Especially in relation to electoral candidates and political leaders, the general public wants information quickly and relatively effortlessly and cheaply. Labels and cues which package information on the basis of beliefs which people already hold fulfil this need. Partisan labels are an obvious example: ordinary people in Germany or the USA or the UK think they know what a Christian Democrat, or a Republican or a Conservative, will think and do. But other cues are used as well. These include physical attractiveness; the late Robin Cook, a leading Scottish politician, ruefully acknowledged that his appearance prevented him from aspiring to become prime minister (*The Telegraph*, 8 August 2005). Other clues are voice or – and this is one of the easiest cues to pick up – sex. Gender stereotypes and naive evaluations tend to lead people to the view that they know how any individual man or woman will behave.

Both men and women leaders seek to exploit, but also suffer from, the ways in which images convey messages through their references and relationships to stereotypes, to other images, to myths and archetypes. Gender is an inescapable element in any portrayal of a person, so gender stereotypes are frequently invoked. Some images may deliberately set out to subvert them, as in the case of the presentation, in both word and graphics, of Margaret Thatcher as the 'iron lady', an image which she sometimes deliberately called upon, for example in the much-quoted sound bite of her speech to her party on 10 October 1980 – 'You turn if you want to. The lady's not for turning' – with its pun on U-turn and its reference to the Soviet characterisation of her as the 'iron lady' and to the title of a 1950s' verse drama by Christopher Fry, *The Lady's Not for Burning*. But Mrs Thatcher was equally inclined to exploit gender stereotypes, for example in her self-presentation as overseeing the affairs of the nation with simple and prudent economy as a housewife should run her household.

An extensive survey of English language sources over a twenty-year period covering ten women prime ministers and presidents matched against their male successors or predecessors found that on average women received less coverage – were less visible within the media – than their male counterparts. Contrary to expectations, however, there were rather few comments on the women's personal characteristics. Nor were they portrayed in stereotypical terms; the image was of women who were 'ambitious, effective' and 'often more confrontational than their rivals' (Norris 1997d: 159). Media coverage operates within specific frames, that is, structures that provide contextual cues and guide the selection, presentation and reception of the material (Norris 1997c: 2). The coverage of women leaders often frames them as 'the first' woman to occupy a particular position or undertake a certain function. This frame may present the woman not only as ambitious and effective but also as an admirable pioneer. But equally, as in the case of Elizabeth Dole, portrayed as the 'the first credible woman candidate', it tends to emphasise that the woman is 'a novelty, an anomaly', deviating from familiar patterns (Heldman, Olson and Carroll 2000: 8).

Moreover, Norris's findings in relation to a few exceptional leaders have not been borne out in other studies of leaders and candidates for leadership at slightly less exalted levels. American studies found that the print journalists devoted notably more attention to the personal lives, appearances and personalities of women than of men. This coverage can disadvantage women. The 'demeaning and personal' comments on Elizabeth Dole during her nomination bid 'would probably not be used when describing male candidates for the highest office in the land' (Heldman, Olson, and Carroll 2000: 2 and 13).

Nevertheless in the United States social pressures have increasingly inhibited downright sexism (though not the subtle 'symbolic sexism' that may still influence media reporting; Heldman, Olson and Carroll 2000: 13) whereas, for example, in France the culture still tends to a greater extent to 'condone male ribaldry and the denigration of women' (Allison 2000: 68). Several French political leaders, such as Elisabeth Guigou and Ségolène Royal, have noted the extent to which a female electoral candidate in France has to put up with insulting obscenities (Sineau 1997: 55). The short term in office of Edith Cresson, the first French female prime minister, was accompanied by a campaign of denigration that was both personal and political. Her appointment produced 'violently misogynistic reactions in the politico-mediatic world' with the persistent implication that she owed her position 'not to her political qualities but to the "intimate" relationship she was alleged to have had in the past with the president' (Jenson and Sineau 1995: 334). Unfortunately, the searing experience of this malignant witch-hunt resulted in Cresson's dismissal of accusations against her behaviour as a European Commissioner as simply further manifestations of the same prejudice. Her failure to take them seriously was one of the main causes of the resignation of the European Commission in 1999.

Trivialisation is a form of 'symbolic sexism' and another possible pitfall for female politicians: the 12 female ministers in the government of the French prime minister Alain Juppé in 1995 were rapidly labelled *les juppettes*, a pun on his name which translates as 'bits of skirt'. A press photograph of the British prime minister Tony Blair surrounded by most of the Labour women members of parliament elected in the female land-slide of 1997 produced the denigratory nickname 'Blair's babes' (Sones 2005: Chapter 7), while the decision by the female ministers who consti-tute half of José-Luis Zapatero's Socialist government in Spain to pose for a group photograph in the fashion magazine *Vogue* in August 2004 to model Spanish-designed garments could also be taken as reflecting poorly on their seriousness and credibility (*The Guardian*, 20 August 2004).

Assignment of responsibilities

The ways in which women can operate within the elite is also conditioned by the types of responsibilities that they are likely to undertake. In busi-ness, even those women who do make it to managerial level tend to be positioned in areas such as human resources or marketing and not in the more prominent and lucrative areas such as finance or production (Davidson and Burke 2000: 2).

Analogous situations abound in political life. And despite the differ-ence in their size and in their political structures, some of the major west-ern countries show marked similarities. A comparison of the United States, the United Kingdom and France reveals that at the time of writing (2006) thirty women have held cabinet or cabinet-level rank in the United States, in France twenty-six, while in the United Kingdom only twenty-two women have ever held cabinet rank, over half (thirteen) of them under Tony Blair since 1997. The shortfall in the United Kingdom may in part be accounted for by the British convention that a minister shall have served an apprenticeship – often a lengthy one – as a member of parlia-ment. The United States and France possess a potentially larger pool since members of the government may be appointed from outside the legislature.

In all three countries, the first women reached governmental level before the Second World War, although in France, where women did not have the vote, they did so only as junior ministers. But the pioneers were very few, and in all three countries almost no progress was made after the Second World War until the mid-1970s (see Box 6.4). Since 1975 there has been no year without a woman in a cabinet-level post in the United States (Center for American Women and Politics 2006a), and there have regularly been female ministers in France since the appointment of

Box 6.4   United States, United Kingdom and France: Women in Government: the Pioneers

The first of these three countries to appoint a woman at cabinet level was the United Kingdom, where Margaret Bondfield became minister of labour from 1929 to 1931. In the Labour government of 1924 she had already been a junior minister (parliamentary secretary). The Conservative government between 1924 and 1929 also had a woman as a parliamentary secretary, the Duchess of Atholl MP. There were four more female junior ministers before 1945. Both Margaret Bondfield and Ellen Wilkinson, who was secretary of state for education in 1945–7, died in office. Ellen Wilkinson (Labour) and Florence Horsbrugh (Conservative) both served quite briefly as secretary of state for education during the 1940s and 1950s, as did Margaret Thatcher in the early 1970s. Barbara Castle was in the cabinet throughout Harold Wilson's terms of office in the 1960s and 1970s, and in 1968 she was joined by Judith Hart. Wilson's successor in 1976 (Jim Callaghan) did not appoint any women.

The first woman to serve at cabinet level in the United States was Frances Harris, Secretary for Labor from 1933 to 1945, followed between 1953 and 1955 by Oveta Culp Hobby as secretary for health, education and welfare. No further female cabinet appointment occurred until 1975.

In France women were appointed to ministerial (though not cabinet-level) posts before they were awarded the vote or could become members of parliament, though with a bias towards posts that were regarded as suitable for their gender. In 1936 the Popular Front government under Leon Blum briefly included three women, Suzanne Lacore with responsibilities for child protection in the ministry of health, Cécile Brunsschvig, responsible for welfare in the Ministry of Education and, for a few months, Irène Joliot Curie, herself a Nobel prize winner for chemistry and daughter of the Nobel prize-winning physicist Marie Curie, with responsibilities for research.

Under the post-war Fourth Republic, one woman, Andrée Viénot, briefly held a ministerial responsibility for youth and sport in 1945 and one held cabinet rank – Germaine Poinso-Chapuis, minister of health in 1947 (Duchen 1994: 53). Not until 1974 (Simone Veil, again as minister of health) was another woman appointed to the cabinet, not least because President de Gaulle (in office 1958–69) was notoriously opposed to appointing women either to his personal staff or to government. He thought they brought personal, emotional and sentimental factors into the cold hard business of dealing with the country's affairs and when his secretary-general (Chief of Staff) asked him to take a woman onto his staff he refused with some awkwardness, saying 'a woman, you know, it's never quite the same thing' (Sineau 2001: 30, fn 2). Only two women held ministerial office under him, in 'suitable' junior posts. Nafissa Sid-Cara, an Algerian Muslim woman who had been a member of parliament for Algiers looked after social affairs in Algeria until Algerian independence in 1962. De Gaulle was astonished when his prime minister Debré suggested her but was willing to go along with the suggestion (Sineau 1997: 47, fn 4). And from 1967 Marie-Madeleine Dienesch held ministerial responsibilities for education and then social affairs.

Simone Veil in 1974. However, like President de Gaulle in France (president 1959–69), Mrs Thatcher (UK prime minister 1979–90) was notoriously unwilling to have female colleagues in government and between prime minister Harold Wilson's resignation in 1976 and John Major's electoral victory in 1992 there was only one woman in the cabinet (Baroness Young in 1982–3).

In all three countries women were initially appointed particularly to posts for which their gender might be supposed to render them suitable, and in particular to responsibilities for labour (in the United States six women have been secretary for labor), education and health. Women continue to be assigned largely to roles in domestic and social affairs rather than to the 'high politics' areas of finance, diplomacy and defence, although with the appointments in the United States of Janet Reno as attorney general (1993–2001), of Madeleine Albright (1997–2001) and then Condoleezza Rice (2005) as secretary of state, in France Michèle Alliot-Marie (2002) as minister of defence, and in the United Kingdom Margaret Beckett (2006) as secretary of state for foreign affairs, precedents have been set.

Conclusion

This chapter has explored the dearth of women in top positions in political life, as political leaders, prime ministers, presidents, ministers and senior officials. It has considered the means by which women may achieve such positions, and the concomitant barriers that may exist, and the conditions under which leadership is exercised. It is important to note that achievement of such positions may place a particular burden upon women. They are likely to be pioneers, or at least distinctive by their relative rarity. Their mistakes will be conspicuous. For some the pressures will eventually become unsustainable. In men retreats from such positions are usually relatively unobtrusive. If a leading businesswoman decides 'to spend more time with her family' or, as in the case of Estelle Morris, British secretary of state for education, in October 2002, admits that she is stepping down because she feels unsuited to the requirements of the office, media comment often carries a sub-text of doubt as to whether any woman would really be suitable for such roles. As Joan Eveline observed:

> Anticipation of her capacities as change agent places a considerable
> burden on the pioneering woman whose token status can mean she

needs to keep proving herself in terms that fit with what Smith (Smith 1999) calls the 'ruling regime'. Unlike many of their male counterparts, few women at the top have the advantage of a wife at home . . . Yet the double burden for the woman leader exceeds the need to juggle public image, job management, household and family arrangements. 'The invisible job' is the pressure on the woman leader to position herself as a path-breaker for other women (Fletcher 1999). Yet the expectation, by both women and men, that the woman leader can always be relied upon to accomplish 'the invisible job' can prove wildly idealistic.   (Eveline 2005)

7

Feminism, Participation and Activism

This chapter turns to women's political participation and activity outside the formal structures of democratic institutions but within the public sphere of private life (see p. 24, Figure 2.1). As noted in the Introduction, the exercise of power, conflict and strategies for resolution exist and emerge not only within the formal systems and institutions of society but also in numerous other situations and events. Women, it is now increasingly recognised, participate extensively in society in political ways (Beckwith 2000: 431). Political participation involves action designed to articulate demands and 'trying to influence the processes of decision-making that ultimately have binding consequences for larger groups or even the whole of society' (Rucht 2006: 111). The notion of participation implies conscious action on the part of an individual person – an actor. Moreover, to be defined as participation, the action has to involve taking part in a collective endeavour: a dinner party as opposed to a solitary meal; a meeting for worship as opposed to private prayer. Given the size of the population of neighbourhoods, cities, states and indeed regional groupings such as the European Union – all levels at which decisions are made – the impact of any one actor, even in collective action, may be small. Political parties, as we have seen, deal with this by aggregating such voices within formal representational politics. However, there are many other forms of activism – not only elections, collective bargaining and formal lobbying but also petitions, letter-writing campaigns, consumer boycotts or demonstrations and similar unregulated activities – in many locations – not only polling stations or courtrooms but also playgrounds or streets. Moreover, there may be differences between campaigning for (or against) a bypass as against toppling a regime (as in Eastern Europe in 1989) or seeking a wholesale change in social structures and attitudes as feminists may seek to do.

Adopting Rucht's categories (Rucht 2006: 111; see also Inglehart and Norris 2003: 100), the discussion below looks at 'non-traditional' political activism: first at the feminist movement, then at institutionalised participation in the trade unions, and finally at non-institutionalised activism by women in politics.

The Feminist Movement

The terms 'women's movement' and 'feminism' or the 'feminist movement' are often used almost interchangeably. For analytical clarity they ought to be distinguished. In both cases we are talking of participation by women in collective activity through groups that are formed exclusively by and for women. Such groups constitute the 'women's movement', that is, women, consciously associating and taking action with other women – in 'community action, social movement and discursive struggles' (Beckwith 2000: 431). These are groups whose 'definition, content, leadership, development or issues are specific to women and their gender identity' (Banaszak, Beckwith and Rucht 2003: 2, fn 3; Beckwith 2000: 437). In other words they do what they do consciously as women. However, women's movement groups fall into two categories, which can be distinguished by their strategies and aims. Maxine Molyneux suggests that the division can be conceived as distinguishing between those groups that are concerned with practical gender interests, often arising from a perception of an immediate need but not challenging existing gender relationships, and those concerned with gender interests which challenge patterns of subordination and have strategic goals related to gender emancipation or equality (Molyneux 1986, cited in Nelson et al. 1994: 18). Groups of the first type can be characterised as 'feminine' (they are discussed below, see p. 164). The term 'feminist' is best confined to groups and activities of the second type. These groups are distinctive in their insistence on an analysis of modern society, states and state institutions as patriarchal, and their campaigning on a number of issues which they regard as fundamental to the reshaping of society in a non-patriarchal way.

First-wave feminism

The development of the feminist movement has been complex and the shape and meaning of its history contested. One widely held approach envisages it in terms of waves. A first wave of feminism developed in what are now the advanced industrial democracies as a reaction to the conditions for women that emerged as the industrial revolution pursued its course and as the implications of the French Revolution became obvious. The new patterns of work and economic relationships confirmed male dominance as did 'modern' legal systems (for example the Napoleonic codes) and habits and expectations of conduct, manners and respectability. In these circumstances movements for women's rights began. Women's organisations tended to develop first in religious and charitable areas: for example, although women were deliberately excluded from the organisations in Britain whose campaigning led to the abolition of the slave trade, in the 1820s they created their own groups to advocate the outlawing not merely of the commerce but of all slavery. It was their experience at the 1840 anti-slavery convention in London that motivated the early campaigners for women's suffrage in the USA. And out of such beginnings came demands for education for girls and women, for changes to their legal status, including reform of divorce and property laws, for rights to employment and indeed access to the professions. In the first half of the nineteenth century, such organisations were strongest in the USA. During the second half of the century, women's organisa-tions working for aspects of the emancipation of women became wide-spread in Europe too (Offen 1998, passim).

Differences in the social and political context in each country led to notable differences in the development of feminism. In some countries (Germany, Russia) class struggle played a prominent role in women's activism, and socialist feminists, working to improve women's position and conditions, believed that only the socialist revolution would produce the changes desired. There was thus considerable tension between two priorities, since feminist objectives were always seen as secondary to the advancement of the class struggle (Anderson and Zinsser 1990: 389). In this way the socialist feminism of the nineteenth century prefigured the dilemma of 'double militancy' and divided loyalties (including the tensions between loyalty to party and to feminist solidarity) that Beckwith defines as a central concern for the twenty-first century women's move-ment (Beckwith 2000: 442). In other countries, particularly the Nordic protestant countries and the United States, bourgeois liberal feminism was stronger. Nevertheless, by the 1880s the word 'feminist' had entered the vocabulary of many languages and 'the growth of a full-blown organised women's movement and the explosion of feminist publications in Western Europe between 1890 and 1914 constitute one of the most significant features of the political landscape' (Offen 1998: 347).

The achievements of this 'first wave' of the feminist movement in the years up to the outbreak of the First World War were very substantial in the fields of political and legal rights, of education, of access to employ-ment. But the huge trauma of a devastating war, of immense burdens of economic and social reconstruction and, in the 1930s, of recession, as well as the polarisation of politics with fascism and revolutionary social-ism at the two extremes, all deflected attention. Moreover 'the majority of politically active women of all nations . . . [between the wars] were not feminists and never had been' (Anderson and Zinsser 1990: 400). Women built on the achievements of the pre-First World War equal rights feminists, but not necessarily in ways which made further substan-tial changes to their social and political status.

The metaphor of waves invokes the notion of peaks and troughs, or even of a breaking and receding before the next wave. So, 'from the late 1920s until the end of the 1960s the women's movement appeared to be a spent political force' (Lovenduski 1986: 61). It is important, however, not to take the metaphor too literally and dramatically. While the political and social circumstances of the time meant that there were no equivalents to the spectacular campaigns of the suffrage movement, equal rights femi-nism continued to make advances, not without struggle. But not usually under a feminist label; the term was rejected as implying confrontation and aggression even by women who would happily have admitted to being in favour of women's rights and would probably fall into the category 'feminist' as defined above (Duchen 1994: 170). Elisabeth Selbert, a Socialist woman representative in the West German Parliamentary Council who, in 1947–8, was largely responsible for successfully mobilis-ing support for the inclusion in the German Constitution of the uncondi-tional statement that men and women have equal rights, said 'I have never been and never will be a feminist' (quoted in Kolinsky 1989: 45). Women gained the right to vote, and admission to training for the senior ranks of the administration in France in 1945, and while 'there may have been no legislation passed [in France] between 1945 and 1965 that specifically focussed on changing women's legal position, . . . there was plenty of discussion over women's "issues" and women's rights' albeit in a rather hostile context (Duchen 1994: 164). The outcomes included the founda-tion in 1956 of what became, in the 1960s, the Family Planning Movement and led, in 1967, to the reform of the law that since the 1920s had banned contraception, and also the 1965 reform of the marriage laws. In the UK in the 1930s, some women campaigned for the end of the marriage bar to employment. The Abortion Law Reform Association was founded in 1936, while female MP Eleanor Rathbone campaigned tirelessly for a system (eventually introduced in 1946) of family allowances to be paid directly to mothers. The campaign for equal pay in the public sector succeeded in the 1950s. Whilst in general the activism of the inter-war and immediate post-war decades falls, in the UK and Germany, for example, into the category of 'welfare' or 'reasonable' feminism (Lovenduski 1986: 72–3 and 101), there was no real ebbing of the tide and the trough was not as low as is sometimes implied (Freedman 2001: 4).

Second-wave feminism

During the 1960s something new emerged, of sufficient extent and intensity to be designated 'second-wave feminism'. The 1960s was a decade of contrasts. In Western Europe the post-war boom seemed, in the advanced industrial democracies, to have banished the pre-war spectres of unemployment and extreme poverty. Adequate housing was in short supply but material conditions for many households were steadily improving. In many countries the welfare state removed the worst anxieties around sickness and old age. In 1957 British prime minister Macmillan told a Conservative Party rally that 'most of our people have never had it so good', thus initiating a slogan that seemed to sum up a mood of confidence, indeed complacency.

Alongside this, however, was a sense, not always very loud but insistent, that things were not right. Young people, in particular, 'with their ideals unsullied by the compromises of hard times' reacted with 'disorganised rebellion' (Bouchier 1983: 51). More specifically, in the United States racial segregation and inequality was contested by the civil rights movement. In Britain, the Campaign for Nuclear Disarmament was protesting about British possession of nuclear weapons, and opposition to the Vietnam war was expressed through demonstrations and marches not only in the USA but also throughout Europe. There was an upsurge of radical leftist and Marxist political groupings. Women were extensively involved in all these actions.

For some women, participation in these anti-establishment, radical movements pointed up the difference between the roles and expectations of men and women even in such groups, and the extent to which their emancipatory discourse contrasted with the constrained realities of women's lives. They, and other women too, were also influenced by two hugely important books. The French philosopher Simone de Beauvoir had published *Le Deuxième Sexe* in 1949, an analytical and, some would argue, unsympathetic, but brilliantly insightful analysis of what it meant to become a woman. It was translated (though not well translated) into English in 1953 and appeared in an English paperback version in 1961. Betty Friedan's *The Feminine Mystique*, which diagnosed a 'problem that has no name', causing women to feel 'as if I don't exist', appeared in 1963 in the United States (Friedan 1965: 18).

Box 7.1　The Greenham Common Women

One of the sites for the deployment of United States Cruise missiles in
Europe was the US airbase at Greenham Common, in Berkshire in south-
east England. The missiles arrived in 1983 and, as a consequence of the
Intermediate Nuclear Forces Treaty of 1987, were removed between 1989
and 1991. In September 1981, 36 women, 4 men and several children
marched from South Wales to the base in protest and some women then
set up a permanent encampment, or rather constellation of campsites,
beside the perimeter fence. This became known as the Women's Peace
Camp (Fairhall 2006). The women used non-violent tactics to protest,
decorating the fence with flowers, needlework and children's clothes, and
attempting to block movement, especially of missiles, in and out. 'Those
prepared to be arrested would lie in the mud in the face of armoured
trucks. When the police pulled one woman from the ground another
would take her place' (*The Guardian*, 9 September 2006). They would cut
open the fence and enter the base. 'Ms Parker said the fine at the time for
trespassing on the base was £25, and so each time someone had a birthday,
their present from the rest of the women would be the £25 to enter the
base. "One woman had a roller skating birthday on the runway – another
went in on her birthday and laid lots of plastic yellow ducks on the
runway"' (BBC 1999). In December 1982 they organised an 'embrace the
base', forming a chain of 30,000 women joining hands around the nine-
mile perimeter fence, and some 50,000 were involved in a similar protest
in December 1983, when part of the fence was demolished and hundreds
were arrested. Participants recalled that it was 'an occasion of grief and

→

In the United States, women's liberation groups began to form from
1967 and in November 1969 a Congress to Unite Women in New York
issued ten demands encompassing equal opportunities, a cessation of
demeaning media images of women, the right to abortion and free 24-
hour childcare centres. The four demands issued by a British national
conference in Oxford in 1970 were not dissimilar: equal pay, equal
opportunities and education, free contraception and abortion on demand,
and free 24-hour childcare (Bouchier 1983: 94; Lovenduski 1986: 75).

The origins and trajectory of revivified feminism across the advanced
industrial democracies were markedly different in different countries. In
Britain the peace campaign, the anti-Vietnam campaign, the student and
radical far Left – in 1966 the New Left Review published Juliet
Mitchell's article, *The Longest Revolution* – industrial militancy by
women (especially the equal pay strike at the Ford plant in Dagenham in
1968) and the lobbying which led to the 1970 Equal Pay Act as well as

➜
triumph' (participant Catherine Taylor, *The Guardian*, 23 September 2006). 'The atmosphere was a mixture of euphoria and desperation. Even if we couldn't change anything we felt we had to do it anyway.' Another remembered the mud and the cold, but also the 'great feeling of solidarity – it was quite a joyous occasion' ('Embrace the base' participants quoted in the *Guardian*, 9 September 2006; see also Harford and Hopkins 1984).

While many women would come for a day or two, some stayed more or less permanently in the camp, in cold, damp and primitive conditions. Men were excluded from the camp and most of the demonstrations. Participants recall the camp as a feminist success: 'We also succeeded in fostering a women-only environment, where women learned that they didn't need to speak or act on men's terms' (Peace Camp participant quoted in BBC 1999).

Press reporting, especially by the more right-wing press, was almost uniformly hostile, if confused and contradictory: the women were '(1) despised for being smelly, flea-ridden and dirty; (2) insulted as . . . peace yobs, screaming harridans or weird lesbians; (3) laughed at for their weakness; (4) pitied as poor pathetic figures in the mud . . . as well as (5) feared and loathed for their brutality, perversion and violence' (Meinhof 1986: 157). Such reporting undoubtedly contributed to a distorted popular image of feminism as unnatural and repellent.

The base was handed back to the British Air Force in 1992 and ceased to be used as an airbase shortly thereafter. The Women's Peace Camp closed in 2000, though peace protests continue at the nuclear weapons research establishment at Aldermaston.

influences from abroad – from the USA and from the May 1968 events in Paris – all played a part. May 1968, when the students involved in the uprising called the whole social order into question and were joined by a general strike of the labour movement, saw the first appearance of new feminist groups in France (Lovenduski 1986: 94). Likewise in Italy, the new feminism began within and around the student movement. In all the new movements a key feature was the emergence of groups within whose intimacy women could share and analyse their personal experience of what it meant to be female in a gendered society. This technique of consciousness raising was a defining feature of the new feminism of the 1970s. And out of this new feminism came publications, women's centres and spaces, and political and campaigning networks (see Box 7.1).

Lovenduski stresses the importance of distinguishing between the established, traditional women's rights organisations, many with a long history and often quite formal and bureaucratic, and the new, less formal, more radical and usually non-hierarchical feminist 'women's liberation' groups, autonomous and 'more concerned to create alternatives than achiev[e] influence' (Lovenduski 1986: 63). This distinction reflects the two strategies which emerged for feminism: emancipatory strategies which emphasise the struggle for gender equality and liberation strategies which stress the need for society to recognise and provide space for gender differences.

Other commentators on the 1970s categorised feminism into three strands: liberal feminism, corresponding in large measure to traditional bourgeois equal rights feminism; socialist feminism, based within an essentially Marxist analysis of a double oppression, both capitalist and gendered; and radical feminism. This not only challenged the gendered structure of liberal democracies but also, without being anti-socialist, the primacy of class-based analysis. Radical feminism contributed the notion of patriarchy to feminist discourse, a notion which other forms of feminism have also adopted. For some radical feminists the only response to patriarchy, which they saw as based within constructs of the family, was the rejection of family (though not necessarily motherhood) and indeed of heterosexual partnerships altogether. But labels are not always helpful, since they tend to lump rather different approaches together under single headings, and at the same time introduce category boundaries between rather similar phenomena (Freedman 2001: 6).

One of the important developments within the feminist movement over the past three decades has been the realisation that the early second-wave feminists tended to view the world through the lenses of white middle-class educated women in the developed world, while in fact most women are not like that. Race, ethnicity, class, sexual orientation and political context (women under state socialism before 1989 simply could not react in the same way as western women (Lovenduski 1986: 63) even if silence did not necessarily imply consent (Nelson et al. 1994: 46)) all condition women's immensely varied responses to the question 'what must be done to make the world a good place for all people, including all women?' Within feminist debate and theorising, the question of what is called 'intersectionality' – that is, the various factors which differentiate women between themselves – has become an increasingly prominent topic.

The feminist movement today

During the 1970s, the feminist movement – which was often rather derisively described as 'women's lib' – in many western countries seemed relatively identifiable, and even cohesive. Whilst the difficulties involved in separating out the effect of social movement organisations from other factors in explaining change are considerable, it can be argued that at least in certain countries, for example Spain, the groups have had an impact in changing the climate and indeed contents of policy-making (Valiente 2003: 31). '[W]omen's movements activities over the [1970s] led to increasingly sympathetic public opinion toward some of the less revolutionary demands of the women's movement' (Banaszak, Beckwith, and Rucht 2003: 20) and across Western Europe it was possible to point to a number of political and policy successes in increased rights for women – the vote in Switzerland in 1971, and in several western countries reforms in the regulation of contraception, abortion, divorce and employment conditions.

The feminist movement (often conflated with the women's movement as a whole) can be characterised as a social movement, which one analysis sees as 'emerg[ing] when a potential constituency can claim sufficient legitimacy to express its claims but is alienated enough to be unable to win much without making a tremendous fuss' (Meyer 2003: 277; see also Nash 2002: 316). An alternative analysis (Melucci 1996; Nash 2002: 320) characterises a movement as

- possessing a specific solidarity;
- in conflict against a specific adversary;
- disrupting social norms for action.

This analysis, paying particular attention to the way the movement has developed in Italy and France, tends to suggest that the adversary in question may be patriarchy or even men in general. This is consistent with the strands of feminist philosophy that have developed strongly in France and Italy and that emphasise notions of female specificity and difference in intellectual, linguistic and cultural terms. And everywhere feminists' identification of patriarchy as the entity to which they are opposed has frequently been simplified into a determination to act as women and against men, who are assumed not to wish to give up the dominance which patriarchy has afforded them.

These analyses help to identify and explain the movement of the 1970s, but can also be used to chart what is taken to be the disappearance, or at least sharp decline, of the movement by the end of the century: 'increased public acceptance and links to other political allies made women's movements in many countries large, diverse and multi-layered . . . in some cases this meant that women's movements became so highly fragmented that they . . . jeopardized their ability to act strategically'

(Banaszak, Beckwith and Rucht 2003: 21). Thus it can be argued that the emphasis on intersectionality and on differences between women, and the growing tendency to act within or at least in alliance with, sympathetic men and institutions (for example, political parties) to further women's interests, have led to a fragmentation of the movement. Feminism becomes a pressure group like any other (Melucci 1996: Chapter 7, cited in Nash 2002: 321). Others disagree: while recognising the continuing existence of different 'clusters' or 'configurations' within the movement – the liberal, socialist and radical tendencies identified above – they argue that what characterises the movement is decentralisation and cultural diversity, not fragmentation, and this has made possible resilience, adaptability and structural flexibility in responding to changing contexts (Mueller and McCarthy 2003: 220 and 240–1).

At the start of the twenty-first century, there is then a real debate about the nature of the contemporary feminist movement and its political role. A number of conclusions can however be drawn. First, the very real achievements of feminist women should not be undervalued or taken for granted. The extent to which policies of which feminists approve have been implemented varies and most feminists would claim that no country has yet achieved all it could or should, but the advances made since the beginning of 'second-wave' feminism have undoubtedly been significant and substantial. Citizenship and employment rights (see Chapters 2 and 9) have been the subject of long campaigns and witnessed some advances. All the countries with which this study is concerned have moved forward markedly in some of the areas which feminists have prioritised, amongst them rights to control their sexuality and reproduction (including access to abortion and contraception), equal employment policy (see Chapter 9), liberalised divorce provision, repression of domestic violence and support for its survivors (Banaszak 2003a: 141). Developments in access to representative institutions have been discussed in Chapters 4 and 5.

There have been instances of retreat or withdrawal in the position of women, especially in Central and Eastern Europe, where they can be ascribed to the difficult necessity to fashion, within the context of transition and democratisation, a genuine and well-founded set of relationships between the three spheres shown in Figure 2.1. In these post-Communist countries, women have largely rejected 'feminism' as it is understood in the West, and the resurgence of conservative nationalistic and religious values has, in areas such as reproductive (abortion) and employment rights (access to childcare), produced a climate with 'a distinctly regressive character' (Molyneux 1996: 248). But this climate comes into conflict with the desire of the states concerned to be perceived as 'modern'. It is one of the achievements of feminists that the concept of a 'modern' state now automatically entails an enhanced status for women, acceptance of the United Nations Convention on the Elimination of All Forms of Discrimination against Women (CEDAW), and for those countries aspiring to membership of the European Union, of the EU's position on the rights and status of women (see Chapter 9 and Molyneux 1996: 254). Both the UN and EU positions are products of campaigning by feminists.

Second, in the West as in Eastern Europe the advances are not inexorable or irreversible. Maybe 'women have been most successful in gaining access to institutions with little power over policy matters' (Meyer 2003: 294) and moreover, as in the United States, it may also be that middle-class women have been the main gainers and poor women have lost out (Katzenstein 2003: 216). A neo-liberal agenda in many countries has resulted in some of the responsibilities for welfare and mitigating economic inequalities which states had taken on being transferred to the economic market or non-elected bodies. Such off-loading frequently means that the burdens of caring are shouldered within families by women who find their economic and social status and opportunities constrained thereby (Banaszak 2003: 1 and 6; Bashevkin 1998; Einhorn 2006: 154). As states reconfigure in a globalising world, and as the globalised political context changes too, women's groups and feminist movements require ongoing vigilance to ensure that what is so readily taken for granted is not diminished or driven back.

Third, the notion of 'women's liberation' has almost entirely disappeared from political discourse, even if emancipatory political projects persist. And the label 'feminist' in its general usage (as contrasted with the specific meaning given to it above) has become an ambivalent one (Budgeon 2001: 23). It is rejected in some countries – as in much of Central and Eastern Europe, but also in France (Ezekiel 2002) – as alien and alienating, 'American' and signifying opposition to a natural, harmonious, not to say seductive, relationship between the sexes. Elsewhere there is talk of 'post-feminism' – an attitude which both suggests that equality has been achieved and also alleges that this equality was in fact a poisoned chalice because it creates the mirage that 'having it all' is possible and produces unhappiness when the promised water turns out to be sand (Budgeon 2001: 13). What it meant to be feminist several decades ago is no longer relevant, it is argued, and moreover feminism carried with it cultural expectations and codes of conduct to which women will no longer subscribe.

'Second-wave feminism' may thus have been absorbed into the eddies and flows of a more confused new century. On the one hand, it has increasingly been 'mainstreamed' not only into political institutions and policy arenas but also into the everyday existence of many women, especially younger women. They may recognise that the changes that would transform society may not have occurred, but they do not question that they should, even if they may in most circumstances expect this to occur through individual rather than collective action. The sixteen and seventeen year olds whom Shelley Budgeon interviewed at the end of the twentieth century felt that individual women should stop listening to the voices in society that told them what they could not do, but argue and insist that they should and would do as they want (Budgeon 2001: 16). Divergences amongst women's groups, stemming from race, ethnicity, sexuality, age, professional speciality or class have weakened perceptions of solidarity. Another divergence runs between insider groups – even individuals – and outsiders, who because of poverty, or status within the state (illegal migrants in the United States, for example, or refugees) or radical or revolutionary ideology, lack the access and resources with which to defend and advance themselves. On the other hand there are still a very large number of situations in which women come together as women to pursue their own personal professional and political interests. The argument that the women's movement no longer exists as a movement is a largely semantic one, highly dependent upon definitions of the term. But that argument should not obscure recognition of the multiple and numerous ways in which the individual and collective actions of women continue to affect, shape and determine the nature and structure of states, polities and localities, and hence of society.

Institutionalised Activism in Civil Society: Women and Trade Unions

Women's activism can occur through participation in the many institutionalised groups outside the formal systems of representative politics. These include trade unions and professional associations and employers' organisations. The main reason for the existence of unions is the undertaking of collective bargaining on behalf of the members. In some countries, even if unions are, as in the UK, linked to one of the political parties, they largely confine their role to the pursuit of their members' material interests. In other advanced industrial countries, functional representation through unions and employers' groups can play as strong a role in certain areas of policy-making as geographical representation. In Scandinavia 'it is powerful [interest] organizations and institutions rather than voters that have become the central gatekeepers in the Scandinavian state system' (Hernes 1992: 76) and these have not been particularly 'women-friendly'. Elsewhere, too, trade unions and employers may jointly run large areas of welfare provision, as in France.

Trade unions may be more or less fragmented, for example by divisions between crafts and skills, although recent trends are towards a lessening of fragmentation, and, for example, unions in Germany have, since their post-war reconstruction, been organised on an industry basis. In countries more marked by a syndicalist tradition (that is, the belief that the working class needed to conquer political power if it were to achieve the amelioration of its conditions), the unions may have general ideological political programmes as well as specific industrial objectives. In such countries, for example France and Italy, the labour movement is divided into competing union federations along largely ideological lines. In these countries the distinction between union and political activity is particularly blurred (Allwood and Wadia 2000: 84).

The extent of female unionism

Their long history and strong institutionalisation turned unions into highly structured organisations. This tendency has been encouraged by the proclivity of states to regulate what may be seen as dangerously conflictual organisations, for example by enforcing secret balloting for leadership positions. The outcome has been bureaucratic, rather formal, hierarchical, rather rigid structures, with in many cases a strongly masculinist ethos. As unions organised during the nineteenth century, many of them excluded women and indeed regarded women workers with hostility since their lower pay undercut male rates. In the early years of the twentieth century, 'the Trade Union movement [in the United Kingdom] was divided in its attitude to women workers and divided within itself' (Boston 1987: 88). In France between the wars, 'much union effort had been directed to keeping [women] out [of employment] . . . Where women were no threat, on the other hand, they were tolerated but no great effort was made to attract them into the unions' (Reynolds 1996: 119)

Where unions did admit women, there was usually a strong insistence on gender segregation in employment and there were very few women in organiser and executive positions even in the UK textile unions where 'women had in some cases been founder members of unions' (Boston

1987: 74). Men's opposition to women, and particularly to equal pay, led in some cases to the foundation of separatist unions, for example in the United Kingdom the National Union of Women Teachers. Eventually (see Chapter 9) the labour movement came rather slowly and reluctantly to support the principle of equal pay, and as the proportion of women in the workforce has increased, so also, despite a somewhat uncongenial environment, have levels of union membership by women (see Figure 7.1), though not in proportion to their representation within the workforce. At least in part, this can be explained by the concentration of many women in sectors where the rates of unionisation have traditionally been low (Garcia and Dumont 2003: 22).

In general, however, the end of the last century and the start of the new one has been marked simultaneously by declining levels of general unionisation – in 19 out of 24 advanced industrial countries studied by Visser union density declined between 1970 and 2003, across the EU, for example, by over eleven percentage points (Visser 2006: 44–5) – and a rising proportion of female membership.

The historic hostility of many male-dominated unions towards women has shifted markedly in recent decades even if 'trade unions do not have feminist sympathies' (*Le Monde Diplomatique*, June 2000 quoted in Garcia and Dumont 2003: 22). This is importantly due to major changes in the nature of paid employment. In the advanced industrial democracies, industrial employment, the bastion of working-class male employment and labour organisation, has diminished. Employment, and the attention of the trade unions, has increasingly shifted to areas in which women form a significant proportion of employees. In the United States,

> [W]omen have made up the majority of new workers being organized for at least the last twenty years . . . [W]omen, and particularly women of color, [have] demonstrated a greater proclivity towards unions than their male counterparts. While the majority of new women workers being organized have been concentrated in low wage service jobs such as nurse aides, home care workers, hotel housekeepers, food service workers, educational support staff, janitors, and day care workers, significant numbers of newly organized workers have included women workers in professional, technical, and clerical occupations in both the public and private sectors. (Bronfenbrenner 2005: 2)

Theories about the level of participation by women in unions are complicated by the difficulty of deciding what constitutes 'participation'.

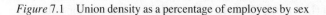

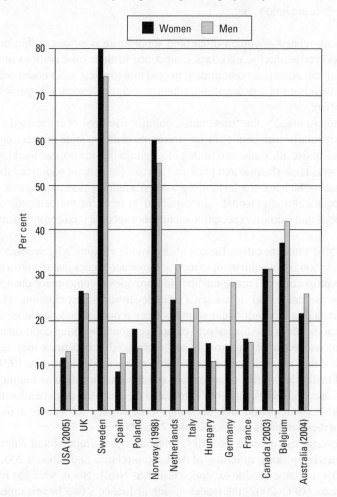

Figure 7.1   Union density as a percentage of employees by sex

Sources: Data for USA from US Department of Labor 2006; Canada from Statistics Canada 2003; EU from Schnabel and Wagner 2005: 19; Australia and Norway from Visser 2006: 46.

Is paying dues and holding a membership card evidence of participation? Most commentators have suggested that participation requires somewhat greater activism, for example attendance at meetings. As Lawrence observes, studies of union participation have tended to concentrate, in the case of women, on why they do not participate, and in the case of men, on why they do (Lawrence 1994: 13). The traditional reasons for failure to participate are held to be:

*   Work-related – women often hold subordinate positions within the working hierarchy, may lack confidence in their own abilities and may not possess a commitment to paid employment as a central part of their life and self-definition, which, it is argued, encourages participation.
*   Union-related – the 'trade union culture' has been characterised as particularly 'masculine' in its jargon, procedures, style of meetings and, above all, venue and timing of meetings outside normal working hours. Their rhetoric and priorities have not in general addressed the issues which are crucial to many women's employment experience.
*   Social-cultural-personal – in particular in terms of the demands of social and cultural expectation on time not spent in paid employment.

Whilst these negative factors still provide reasons why women's unionisation is not equivalent to men's, Lawrence argues that the growth in the proportion of female membership provides arguments for change within the union and in women's attitudes towards participation. The importance to any individual woman of her economic independence is likely to result in a willingness to campaign around working conditions. Where women work in strongly sex-segregated occupations they are likely, if they are organised at all, to participate actively (Lawrence 1994: 18). Finally the women's movement, and the dissemination of feminist ideas since the 1970s, have both prompted the unions to pay attention to women's participation and motivated some women to become active within their unions (Lawrence 1994: 17 and 21).

Nevertheless, women are still substantially under-represented within the decision-making structures of the Unions (Garcia and Dumont 2003: 22), despite some notable exceptions, such as Nicole Notat, who was for ten years (1992–2002) the leader of one of France's two largest union confederations (the Confédération Française Démocratique du Travail – CFDT), Brenda Dean, secretary general of the UK union for clerical and ancillary workers in the printing trades, SOGAT, from 1985 to 1993 and Sharan Burrow, president of the Australian Council of Trade Unions since 2000 and of the International Confederation of Free Trade Unions since 2004. The reasons for this are much the same as those which explain the absence of women from senior positions in other spheres (see Chapter 6).

The impact of women in unions

Evidence for the impact of increased proportions of women in the unions is complex. As Chapter 9 demonstrates, the labour movement did play a role in the battle for equal pay. The impact of the feminist movement has led to the creation of women's departments and/or women's committees. A survey of union federations across Europe affiliated to the European Trade Union Congress showed that in 2002 all of them had either a women's committee or a women's department in their central organisation, or both, and just under half of them held women's conferences (Garcia and Dumont 2003: 47).

Unions need to identify the priorities which they wish to pursue. Some outcomes, for example more flexible hours or better leave conditions, may seem disproportionately to benefit one group of workers rather than another but, as was observed in relation to a campaign in the 1950s by bank workers to end compulsory Saturday morning working, both men and women favoured that outcome. What differed was the use to which Saturday mornings might be put. There are two points of view: the first is that unions have seen themselves as standing for the interests of the working class, but that 'men's interests . . . have been accepted as "class interests" and women's interests dismissed as "sectional interests", [so] to promote women's concerns appears to be promoting disunity' (Allwood and Wadia 2000: 85; Munro 1999: 197–8). 'Women's issues' can be hived off as either irrelevant to the world of paid employment or, at best, as peripheral (Bono and Kemp 1991: 274; Garcia and Dumont 2003: 23), despite the efforts of women in the unions – for example Italian feminist collectives and female shop stewards in the 1970s – to introduce into the union platforms specifically female issues such as flexible working hours (Della Porta, Kriesi and Rucht 1999: 53). At the same time the union discourse of equality promotes the notion of treating everyone the same; 'any recognition of a diversity of interests would undermine this basic feature of trade unionism' (Munro 1999: 197–8). That is the point of view expressed by Lawrence, who found that her interviews with shop stewards (union organisers) showed that the similarities between the bargaining priorities of men and women were greater than the differences, with pay increases for the lower paid (even though this might affect more women than men) and service conditions ranked highest by both.

Nevertheless, the growing importance of female membership has obliged trade unions in Western Europe and the English-speaking advanced industrial democracies to reconsider their approaches. On the one hand, women have proved willing to become involved in industrial disputes and actions. In the United Kingdom as far back as the nineteenth century, the 1888 strike for better pay and conditions by the 'matchgirls' (makers of fire-lighting matches) had both an immediate and a long-term impact on the development of unionism (Boston 1987: 48–51). The massive strikes of 1936 in France, which often took the form of occupations by the workers of their workplaces, were strongest in the least unionised sectors of industry where there were high proportions of women workers. Women participated substantially and strongly in the strikes, albeit on men's terms, and within the union movement 'more women did suddenly become visible' (Reynolds 1996: 124), for example as delegates to union conferences. In France after the Second World War, 'a massive strike of metalworkers in St Nazaire [in 1967] . . . was joined by women office workers putting forward specific demands' (Allwood and Wadia 2000: 87) and in 1968 at the time of the 'May events' which included a general strike 'women constituted a sizeable proportion of the strikers and demonstrators' (Allwood and Wadia 2000: 87). In the United Kingdom, one of the striking features of women's union activism has been the willingness of women of varied ethnic origin to take part. For example, women of Asian origin were very heavily involved in two of the highest profile disputes in the UK over the past three decades, the 1976–7 strike at the Grunwick photo-processing plant and the 2005 Gate Gourmet strike of airline food processors.

On the other hand, particularly during the 1970s, growing feminist consciousness began slowly to cause the unions to pay attention to issues that previously had been dismissed as belonging entirely to the private sphere. In France, Italy, the United Kingdom and the United States, unionised women pressed their unions to campaign on issues such as abortion rights and healthcare. The Coalition of Labor Union Women, founded in 1974 in the United States, saw involving more union women in such campaigns as one of its key aims, and continues to campaign on issues such as the availability of contraception (Coalition of Labor Union Women 2006).

The 1980s and 1990s, however, were almost everywhere difficult times for unions. In the United Kingdom, Margaret Thatcher's government passed a raft of legislation restricting union activity and, in 1984, embarked upon a major confrontation with the miners, who took strike action over proposals to close many of the pits. Although this began as a classic male-oriented industrial dispute, the women of the mining communities steadily organised to support the strike. As they organised money-raising, and the provisioning, cooking and distribution of food, as well as links with supporters across the country, they 'transformed not only the strike but . . . the lives and politics of the women themselves . . . they established an autonomous and influential role for themselves as insubordinate women against the values of the Thatcher government' (Coote and Campbell 1987: 179). While the experience undoubtedly had a transforming effect on many of the women involved, it did not herald a new era. The longer-term trends of industrial reconstruction and globalisation have emphasised the vulnerability of all workers. In Europe, the European Union has encouraged the discourse of social partnership and compromise. Allwood and Wadia argue that in France the changing context resulted in one of the leading federations, the CFDT, despite being led by a woman, 'back[ing] employers and government against the interests of its traditional constituency and against the interests of women' (Allwood and Wadia 2000: 104). Similarly in Italy one observer laments the 1980s as a period of a declining sense of solidarity which led feminists to act outside union structures (Bono and Kemp 1991: 278).

Nevertheless, women's sections and committees persist, and trade unions in general have been increasingly alert to, and successful in pursuing, issues of equal pay, equal treatment and equal opportunities. The Australian Confederation of Trade Unions has achieved advances on equal pay, parental and personal carer leave through pursuing test cases in the courts. The European Trades Union Congress 1996 framework agreement with the employers on parental leave formed the basis of the EU parental leave directive. The prevention of sexual harassment (defined by the European Union as the protection of dignity at work) is also an area where individual unions and union federations have been active, for example in the United States and the United Kingdom. Trade unions, then, have in recent decades become a key arena for political activity by women, one in which women are increasingly active, though equally, as in formal politics, an arena where women are far from being proportionately represented in leading positions.

Non-institutionalised Activism

Whilst trade unions are deeply enmeshed in the structures of the state, the public sphere of private life is further constituted by a huge range of associations. People come together on a voluntary basis to undertake some kind of action together: faith groups worship (and do many other things as well); sports clubs play sport; choirs sing, and so on. 'Women may be more active in these alternative channels than via traditional modes of political expression' (Inglehart and Norris 2003: 111).

The interest taken by political scientists in the contacts and associations within which people are enmeshed has grown with a developing
debate about the impact of 'social capital'. This is constituted by the
'relationships of trust and reciprocity' built up by 'patterns of formal and
informal sociability' (Lowndes 2004: 45). It is argued that where such
capital is abundant the result is strong democratic and economic performance and good government (Putnam 2002). Concentrating on informal
as well as formal activity might serve to shed new light on the political
activity of women, but, as Vivien Lowndes has forcefully suggested,
analysts of social capital have ignored gender dynamics and this lack of
interest 'tended to produce male bias rather than gender neutrality. In
operationalising concepts within the social capital debate, attention has
focused disproportionately upon male-dominated activities' (Lowndes
2004: 47).

Data from the UK and the USA support Inglehart and Norris's findings that women worldwide were markedly less likely than men to belong
to sports and recreational associations but more likely to belong to associations for education, arts, music and cultural activities, to religious
organisations, and to those concerned with health or social welfare, for
example for the elderly. Women on the whole have no less social capital
than men but 'women and men tend to have different social capital
profiles, with women's social capital being more embedded in neigh-
bourhood-specific networks of informal sociability' (Lowndes 2004: 54).
Local, supportive networks of neighbours, mothers at the school gate,
family and friends can give rise to concerted and political action when a
specific issue arises, as can group membership (see below). Examples of
struggles for community improvement and lobbying for policy change.
include the women of the UK mining communities referred to on p. 160
and the women of Niagara Falls in the USA who fought against dioxin
pollution (Kaplan 1997: 15ff).

Non-institutionalised political participation by women, outside the
strategic and focused activity of the feminist groups discussed above, see
p. 149, thus takes place in a multiplicity of groups. These fall into two
types: first, there are groups and associations in which women are
involved, sometimes as a majority of members, but which none of the
members would regard as 'women's groups' and nor would they regard
their activities as involving 'women's issues'. Beckwith speaks of
'women in movement', active in groups the content of whose action is
not particularly gender-related and where men are present and indeed
usually predominate in the leadership (Beckwith 2000: 437). There is
considerable evidence for the participation of women across the world in

class-based movements, or revolutionary movements. Nationalist or resistance movements also involve women, who frequently have more freedom to act than do men, who may be more liable to surveillance and violent repression (Klugman 1994: 657, fn 11). Women in the French Resistance between 1940 and 1945 (Schwartz 1989; Weitz 1995), Polish women from the Solidarity Trade Union when it was banned between 1981 and 1983 (Penn 2005), and South African women under apartheid, both the white middle-class women of the Black Sash anti-apartheid movement and the Black women of the ANC and its armed wing, the Umkhonto we Sizwe (Klugman 1994), are examples of such activism and there are many others. But women are also involved in smaller-scale grass-roots activism. Faith communities, residents' and community associations, conservation groups (whether for nature or heritage) and parent–teacher associations are all examples of such groups. Whilst feminism and its political role have been much studied, the role of women in other groups is seriously under-researched. It is not difficult to find anecdotal evidence: in the author's local Residents' Association, much concerned with local political issues such as conservation and local development, tree preservation and traffic management (speed limits, parking), the current chair and the majority of the committee are women. Clearly active and vigorous political participation by women is occurring here, and women are having an impact upon local policy-making. But the overall scale of this across industrial democracies is unclear, although Inglehart and Norris assert (Inglehart and Norris 2003: 112) that community associations tend to be male-dominated.

One area where women's participation has been considered is the emerging environmental and ecology social movement of the 1970s. In both France and Germany women took leading and prominent roles in some of the 1970s' environmental protests – for example in 1980 women led the protest against the development of a nuclear reactor at Plogoff in Brittany (Allwood and Wadia 2000: 163) – and were key figures in the development of Green parties (see Box 7.2). But Allwood and Wadia's conclusion in respect of France holds for other countries too: we simply do not know whether women were in fact more active in such groups than in others, or than in mainstream political parties (Allwood and Wadia 2000: 163 and 167).

Grass-roots, practical, small-scale campaigning, not just on environmental issues, may well be the largest, most widespread and most effective form of political participation by women. How that participation compares with that of men is impossible to state, not least because of the difficulties of measuring such levels. We have some evidence on

**Box 7.2   Women and Environmental Activism: Two Portraits:
Petra Kelly and Dominique Voynet**

Petra Kelly, 1947–1992, was educated in Germany and in the United
States to which she moved with her mother and stepfather in 1960 (retaining her German citizenship). She took a BA degree in international relations at American University in Washington, and an MA at the University
of Amsterdam in 1971. Then until 1983 she earned her living in the administrative services of the European Community Economic and Social
Committee. From the early 1970s she became involved in the German citizens' initiative groups *(Bürgerinitiativen)* for environmental protection,
protesting in particular against the proliferation of nuclear power reactors,
and in the peace movement. This led her into traditional politics more
broadly. She headed the German Green list in the 1979 European
Parliament elections and in 1980 was a founder member of the German
Green party. She became a member of the German lower house of
Parliament *(Bundestag)* in the 1983 general election and retained her seat
until 1990. She was very prominent as a spokesperson for the Greens and
as an activist, thinker and writer in the causes of environmental protection,
peace and disarmament. She was murdered in 1992.

Dominique Voynet, born 1958, qualified and worked as a doctor, specialis-
ing in anaesthetics. From her student days onward she was active in the ecology and anti-nuclear movements, and in the peace movement. In 1984 she
was one of the founder members of the French Green party *(les Verts)* and
between 1989 and 1991 represented them in the European parliament. She
was a Green Party spokesperson after 1991, and in 1993 was instrumental in
the decision that the party should accept electoral alliances, though only with
parties of the Left. In 1995 she stood as their presidential candidate, obtaining
3.32 per cent of the first ballot vote. In the 1997 general election an electoral
agreement with the Socialist Party meant that she was unopposed by that
party in a constituency in the Jura and was therefore elected to parliament.
From 1997 she was minister for regional development *(aménagement du
territoire)* and the environment in the Socialist government, resigning in
2001. In 2004 she was elected to the upper house (the Senate) of the French
parliament. She was the official candidate of the Green Party for the 2007
presidential election, obtaining 1.57 per cent of the votes cast.

membership of groups but none on intensity of involvement, energy of
activity and extent of influence, which would enable a gender-based
comparison to be made.

Second, there are 'feminine', but not feminist, groups. Such (feminine) women's groups include those which encompass both sociability
and, usually, personal development and charitable activity: examples

include the Soroptimists International or the Women's Institute in Canada and the United Kingdom and the Countrywomen's Association of Australia. Some are faith-based, for instance the World Union of Catholic Women's Organisations, the Anglican Mothers' Union, with particular strength in Africa, or the International Council of Jewish Women. There are also nowadays in all countries very many groups for women with specific qualifications, such as women university graduates, or specific professional interests, for example women in media, or science and engineering, or policing (Katzenstein 2003: 211–12). Many of these groups regularly or sporadically become involved in political action and campaigning. Indeed, one very long-standing and almost archetypally traditional group, the UK Women's Institute (WI), claims on its website that '[w]orking together through the WI, with its long tradition of informed dialogue with government as a mature and responsible organisation, women can continue to make a difference in this high-tech and fast-moving decade' (http://www.womens-institute.org.uk/archive/indexpresent.shtml, accessed 10 August 2006).

Such groups have begun to develop in Central and Eastern Europe. For instance, in Lithuania and the Czech Republic, where there were 59 women's groups in 2000 (Sloat 2005: 439), and in Romania, where there were 73 at the same date (Chiva 2005: 90), the 1990s saw the emergence of women's clubs, societies, study centres and self-help groups. Some of them are quite conservative, concentrating on supporting women in their traditional domestic roles (Chiva 2005: 91). In Romania as elsewhere there are also, for example, organisations for women in particular professions. In many Central and East European countries women's groups have developed as non-governmental organisations filling gaps in welfare left by the demise of the Communist state. '[W]omen's unpaid labour – often of women made redundant who have difficulty finding re-employment . . . provides social supports such as childcare or care of the elderly. This labour remains invisible, simultaneously depended upon yet unrecognised by state agencies. Women's NGOs and grass-roots activist groups are filling the vacuum where the state has withdrawn from public service provision' (Einhorn 2005: 12). However, they suffer from the context of the deep distrust of feminism and emancipatory politics that was a legacy of the previous regime and moreover have often been funded by Western European money which is now being withdrawn.

Scarce financial resources cause competition between women's NGOs, whose efforts are often fragmented and disjointed. Cooperation is limited, usually the result of shared interest in a particular topic (e.g., abortion, Roma) or due to the efforts of an umbrella organization. The idea that women should support women to achieve common objectives is not widely held, and ... further hindered by the failure of many women in government and the civil service to recognize gender as a political issue. (Sloat 2005: 448)

Women's groups in Central and East European countries are neither engaged with the political institutions nor with the majority of women, since they are generally confined to the middle-class and well-educated (Chiva 2005: 91). Nevertheless, despite these contrasts between the West and Eastern Europe, it is important to recognise the contribution which such groups are making to the revival of civil society in these countries.

The example of Central and Eastern Europe also underscores the importance of observing Karen Beckwith's injunction to resist both any 'impulse to identify (any) women's activism as part of a women's movement and [any] eagerness to recuperate (almost any) women's activism as feminist' (Beckwith 2000: 435). This tends to blur the very real differences between women and equally to obscure the divergences between and potentially even conflicts within what women define as their interests and their objectives. For example, in Argentina during the economic crisis of the 1980s, middle-class women attempted to protect their economic status on a gendered basis through consumer groups, in moves that could work against women of other classes (Beckwith 2000: 436; Del Carmen Feijoó 1994: 66). In the United States, groups such as Concerned Women of America and the Independent Women's Forum speak for conservative women within the policy process but in, respectively, opposing abortion rights and rejecting affirmative action, distinguish themselves sharply from feminist groups (Schreiber 2006). Traditional women's groups, whose objectives may be far from concordant with those characteristically advocated by feminist groups, must nevertheless be recognised as part of a movement concerned with the welfare and position of women in society. Some scholars use a definition of the women's movement which excludes them – for instance in her research on 26 women's groups in Florence in the 1990s, Valenza classified only thirteen of them as part of the women's movement, using criteria related to self-perception, previous affiliations of the founding members, organisational history and networking with other groups (Della Porta, Kriesi and Rucht 1999: 49). However, this classification seems to stem from a narrow conception which conflates 'women's' with 'feminist' and in consequence is liable to overlook or underrate the substantial political role that women can play in feminine, and indeed women-in-movement, groups.

As the discussion in Chapter 4 revealed, however, women convert their social capital into formal political engagement less often than men do. Lowndes suggests two reasons: first, women may be spending their social capital simply to 'get by' – to facilitate the complex management of their everyday responsibilities – and, secondly, that successful engagement in formal political activism may depend on the personal support mechanisms that women, using all their resources, provide for men, while they themselves 'do not know how to make wives of men' (Apter 1985: 10). Lowndes observes: 'In my own experience, male parent [school] governors make productive use of their female partners' informal "school gate" knowledge when debating and taking decisions in meetings. At the same time, those partners are providing practical support to male governors through babysitting at home – or using their social networks to arrange such care!' (Lowndes 2004: 59).

8

Do Women Make a Difference? Political Theory and Political Practice

On 10 December 1997, the members of the UK House of Commons voted on a government proposal that would entail a cut in the benefit payable to lone parents not in paid employment and consequently have an, arguably deleterious, impact upon lone parents who chose to care full time for their children, the large majority of whom were women. This therefore looked like a women's issue, and a policy which women MPs should, if they were acting for women, oppose. In the event, 47 Labour MPs did vote against their own government on the proposal but amongst them was only one woman. There was an instant outcry from the more liberal and feminist media commentators (Lovenduski 2005: 155). What was the point of struggles to achieve descriptive representation (see Chapter 4) – which had seemed to be bearing fruit, when earlier that year the proportion of women members increased from nine to eighteen per cent – if substantive representation did not follow? This criticism was narrow and for reasons that will be further explored below, unfair. But the episode serves to point up a key question: what, if any, difference does women's participation in political life make? Are the things women do different from those things that men do, and do they do them differently? If so have they had a discernible impact upon the outputs of the political process? This chapter considers, first, the ways in which women might be expected to make a difference, and second, the ways in which the conditions within which they operate constrain or facilitate their capacity to do so.

Underlying the discussion is a key assumption: that the presence of women to any significant extent in public political life is a new phenomenon, new enough for the present to be discernibly different from the past. Certainly there is still an element of surprise attached to the presence of women within political institutions where they are assumed not to belong (Puwar 2004: 71; and see Chapters 4 and 5). Changes in society and changes in political life have an interactive relationship in all polities.

Because of the differences between men's and women's experiences within society, shifts, even if relatively small, in the relative proportions of men and women engaged in any activity are likely to result in change. But that change will be shaped and conditioned both by the proportions involved and by the institutions within which it occurs.

Doing Things Differently

The question thus arises whether the shape of political life has changed, is changing and may continue to change because women's presence and voice are more important within it than before and because they, for whatever reasons, in practice behave differently from men. Changes might include:

- politics might become more honest and less corrupt;
- politics might be undertaken more conscientiously;
- political style might become less aggressive and combative;
- policy might become more socially progressive;
- the ways in which political matters are expressed in speech might become different and more diverse.

Evidence can be found both to support and to undermine many of these hypotheses, and they are examined in turn below.

Politics might become more honest and less corrupt

There is a stereotypical image of women that suggests they have more integrity and are more principled than men and less implicated in corrupt networks. Politics in which more women are involved might, it is some-times suggested, therefore become more honest and less corrupt. 'Such a view is seductive in its touching faith in the intrinsic "goodness" of women – what other position is possible when thinking of motherhood, babies and apple pie?' (Ross 2002: 190).

The salience of this image is demonstrated by the fact that the tendency to turn to women leaders when parties are in particular difficul-ties (see Chapter 6) can be explained in part by a perception of a lower likelihood that they will be embroiled in close networks of 'men only' relationships that might have turned unhealthy, whether through back-ground, business or social activities. One example was the appointment of veteran woman MP (and first Italian woman cabinet minister) Tina

Anselmi as chair of the parliamentary commission of enquiry into a major financial and political scandal in Italy in the early 1980s. In the 2006 elections for the regional presidency in Sicily a female candidate, Rita Borsellino, attracted support because she was 'an outsider. Someone with no political debts to pay' (*Guardian Weekend,* 13 May 2006). However, her programme, including spreading an anti-mafia culture, failed to secure her victory in the election. Likewise the choice of a woman party leader has not always (Mrs Thatcher is perhaps the striking exception) proved a cure-all for the party's ills.

This notion can be criticised first, because it falls into the 'essentialist' trap of attributing particular qualities to women arising from their sex. There is, as we have seen, an argument for the view that reproductive capacity and/or gendered experiences may induce priorities, interests and perspectives in women which differ from those of men. Carol Gilligan argues that sex affects psychological orientation in ways which result in *approaches* to morality which differ between men and women, but none of these arguments support the view that there might be differing *levels* of morality between men and women. Nor is there, second, particular empirical evidence to back up such a view. Prominent women have not been immune to accusations and allegations of corruption and wrongdoing, even if this can be seen as an unavoidable part of political combat. Some such charges have been substantiated – the case against Dame Shirley Porter, the leader of Westminster Borough Council in the UK, was upheld in the courts. In other cases the allegations cloud careers: the position of Edith Cresson, former prime minister of France, in the events that brought about the resignation of the European Commission in 1999 is one example, while charges of various kinds hang over Benazir Bhutto, former prime minister of Pakistan. Finally, the assumption of higher moral standards places additional burdens on women, as we saw when discussing women's experiences before the criminal law. An Australian woman politician interviewed by Karen Ross told her that 'she did not mind being called to account, but she objected to the fact that different standards were expected of her' (Ross 2002: 190).

Politics might be undertaken more conscientiously

The notion that politics in which more women are involved might be undertaken more conscientiously arises from a widespread perception, uncovered in surveys of women legislators in several countries, that women work harder than men, and may be more conscientious. In the French National Assembly 'everyone agrees that the women do much more work than the men, both in the Committees and in the plenary debates' (Abelès 2000: 33; author's translation cited in Green 2004: 189). Rosenthal reports a representative from Arizona commenting 'no matter the party, . . . the women work harder' and one from Ohio added, 'we [the women] are more willing to take on committees that require more work' (cited in Rosenthal 2005: 206–7). Linked to this perception of women as conscientious is a view that women may be task-oriented; that is, they may be particularly focused on 'getting the job done', 'getting their agenda completed' (Rosenthal 2005: 205). Mary Buckley found that women in the post-soviet Russian parliament claimed that they were more conscientious, more hard-working and more pragmatic than the men (Buckley 1997: 173; cited in Stokes 2005: 33).

Some empirical evidence supports these perceptions. In state legislative assemblies in the USA, the time which women (surveyed by Epstein and his colleagues) reported spending on eight different activities was in all cases greater than that reported by men (Epstein, Niemi and Powell 2005). Manda Green investigated such claims for the French National Assembly by looking at actual attendance by women representatives in 1999 and 2000 and found, for example, that across four very different parliamentary committees (which are key legislative bodies within the French parliament, as in many continental European parliaments and in contrast to Westminster) women constituted 12 per cent of the membership and 17 per cent of the attendance and their attendance was more regular (Green 2004: 191).

Political style might become less aggressive and combative

The perception that, as several of Sarah Childs's MP interviewees stated, between women 'there is less aggression and more co-operation, teamwork, consultation and willingness to listen' (Childs 2004: 10) is a widespread one. It finds some empirical support. Epstein and his colleagues found that US women state legislators seemed in general to be 'more committed team players than men' and their approach appeared 'to be more conducive to co-operation than that of men' (Epstein, Niemi and Powell 2005: 101). 'I am less interested in scoring for the sake of it and more in consensus', a female member of the European Parliament told Hilary Footitt (Footitt 2002: 53–4). Similarly, a French MP commented to Manda Green on the team-working experienced within the National Assembly's Women's Delegation 'because it has a majority of women' (Green 2004: 275, author's translation).

This analysis can be criticised, however. As one female politician pointed out, there is no intrinsic reason for women to be associated with the 'niceness' and 'goodness' to which rejection of aggression is linked, and many female politicians have been 'hard and tough and played the game like one of the boys' (British MP quoted in Childs 2004: 182). French women politicians have been characterised as being willing to fight very hard for political position, willing to use cunning, tactics and wild promises (Belloubet-Frier 1997: 63–4). Betty Boothroyd, a long-serving female MP who became Speaker of the UK House of Commons, dismisses the complaints of female members about the adversarial, tactical and aggressive nature of House of Commons debates as a failure to understand both the nature of parliament and the role of the opposition (Boothroyd 2002: 437). A close examination of the speech of members of the European Parliament caused Hilary Footitt to conclude that both men and women 'share common notions of engaging in politics as a fight'. However, 'women imagine a less confrontational and a more personal and defensive fight. They engage with politics as a site of cure rather than a site of problems . . .' (Footitt 2002: 74).

Policy might become more socially progressive

This hypothesis arises from the suggestion that women in general, and women legislators in particular, tend for a variety of reasons to be more socially progressive than their male counterparts. This suggestion arises most strongly in the context of the United States where the political system allows for the expression of individual policy preferences.

For the United States there is some empirical evidence. Research there suggests attitudinal differences on average between male and female state legislators. Women representatives were, for example, notably more likely than men to oppose the death penalty and to oppose tax cuts if they would mean cutting public spending (Epstein, Niemi and Powell 2005: 102). The researchers needed to disentangle the effect of partisanship and of geography (to ensure that the differences are not simply due to women being systematically more often elected in more liberal states and for more liberal districts) but still found that statistically 'even relative to their constituents and other legislators of their party women legislators are more liberal than men' (Epstein, Niemi, and Powell 2005: 104).

Mercedes Mateo Diaz used similar techniques to try to gauge how closely aligned male and female representatives in 10 of the EU states were to the views of their voters. Using measures of left/right alignment, she found that women MPs placed themselves on average more to the left than did either male MPs or male and female voters (Mateo Diaz 2005: 190).

In a context which affords individuals scope for policy initiatives (see below p. 183), Swers found that women legislators were more likely than their male colleagues to sponsor bills on 'feminist' issues such as breast cancer policy and measures to combat violence against women. On social policy the difference between men and women was much less marked (Swers and Larson 2005: 115–116).

The assertion that women are more socially progressive is clearly linked to the further assertion, discussed below, that women talk about politics in a different way. If, as both Kathlene and Footitt find, women tend to talk about politics in terms of interconnections, of plurality and diversity, of people, not abstract citizens, and to think of policy in terms of long-term and multi-faceted solutions (Footitt 2002: 152; Kathlene 2005: 216 and 228), then their orientation may indeed appear to be socially progressive. However, the extent to which this tendency can be discerned and measured differs between, for example, the United States with its rather loose structures of party ideology, and the much tighter and more disciplined ideological structures of partisanship elsewhere. It is, as the discussion of the contexts of politics below seeks to argue, far from evident that the arrival of more women representatives would *in itself* produce a more socially progressive policy orientation, or indeed has even in the USA necessarily done so (for example, see Dodson 2006: 249–50).

The ways in which political matters are expressed in speech might become different and more diverse

This hypothesis stems from the self-perception of a number of women politicians, shared by women managers in commerce and industry, that they use a more direct and straightforward language than men. Male MPs, said one of Sarah Childs's interviewees, 'always do want to say it again' while women were, said another, 'not prone to political babble [and] jargon' (Childs 2004: 184). 'Women speak less and act more. They have no time to waste on endless bla bla', said a woman MEP from Luxembourg (Footitt 2002: 54). According to a male French senator, women are more authoritative, more concise, more determined (Belloubet-Frier 1997: 64).

Investigating these claims, Kathlene found that women chairing committees in American state legislatures spoke less, took fewer turns and made fewer interruptions than male comparators, and male committee members 'spoke longer, took more turns and . . . made and encountered more interruptions than did women committee members' (Kathlene 2005: 226). Hilary Footitt, using the concept of 'language' in a broad sense to cover the ways in which women's communication in writing, and – especially – speech, situates, frames and expresses political activity, observes that there are 'some languages of politics commonly spoken by women . . . which are different from the languages men more normally speak' (Footitt 2002: 147). She is careful to nuance her observations by arguing that there is a variety of languages used by women and by men, but some which women have a tendency to use more often than men do. Women MEPs used a vocabulary for citizenship which encompassed 'plural and overlapping identities' and insisted on dialogue, on personalising and embodying citizens, and they imagined a Europe that was a matter not so much of structures and frameworks as of diversity and movement.

Context is Crucial: Political Opportunity Structure

Seeking to analyse the conditions under which groups and movements can have a political impact, political scientists have developed the concept of political opportunity structure. This seeks to identify the features within the political culture and institutions of any society which facilitate, or alternatively constrain, the ways in which groups seeking to influence political decision-making can emerge and take action collectively. The components of political opportunity structure are, first, the historical backdrop against which such action takes place; second, the resources which a group can deploy; and third, the nature of the political regime within which action is attempted and the extent to which the group may be able to change its structures. These features have been implicit through the discussion above and are further discussed below.

Historical backdrop: the gender regime

The historical backdrop against which women's action within the political sphere takes place is one of exclusion (see Chapter 2). This has influenced the gender regimes of political life and institutions; that is, its 'gender ratios, gender status, norms of occupational appropriateness, patterns of resistance and intrusiveness' (Lovenduski 2005: 143). They have largely been shaped around male expectations, habits and customs, in every detail from the nature of the building and its fixtures and fittings to the tenor of discussion and the conduct of proceedings. The debate about the 'modernisation' of the House of Commons' archaic timetable arrangements (see Box 8.1) was 'framed in a complex set of arguments in which concern about democracy and accountability was cross cut by considerations of professionalization and representation' but the gender dimension was played down (Lovenduski 2005: 171) as a tactical concession to the 'institutional sexism' of the House of Commons. Women very often face issues of tactical compromise of this sort. The impact that women can have is hence very dependent upon the other components of the political opportunity structure – resources and institutions.

Resources

Presence and critical mass: Whilst formal exclusion has now generally been overcome, it has left a constraining legacy which is also linked to the resources which women can deploy. One resource is numbers – opportunity and ability to act may change as more women arrive.

There are two key approaches to the impact of the arrival of women within political life; they are similar but not quite the same (Mackay 2004: 101). The first is the argument that presence is important. Anne Phillips, arguing for the politics of presence, suggests that women's presence within institutions, in growing (if small) numbers, has a double impact: first, a symbolic one because their presence symbolises justice for all members of society and the inclusion of all citizens within the life of the polity; and, second, at least the possibility that a distinctive voice will be heard (Phillips 1995: 39–44). Women are diverse; their interests, Phillips argues, are not necessarily 'transparently obvious to any intelligent observer' (Phillips 1998: 234), but within the gendered societies of modern states they share life experiences which differ from those of men. Moreover, their mere presence within a previously almost exclusively male institution disturbs and disrupts even if, as some would argue, 'much more than the existence of these [female or ethnically different] bodies in predominantly white and male spaces is required' (Puwar 2004: 66). This approach, however, does not downplay the potential differences amongst women, as well as between women and men.

The second approach to the arrival of women within political institutions is the argument that it is not so much the presence but the proportion of women in any particular organisation that matters. These arguments draw upon two key studies. In 1977, Rosabeth Moss Kanter studied a business corporation within which the few senior women 'often found themselves alone among male peers' and noted '[w]hat happened around [the corporation's] women resembled other reports of the experiences of women in politics, law, medicine . . . who have been the few amongst many men' (Kanter 1993: 207). She argued that once the proportions of any visible minority in a group have 'reached ratios of perhaps 65:35 . . . minority members have potential allies among each other, can form coalitions and can affect the culture of the group' and that in a balanced group with a better than 60:40 ratio group identification with a particular type (no longer a minority) ceases to be a key factor in determining group dynamics (Kanter 1993: 209; see also Lovenduski and Norris 2003).

Kanter's work has been very influential, and was drawn upon in the second key study, by Drude Dahlerup, when in 1988 she considered, in the light, in particular, of experience in Scandinavia, the possibility that what occurred was analogous to the achievement of a 'critical mass' in a physical situation, which allows a 'chain reaction' to take off (Dahlerup 1988: 276). Dahlerup acknowledged the limitations of the analogy, admitting that context is crucial. Physical chain reactions occur in a vacuum, and it is very difficult in human affairs to isolate the impact of changing proportions from that of other contextual factors, or to control for it by comparisons across historical periods or national boundaries. Dahlerup has often been represented as asserting that critical mass, which would spark off key changes in politics, would occur when the proportion of women reached about 30 per cent (see Mateo Diaz 2005: 122; Studlar and McAllister 2002: 235). In fact her formulation was less precise (although she has argued for quotas for women at the 30 per cent level or higher) and she identified what she termed 'critical acts' – the exploitation by women of whatever positions they had obtained and whatever means were open to them – as being likely to have more specific effects in areas of concern to feminists.

Nevertheless, the concept has been widely utilised, for example in support of increased representation by women and to suggest both that, once a certain level of recruitment of women to elected office or government positions had been achieved, it would become self-sustaining so that the proportions would be unlikely to fall back, and alternatively that the achievement of a critical mass would produce changes in legislative output (Norris 1996b: 94). The various notions of critical mass have been much debated and much criticised, not least because Kanter's and Dahlerup's early formulations have been misinterpreted or misapplied (Childs and Krook 2006: 2).

First, one application of the notion of 'critical mass' has been the suggestion that the proportion of women in representative bodies will rise at an accelerating rate rather as a chain reaction takes off. Hence, the notion is used as one of the arguments underpinning the advocacy of quotas for the representation of women, on the grounds that this will start the 'take-off'. This argument has been challenged in two ways. First, it has been suggested that where the process of achieving representation has been unhurried and incremental, as in Scandinavia, the dynamic may differ from that experienced where there has been a sudden and possibly enforced increase (Dahlerup and Freidenvall 2005: 27). Second, extensive statistical study of 20 industrial democracies over some 50 years found no evidence of acceleration (Studlar and McAllister 2002: 247–8).

A second related application of the notion is the suggestion that, above a certain proportion, the presence of women in representative assemblies will be self-sustaining. This helps to support the suggestion that quotas are a necessary but temporary measure and the presence of sufficient women will ensure a change in political culture such that the old prejudices and barriers will be unsustainable, at least in established liberal democracies. The fall in proportions in Central and East European countries since the 1980s is, on this argument, the result of the legacy of non-democratic regimes. The expectation that change will be self-sustaining surely incorporates an element of the 'politics of optimism' (Childs and Krook 2006: 8) in its assumption that there will be no backlash. The advent of women in even double-figure proportions in most representative assemblies is too new a phenomenon to allow substantial empirical testing of this hypothesis: it is the case that the average proportions have been rising steadily since the early 1970s but there have been cases of some decline, usually as a consequence of the party configuration of the assembly, and it is certainly too soon to assert that the figures are rising steadily or are even stable over the medium to long term.

Third, it is assumed that the achievement of a critical mass will improve the working conditions for women operating in representative assemblies. There is substantial qualitative evidence of the difficult conditions experienced by women, as they appeared in small numbers and like 'space invaders' (Puwar 2004) in the male spaces of, for example, the Canadian, French or British parliaments (Freedman 1997; Trimble 2006: 128–9). There is also some evidence that, even if some institutions tend to be markedly resistant to change in their practices and routines (see Box 8.1), as women's numbers have risen the most egregious instances of sexist insult have diminished if not disappeared (Green 2004: 109; Sones 2005). But the level at which change occurs is debatable: Mateo Diaz found that even a relatively small proportion of women (she suggests ten per cent) can start a process of acculturation and spillover by which the values and agenda of the body may change (see

Box 8.1   Women and the Working Practices of the House of Commons

Any change in the working values of the House of Commons as a consequence of the doubling, in 1997, of the proportion of women members
might have manifested itself in change to the rather bizarre working hours
and in child-friendly practice.

Working hours: These derive from the practices of the nineteenth century
when unpaid MPs required the morning to attend to the affairs from which
they acquired their income. The House therefore began its meetings
(except on Friday) in the afternoon and the main vote of the day, at which
MPs' attendance was required, took place at 10 p.m. There was pressure
for reform which increased after 1997. However:

- women and men were both divided about the desirability of change;
- some women were reluctant to criticise the status quo lest they appear
  to be suggesting that they were not up to the job (Childs 2004: 66);
- some proponents of reform feared that clear support from women
  (especially newly elected women) might devalue the proposals in the
  eyes of longer-standing members. This was perhaps 'an after-effect of
  the post-1997 backlash against women MPs' (Lovenduski 2005: 173).

In the event, following reform in 2002, partially reversed in 2005, changes
have been minimal. The House continues to sit in the afternoon and
evening on Monday and Tuesday and sits from mid-morning until early
evening on Wednesday and Thursday and earlier on Friday but later and
indeed late-night sittings are still possible.

Childcare: In 2000, members were told that they might not take their
babies into the debating chamber, the division lobbies or the committee
rooms. Babies could consequently not be breastfed during the meetings of
committees of the House. A deputation of female MPs sought unsuccessfully to persuade the Speaker, who decides such matters, to change the
ruling, thereby making the House more women-friendly and less 'ante-
diluvian'. The view of the Speaker – the first woman to hold the post – was
that breastfeeding during committee meetings 'was not conducive to the
efficient conduct of public business' and that Commons sittings did not
provide 'the calm environment babies needed when they were being fed'
(Boothroyd 2002: 436).

Box 8.1), and as the proportions grow to 20 per cent the likelihood of
change increases (Mateo Diaz 2005: 230).

Fourth, a crucial assumption often made about critical mass, indeed,
according to Childs and Krook (Childs and Krook 2006: 15), what is
often taken to be the only claim made by the principal theorists, is 'that

[rising numbers of women] would enable women increasingly to formulate supportive coalitions among one another to promote feminist-oriented change' (Childs and Krook 2006: 15). The logic underlying this assumption is both understandable and complex: it seems almost self-evident that numbers must matter, and scholars speculate about what *might* change if numbers rose (Dahlerup 1988; Mansbridge 1999; and see Childs and Krook 2006). However, Dahlerup's research showed that the move from a small to a large minority had *in fact* resulted in no more than some diminution in stereotyping, that some new role models emerged, that the social conventions of the parliamentary organisation changed a little, and that open opposition to women politicians did disappear (Dahlerup 1988: 295). Paradoxically, it may even be that feminist policy initiatives may have greater chance of success, and that women may be more effective, when their proportions are smaller. This paradox can be explained because when the proportions are small the habits of the organisation have not been unduly disturbed by the arrival of the 'space invaders', and so the few women who are present have less fear, anxiety and resentment – in a word, backlash – with which to contend (Childs and Krook 2006: 8).

There are two further reasons why larger numbers may not necessarily lead to feminist-orientated change. First, female politicians may not agree or make coalitions with each other. UK prime minister Mrs Thatcher constitutes one example; she proclaimed herself a 'conviction politician' and showed no propensity to form alliances to further women's interests. Secondly, even where there is agreement that certain issues are of particular importance to women, partisan loyalty or personal ideology may lead two women to come to very different views about what the policy implications should be (Childs 2004: 101). The events cited at the start of this chapter illustrate this, and other examples may be found in the United States where women legislators have in some states supported the tightening of the abortion laws with arguments, contested by feminists, that the 'pro-life' approach reflects 'female' values of respect and support for the family, and care for children.

It is possible to argue that the achievement of certain proportions may not be a trigger for, but rather a consequence of, a whole complex of social and attitudinal changes amongst both elites and the general public, and amongst both men and women. So both an increase in the number of women in formal politics and policy changes which further the demands made by feminists may both be the result of broader social changes (Mateo Diaz 2005: 122).

Safe space: Alongside their presence and the potential impact of their numbers, another resource which women can deploy is the creation of what can be conceptualised as 'safe spaces' within which women, and possibly men who share their values, can develop their ideas despite a hostile environment. '[T]he validating presence of other women legislators is an important precondition for women to act on parts of their agenda that differ from those of their male colleagues' (Green 2004: 225). Given the negative connotations of categorisation as 'feminist', safe spaces should allow women to pursue substantive action on issues affecting women whilst being protected from denigration (Childs 2001: 181). They can provide a framework within which co-operation may be possible across partisan and sometimes gender boundaries and solidarity and confidence for those who seek to promote 'women friendly' measures. Indeed such an institutional 'haven' for gender solidarity within, not outside, the gendered institutions may ultimately be more effective than the achievement of critical mass in promoting change.

A number of examples of such safe spaces can be identified. One is the women's caucus within the US Congress. This was created in 1977 by 15 congresswomen and by 2006 membership numbered 63. Between 1981 and 1995, as the Congressional Caucus for Women's Issues, it was open to both men and women, but changes in the House's procedural rules that year led to it being transformed into a women-only membership association. It has always been a bi-partisan organisation, co-chaired by one Democrat and one Republican woman. It has had a particular interest in, and influence on, issues of women's health, women's social security, sexual harassment and violence against women and claims a number of laws in these and related areas as the results of its activity. In the British parliament, the parliamentary Labour Party women's group constituted a small body in which female Labour MPs discuss women's issues, but with a view to influencing government policy, so it meets with ministers: opinions about its effectiveness vary, even among the cohort of women MPs (Childs 2004: 138). Both these bodies exist on the periphery of legislature procedures. In France, the Delegations for Women's Rights of the National Assembly (National Assembly 2006) and the Senate are formal parts of the parliamentary structure established by law at much the same time as the parity amendment to the constitution (see Chapter 5): the two initiatives were closely linked. The delegations are composed of men and women MPs (though women have, unusually, been in the majority and in 2006 the ratio was 27:9) who are nominated by the party groups proportionately to their presence in the assemblies. The National Assembly delegation has demonstrated its effectiveness; most of the laws

Box 8.2   Women's Committees in United Kingdom Local Authorities

In 1981 the Labour Party took control of the Greater London Council, and in 1982 a women's committee was established, starting with an attempt to involve the women's movement more widely through the holding of open meetings and the setting up of independent working groups which would formulate policy ideas on 'the working principle that women are the experts in what women want' (Lovenduski and Randall 1993: 194). Their activities included, for example, policies to improve women's safety in and outside the home, development of childcare facilities and training opportunities for women and the promotion of women's cultural activities. This committee was followed by others in some of the Labour-controlled London boroughs, and elsewhere, for example in Birmingham, Leeds and Bristol. At their peak, nearly eleven per cent of UK local authorities had committees with explicit responsibility for women (Stokes 2005: 188). However, the committees proved very vulnerable. They proved to be

- too readily characterised – and caricatured – as the emanation of the 'loony Left' – wasteful, impractical and radically feminist. This was one of the features that made possible the Conservative assault on the GLC, which led to its abolition in 1986 and the consequent disappearance of the pioneer women's committee;
- too caught within the politics of the Labour Party: they were opposed both by the traditional anti-feminist trade union old guard (Lovenduski and Randall 1993: 206) and by the 'modernisers' who saw them as one of the 'way-out' features that were making the party unelectable. For example, in Birmingham the committee was blamed for contributing to electoral losses in the 1987 local elections and abolished;
- open to conflict and difficulties in relation to differences between the women whose interests they were intended to further. Women of colour and white women, young socialist feminists and older female politicians who had fought their way through male-dominated structures, lesbians and heterosexuals, all had different approaches and expectations.

By the 1990s, the high profile roles of women's committees had largely disappeared. Routine had replaced enthusiasm and innovation, budgets had been cut and work had often been absorbed into other departments. In 2006, for example, Camden Council, where one of the first London borough women's policy committees was created, had no such committee, but did have an equality policy, as all public bodies must under the Race Relations Act, an executive member for Social Inclusion, Equalities and Regeneration, and a stakeholders group.

which they have examined had moved further towards equality by the time that they were passed. It seems to be based upon practices of team-working, including cross-party and (occasionally) cross-gender co-oper-ation, on partnership with other parts of the legislative structure (since they are dependent on the leadership of the Assembly or the chairs of the standing committees for referral to them of texts for their consideration) and on an emphasis on a practical task-force approach. The delegations act as a safe space in Childs's terms because 'the existence of a formal "place" within the Assembly for equality implants a nucleus of legitima-tion in [MPs'] minds' (Green 2004: 318), perhaps particularly when, as between 2002 and 2007, it is chaired by an active Centre-Right female MP, Marie-Jo Zimmerman.

Another example of such safe spaces was the Women's Committees set up in a number of UK local authorities, most notably the Greater London Council, in the early 1980s (see Box 8.2). They epitomised an alliance between second-wave feminism (see Chapter 7) and the Left, and were both highly active and highly visible in promoting feminist causes. But the fate of these committees clearly illustrated the weak-nesses of 'safe spaces'. First, the existence of 'safe spaces' can be seen as legitimating the failure of any other parts of the system to handle issues related to women's interests. Second, even when men are included, they tend to disengage as a consequence of embarrassment or, sometimes, a feeling of intimidation. Third, the women involved may be caught up in the internal affairs of the committee and fail to communicate outside it, and equally risk not being heard when they do (Green 2004: 295–6 and 305). Fourth, the arrangements are often dependent on the goodwill of the party managers for their existence.

Institutional constraints and behavioural impact

The institutional structures of politics, which form the final component of the political opportunity structure, comprise not only the location, build-ing, formal rules, powers and sets of relationships with which any politi-cal body – supranational, national or local assembly or executive, trade union, association and so on – is endowed, but also routines, procedures and informal expectations. They incorporate expectations and norms about how individuals within any political structure should conduct themselves and what solutions are imaginable. 'An institution such as parliament has a strong regulating capacity, its own logic, a strong iner-tia, very little room for innovation and many ways to socialise or assimi-late "dissidents"' (Mateo Diaz 2005: 225).

Scope for policy initiation: Women may be more able to make a difference in institutions which are accustomed to according individual
members scope to sponsor or initiate policy. In a system such as the
Congress and State legislatures of the USA where there is a strong separation of powers between legislature and executive, coupled with a relatively weak impact of party programmes, members of the legislature are
involved in policy formulation as the proponents and sponsors of bills. As
Lovenduski and Norris point out, 'roll call analysis [that is, examination
of voting patterns as a way of estimating the impact of women's behav-
iour] is perhaps better suited to the US Congress [than other legislatures]'
(Lovenduski and Norris 2003: 90). Members of Congress have some
autonomy and ability to 'construct their legislative portfolio' and 'determine their legislative priorities' (Swers and Larson 2005: 115 and 116).

This ability, in the case of women, is affected by two factors. One is
their partisan status. 'When moderate Republican women were in the
minority party they could more easily support feminist initiatives . . .
[than] when . . . they were part of a Republican majority caucus in which
social conservatives were a key constituency . . . [They] had to focus on
social welfare initiatives that were less likely to alienate Republican
colleagues' (Swers and Larson 2005: 115 and 116). The second factor is
their position in party and congressional offices, for example within the
committee structures discussed below. Without positions of power
within their parties and the committees, women may not be able to be
involved in the detailed policy design; for example, in relation to policy
on abortion in the early 1990s, all women in Congress could do was make
speeches on the floor of the house, which failed to inflect the details of the
policy which was negotiated within committees (Swers and Larson 2005:
113). The election of Nancy Pelosi as the Democrat leader in the House
of Representatives in 2003, and in 2006, when the Democrats just gained
a majority, as its Speaker, and of Deborah Pryce to the fourth-ranking
position in the Republican Party, has enabled them to promote the position of women within their party structures. Other legislative systems,
where policy-making and the legislative agenda is largely monopolised
by the executive and controlled by party discipline, provide much less
scope for initiatives by women.

New assemblies: Another institutional framework which may provide
scope for initiatives by women is that offered by very new legislative
assemblies, especially those where women have from the start been
strongly represented. This is not the case in all new assemblies – the
assemblies of former Communist countries could in many respects be

described as 'new', since they operate under a transformed political structure, but women's representation in them has been low. However, the regional assemblies of Scotland and Wales have from the start been characterised by rather high levels of female representation. And from the design stage women worked to ensure that they achieved equal standing for men and women, and a statutory framework that required the promotion of equality of opportunity and were, in the words of one female Welsh Assembly member, 'set up in such a way that it was very difficult for anybody to do anything else' (quoted in Chaney 2004: 288). '[F]rom the very outset with these [equality] issues at the forefront, they weren't afterthoughts, they were really mainstreamed in the way that the place was set up, in terms of the legislative framework' (Welsh Cabinet member quoted in Chaney 2004: 288). This has ensured, for example, that the operating procedures of the Scottish parliament have from the start been notable for their attention to the concerns of women. The parliament timetable is geared to normal working hours and takes school holidays into account (Brown et al. 2002: 76). 'Equal opportunity' is one of the key principles of operation for both the Scottish parliament and the Welsh Assembly. Both have set up committee systems with a pre-legislative consultative process which more closely resembles some continental European models than that of Westminster and provide substantial opportunities for a consensual style of politics. The institutional design has come into operation with high proportions of female representatives (see Chapter 5) and taken together these features, achieved as a result of pressure and lobbying both from women within the political parties and from the broader women's movement, have made it possible to claim that 'enhanced influence for women in the policy-making process has been achieved' (Brown et al. 2002: 82 and see Chaney 2004: 299).

Partisan discipline:　Whether in long-standing or in new institutions, partisan discipline is a key feature that structures what representatives can do. And parties are (see Chapters 4 and 5) themselves gendered structures, if only because in very many cases they pre-date the relatively recent emergence of women onto the political scene. Women representatives consequently experience tensions between their party identity, which imposes loyalty and discipline, and their gender identity, which might lead them to seek to 'act for women' (Childs 2002: 151). A telling example occurred in Australia in the 1990s, when the number of women in the federal parliament rose, but the number of interventions on issues such as domestic violence and parental leave diminished. The rise in numbers mostly resulted from the return of female members of the right-wing coalition parties, then in government. The coalition was broadly 'anti-feminist' and 'were positioning themselves as "governing for the mainstream" undistracted by "special interests" . . . [so] Coalition women parliamentarians were particularly anxious to avoid the career-threatening implications of being identified as advocates for women' (Sawer 2002: 9). Dodson reports that Republican women in the US Congress 'feel that consorting with women's groups tags them as disloyal to their party' (Dodson 2006: 192). Partisan loyalty structured the responses to the issue of benefit for lone parents referred to at the start of this chapter, and at the end of the first term of the new Welsh Assembly, with its high proportion of women members, Paul Chaney found that early movement towards a more consensual style had been 'held back and undermined by party politics' (Chaney 2004: 294).

Sarah Childs and Philip Cowley have identified the extent of party loyalty amongst the new women Labour members in the 1997–2001 parliament. They were notably less likely to vote against their own government than men or longer-standing women. Careful statistical analysis dismissed most of the facile explanations for this – that the new women were too young or too inexperienced to rebel, for example – and found that, when all other factors had been taken into account, the difference between men and women was very small, but not inexistent. Perhaps the most plausible explanation, the researchers hesitantly concluded, and the one preferred by the women concerned, was that they saw no reason to undertake futile gestures of disloyalty when to do so would only reinforce the 'macho' politics of confrontation (Cowley and Childs 2003: 363).

Working behind the scenes: committees, questions and motions

Participation in formal politics is by no means limited to sponsoring new legislation or acting outside partisan guidelines in voting for (or against) new proposals. Parliaments provide a variety of arenas within which representatives' voices can be heard, and women may potentially have an impact. For example, many of the women who voted against the cuts in UK lone-parent benefit discussed above subsequently argued that their behind-the-scenes outrage and pressure for better policy resulted quite rapidly in policy adjustments which were more advantageous to disadvantaged women than the previous regime had been (Sones 2005).

Committees provide one arena for such activity: the status of the committee and the opportunity it provides for policy impact condition the roles which women can play. In legislatures in which specialised committees play a key role in pre-legislative discussion, there is a hierarchy of status: committees concerned with foreign policy, finance and economics carry greater prestige than those concerned with education, health and similar social matters. And as with assignment to executive posts (see Chapter 6), so the assignment of women representatives to committees, generally decided upon by party leaderships, with MPs' own preferences sometimes playing a part, tends to reflect a gendered approach to status. In France, for example, after 1997 women were present in all the committees, but in a tiny and marginalised minority, in terms of both numbers and seniority, in finance and defence (Green 2004: 125–38). In contrast, in the 1997 parliament (10.9 per cent female members), they made up 18 per cent of the membership of the social affairs committee and in 2004, with 12.3 per cent in the parliament, the proportion was 26 per cent (Green 2004: 155 fn 34). The social affairs committee along with trade and industry was nicknamed 'the dustbin' but this dismissive attitude to social affairs did not necessarily reflect either its workload or its importance in terms of domestic policy-making.

Belgium and Sweden provided similar examples: as one Belgian MP told Mercedes Mateo Diaz, 'Most female parliamentarians . . . are in the committee of health and social affairs, in the "soft committees" ' (Mateo Diaz 2005: 131). In these two cases, however, as the proportions of women in the parliament grew markedly, so the distribution of women across the various categories of committee became somewhat more even. The explanations for gendered distributions are not necessarily straightforward. In Sweden there was, in almost every case which Mateo Diaz explored, a connection between MPs' previous areas of interest and their committee assignments, so the distribution reflects the gendered divisions of labour within the wider society. In Belgium, there was more evidence of gendered and 'unfair' committee assignments, while in all three countries (France, Sweden and Belgium) the perpetuation of incumbents within the committees and seniority within the parliament affected the chances of women achieving assignments to the committees which they preferred (Green 2004: 147; Mateo Diaz 2005: 132–3). However, since the outcomes form part of the formal legislative process and are therefore subject to partisan constraints, the specific impact of female members is hard to discern.

There are other committees, either permanent or temporary, which scrutinise both policy-making and policy implementation and make reports. For example the French National Assembly sets up committees of enquiry and special committees, Australia and the UK and other 'Westminster-type' parliaments have select committees, and the very powerful United States' Congressional committees act as both pre-legislative and scrutiny committees. These may provide an arena where women's voices can be heard to some effect. The presence of a woman on the House of Commons select committee on defence after 1997 opened up its agenda; 'this used to be a committee for boys with toys and now it focuses on service families' lives and personnel issues and so on . . .' (quoted in Ross 2002: 200). In France, women MPs found participation in temporary committees rewarding, and when 'it involves issues that concern them . . . they not only seek seats in the temporary committees . . . but they also participate more actively than their male counterparts' (Green 2004: 173). Another example can be found in the 103rd Congress in the United States where, 'when women found at least some bipartisan common ground on . . . health care reform, it was those women of the majority with seats on the committees handling health care reforms who were critical conduits' for inserting women's values into the legislative process (Dodson 2005: 138).

Other arenas for women's voices exist in most legislatures. These include questions to the government. Matching women with male comparators, Green found that in the 1997–2001 parliament in France women posed more questions than did comparable men, and that although they asked questions across the full range of governmental activity, a higher proportion of their questions than of the men's related to social and cultural affairs (Green 2004: 208–10). However, the posing of the questions was quite strictly controlled by the parliamentary parties and the party managers chose to highlight their female members as a deliberate public relations strategy. Similarly the UK House of Commons device of 'Early Day Motions' allows members to express their views on a very wide range of issues. Research on the 1997 parliament showed that women (or rather Labour women, who made up the large majority of female members) expressed their views by signing such motions overall less often than men, but were more likely than their male comparators to sign motions that could be categorised as related either to 'women's' or to 'feminist' concerns. It is possible that the act of signing such a motion is one visible expression of a general tendency for female members to act 'for women' in the 'behind the scenes' work of legislatures (Childs and Withey 2004: 562–3).

Altering the terms of discussion

An Oslo town councillor told Drude Dahlerup that a consequence of a female majority on the council was 'that men have started taking an interest in matters that only women considered before' (Dahlerup 1988: 292). Women's health, or childcare, or the conditions of life for families of members of the armed services, and gender equality in general become matters about which serious discussion is deemed appropriate. 'Gender equality has become more mainstream' (Mateo Diaz 2005: 229). This is what seems to have occurred in Scandinavia. An attitude survey of candidates and elected members standing in the British general election found that women of both major parties were on average significantly more supportive than the men of their parties of measures for affirmative action and gender equality. Lovenduski and Norris suggest that these attitudinal differences are crucial to potential change: party discipline and 'the culture of party unity' (Lovenduski and Norris 2003: 98) suppress differences between men and women in many policy areas and much behaviour, but the divergence in the average values on issues related to women's autonomy might shift the ways in which legislation and implementation is scrutinised and policy priorities debated. A higher proportion of female representatives may shift the range of issues which get discussed, even if their attitudes to those issues may be widely divergent. Work in the United States suggests that this is particularly likely to occur if women representatives can draw on strong support from groups within civil society (Dodson 2005: 134).

The Nature of Women's Impact: Acting for Women?

This chapter has argued that despite institutional rigidities, discouragement and backlash, as female representation has risen values and priorities have begun to change. There is, however, a need for caution since it is so difficult to disentangle political and general social changes. However, a change in subjects of discussion does not necessarily mean a change in outputs. Do women representatives and politicians represent and act for women?

The notion that women might make a difference by 'acting for' women is predicated upon the idea that they have concerns and interests that are different from those of men (see Box 4.2). What might those interests comprise? At the most broad and general level, some theorists would argue that everyone has an interest in the establishment of a society that would be just and humane for all human beings. Theorists of interests within society, most notably, but not exclusively, Marxian theorists, have seen conflicting interests within society as fundamentally economic and social, deriving from different relationships to economic resources and productive activity. The result is politics based upon divisions of class and in certain polities, race and ethnicity. A number of feminist theorists, however, now argue that an equally fundamental, but cross-cutting, division derives from differing relations to *reproductive* activity (Sapiro 1998: 166). Women, as Diamond and Hartsock for example argue, have created survival strategies 'in response to their powerlessness' but these may differ between different races and classes (Diamond and Hartsock 1998: 199). The role of women specifically is to ' "act for" women in identifying "invisible" problems affecting the lives of large numbers of women' (Diamond and Hartsock 1998: 198).

The identification of reproductive activity as being key to the distinctive interests of women may help to define their content. This will comprise concerns around three areas in particular: the welfare, health and upbringing of children (including the family as the place where this takes place); care more generally, including housework, healthcare and indeed social policy in a broad sense; and women's bodies and sexuality, including issues such as reproductive rights (for example fertility, assisted conception, contraception and abortion), violence against women (especially domestic violence), rape, sexual exploitation and prostitution. To these three fundamental areas a fourth may be added: issues around the status of women as it has developed within gendered societies: these would include the citizenship rights discussed in Chapter 2 (including access to education and the labour market, social security, the impact of marriage and property ownership).

The identification of these interests as being particularly salient for women carries implications, risks and controversies.

First, the identification of certain issues as 'women's issues' does not imply:

- either that men take little or no interest in these matters
- or that men and women cannot agree upon how they should be tackled within a good and just polity
- or that women will agree with each other about what stance should be taken in relation to them and how the issues that arise in these areas of concern should be tackled.

Second, such an identification does present certain risks and costs to those seen to be concerned with such issues. Within gendered, masculine institutions, the areas of concern that are identified as being 'women's issues' may be marginalised or devalued. Consequently, those who are concerned with them, especially if they give the impression that is all they are concerned with, may be characterized as not 'having any depth' (woman MP quoted in Childs 2004: 127). Second, there is 'an implicit elision between "women's issues" and "soft issues" '. Perhaps this explains why French women MPs have a 'love–hate' relationship with the social affairs committee to which so many are assigned (Green 2004: 151). Men may turn away from concern with such issues, some of which at least (education for example) they would have been compelled to tackle had women been even more sparsely represented. Thirdly, men may take the view that as the representation of women improves, then these are matters that men 'don't have to worry about' (woman MP quoted in Childs 2004: 128). They may feel that 'women's presence absolves them of this responsibility' (Childs 2004: 128). Finally, the marginalisation of women's issues and the characterisation of them as 'soft' may, in ways reminiscent of the insistence of some prominent women that they are not 'feminists', cause women themselves to attempt to distance themselves from women's issues and consciously seek to avoid any obligation of substantive representation. Certainly a number of Childs's interviewees suggested that too close an identification with women's issues might harm, or at least would not further, their political careers.

This final risk is linked to the controversy surrounding these issues. As we have seen, the very notion that women may have distinctive interests is controversial. Many people, including women, are not prepared to subscribe to the notion that personal, social and economic life is struc-tured by gender, and hence are not prepared to recognise any issues as pertaining more importantly to women than to men or to accept a feminist viewpoint (Ross 2002: 189; Sawer and Simms 1993). Given the extent of the controversy and in particular a context where the term 'women's issues' implied a limited and devalued set of matters, it is scarcely surprising that both Sarah Childs (Childs 2004: 126) and Karen Ross (Ross 2002: 189) found that many interviewees in the UK, in Australia and in South Africa were cautious about referring to them. In general, Childs found, they preferred to talk of 'issues which have an impact on women': one of her interviewees stated 'there is no issue which is not a person issue, no issue that is specifically a woman's issue' (Childs 2004:

126). In France, the women's rights delegation has been careful not to be seen as a women's lobby and to make recommendations where they felt that men's rights were being limited, as in the case of legislation on divorce settlements (Green 2004: 248).

The dilemmas of policy content

Politicians never claim to be acting 'against women', even when they make a virtue of opposing 'women's liberation'. The proponents of lone parents' benefit cuts (see p. 168) argued that in increasing the incentive for women to find paid employment they encourage them to greater autonomy and prosperity. Feminist women can point to substantial legislative and policy changes in the advanced democracies in the directions which they advocate (see Chapters 7 and 9). The visibility and activism of women in politics have aided these changes, as has the input of feminist men (Chaney 2004; Mackay 2001). But 'clashes will occur about the meaning of women's status in politics and the family and about . . . the role of government in women's lives . . . [F]eminist and conservative women's organisations battle over whose stories about women are most representative' (Schreiber 2006: 149) and a roll-call of recent activities linked to women's interests in the US Congress (see Box 8.3) reveals the variations.

We can thus say:

- Women give birth to and suckle babies. In the gendered societies of industrial democracies they still have primary responsibilities for care of the young, the old, the disabled and the sick. They undergo socialisation and life experiences which differ from those of men. Women can and do wish to see the ordering of society changed where it fails to take issues which arise from these features into account.
- But there may be very considerable differences about how society should be changed: for example policy related to families has in some countries been very much the preserve of the right-wing parties. Whilst those who are 'attitudinally feminist' may place an emphasis on women's autonomy, others may wish to emphasise support for a more traditional and dependent female role, and protection rather than autonomy (see also Chapter 9, and for an example see the discussion of French Gaullist policy towards women and the family in Opello 2006: 51–7).

Box 8.3   Recent Examples of Women Making a Difference in the US Congress

- Congresswoman Heather Wilson's fight against Congressional attempts to further limit the jobs military women can hold
- Bi-partisan efforts to advance human rights for women and children in Afghanistan and Iraq
- Republican Congresswoman Deborah Pryce's effort to secure more money for the fight against child abuse
- Republican women's success in securing additional funds for childcare block grants
- Bi-partisan support for campaigns to assist people to stop smoking
- Bi-partisan support for the Patient Navigator, Outreach, and Chronic Disease Prevention Act, to assist people to access healthcare
- Republican women's efforts (unsuccessful at the time of writing and opposed by Democrat women and the National Organisation of Women, see http://www.now.org/issues/economic/050103familyflex.html) to change labour laws to allow workers to choose between paid overtime or compensatory time (time off in lieu) so as to accommodate family needs
- Republican women's efforts to rally support for President George W. Bush's conservative women judicial nominees

Source: Data from Dodson 2006: 266, fn 1.

Conclusion

This chapter has argued, first, that the political opportunity structure in general constrains strongly visible or rapid change resulting from the appearance of women within formal politics. Within the structure the traditional gender regime and the nature of the institutions provide the major explanations for the persistence of the political status quo, rather than the limited proportions in which women are, in very many cases, present. Second, the difficulty in discerning clear indications of women acting for women stems from divergences of views as to what doing so would imply. The societies of modern industrial democracies have changed, and many (but not all) of the new policies and policy changes have been, in the eyes of many (but not all) women, beneficial to their status. As Joni Lovenduski remarks (Lovenduski 2005: 179), it is impossible to prove the hypothesis that these changes have resulted from the growing role of women in politics – but equally it cannot be disproved.

9
Women's Policy: the Case of Equal Employment Policy

Many of the strands of women's political action discussed in the preceding chapters come together when the issues of equal pay, equal treatment and equal opportunities for women are considered. This chapter is therefore a case study of what may, for convenience, be called equal employment policy. These are issues which are at the heart of feminists' claims for the status, integrity and autonomy of women. 'Equal treatment or sex discrimination law has an important cornerstone function' (Forbes 1996: 163; Shaw 1999). Since these issues relate to women's participation in the economic life of society, they have a reciprocal relationship with citizenship (see Chapter 2). Moreover, equal employment policy has attracted the concern of international bodies, so that nation-states are subject to pressures on policy-making not only from internal groups but also from external bodies.

The operation of an equal employment policy depends on three factors. First, the desirability of equality must be recognised in principle, so that it is strongly justified and widely supported. Second, there must be a legal framework to prescribe what must be done. Equal pay has often been a starting point. What is more widely at stake is access: access to paid employment, access to position and opportunity, and access to services and resources, which require both negative and positive action. Legislation, with a few exceptions, provides for negative action, requiring the removal of formal, legal, regulatory and procedural barriers. Positive action – actually offering women jobs or promotion – has to come from employers. The third requirement of an equal employment policy is processes – arrangements for action to implement the policy which may also support 'the development of attitudes, mind-sets, and social habits and lifestyles that promote access and opportunity' (Forbes 1996: 166).

Claims for equal pay for work of equal value proceed from principles which may be derived either from classical liberalism, or from a more radical Socialist or Marxist view, but they converge on fundamental principles of equality, social justice, and, more recently, respect for diversity (Forbes 1996: 166). But even today they are not uncontroversial. First, they pose dilemmas of equality and difference: are women in employment to be treated 'as if they are men' or are they sufficiently different to require different, possibly protective, treatment? For example, the German Constitutional Court, for two decades after the legal assertion of the principles of equal pay and equal treatment, interpreted these as permitting what it called 'functional differentiation' (Marx Ferree 1995). Second, conservatives argue against the 'social engineering' involved in provoking change in social structures and attitudes, preferring on the one hand a justification for equal employment policies by a 'business and economic rationale', and a discourse of merit and competitiveness which simply requires the negative abolition of barriers, and on the other the preservation of stable social structures (Forbes 1996: 167).

Such policies have a history. The chronological stages in the development of equal employment policy have been:

* special protection
* equal rights
* non-discrimination
* equal roles and opportunities
* and, most recently, mainstreaming (Reinalda 1996: 208; Rees 1998).

This chapter examines the current position of equal employment policy in the leading industrial democracies, and looks at the policy and legislative trajectories which have brought it about.

In the Beginning

As industrialisation developed in the states that were to become the post-industrial democracies during the nineteenth century, two paradoxical trends developed: women (and children) were exploited as labourers in the developing mass production systems, while simultaneously within bourgeois society the norms of respectability which developed increasingly confined women to the private sphere. The divergence between paid and unpaid employment increased, and the nature of women's paid employment, which kept them in the public sphere of the economy, became both more visible and a cause of concern (Frader 1998: 306–7). However, the idea of equal treatment and equal pay acquired little purchase. The women's movement had other priorities (property and divorce rights, access to education, political rights) and working-class men used the notion that men required a 'family wage' to enable them to support a wife and child as an argument for better pay. Meanwhile both middle-class observers and left-wing critics of capitalism such as Friedrich Engels 'assumed that the right to provide subsistence to the family was a male right, and that women's [paid] work was either "unnatural" or a perversion of women's maternal duties' (Frader 1998: 306–7). The consequent devaluation of women's paid work meant that the orientation of most political action in relation to women's economic status and activity until after the Second World War was essentially paternalist and protective. In prohibiting night work, or limiting hours, for example, it emphasised difference, not equality.

Employers exploited this devaluation and there was little challenge to this from the trade unions, in which women were under-represented (see Chapter 7). The arguments for the male 'family wage' generally prevailed, despite fears that lower paid women would undercut men. One response was to try to keep women out of male sectors of employment, and this was what occurred very widely. The segregation of male and female employment suited both the male unions and the employers who, when new machinery was introduced, could employ women to undertake the 'new' jobs and reduce the wages bill (Anderson and Zinsser 1990: 292–3; Boston 1987: 41–2). Crisis briefly overrode difference. The First World War saw the suspension of protective legislation and governmental exhortation to employers to ensure that jobs continued to be paid at previous rates even when the absence of the men meant they were now being done by women. This would protect the men's conditions when they were again available. These urgings went generally unheeded (Anderson and Zinsser 1990: 296). Nevertheless, the wartime crisis left one legacy. The Versailles peace treaty contained a Labour section, which set up the International Labour Organisation (ILO) and included an Article (427) embodying general principles for workplace rights and conditions, amongst them equal remuneration between men and women for work of equal value. However, as the chronology set out above implies, the ILO's early activities were initially geared to difference and protection – they included conventions on maternity protection and nightworking by women (International Labour Organisation 2006). ILO provisions were motivated in part by some concern for social justice combined, in the aftermath of the

Russian Revolution, with fears both for the social stability of states if there were not a modicum of social justice and for the competitiveness of individual countries if they had to act individually (Anderson and Zinsser 1990: 296; Galbi 1993).

After 1945 and within the context of the restoration and guaranteeing of human rights, as well as recognition of the role of women in both resistance and reconstruction, the preamble to the UN charter reaffirmed faith in 'the equal rights of men and women' and its first article mentions sex as one of the factors which must not lead to distinctions in respect of fundamental freedoms and human rights (Judt 2005: 565). The Universal Declaration of Human Rights was adopted by the UN in December 1948. Article 2 forbids 'distinction of any kind, such as race, colour, *sex*, language, religion, political or other opinion, national or social origin, property, birth or other status' (emphasis added). The ILO was reconstructed as a UN agency and its principles restated in the 1944 Declaration of Philadelphia including a commitment to equal opportunity. In 1951 its one hundredth convention, which was accompanied by a recommendation, covered equal remuneration. Any individual country is only bound by a convention after that state has ratified it, and the ILO has no enforcement mechanisms, so the principles and convention had no more than a declaratory and moral effect. Equally, at the same period the new constitutions in France, Italy and Austria and the basic law in West Germany included references to equality between men and women (von Wahl 2005: 84).

Frameworks for Policy

Equal employment policy, as it has emerged in the latter half of the twentieth and the early twenty-first century, has been set within political frameworks, utilised in different ways and to varied effect across developed industrial societies. These frameworks are:

• overarching grand designs at international level;
• overarching grand designs at national level;
• specific national legislation;
• collective agreements.

Each is considered below.

Grand designs: international institutions: the United Nations and the European institutions

The United Nations established a Commission on the Status of Women in 1946, initially as a sub-committee of the Human Rights Commission, but under pressure from women activists it soon became a full-standing commission (United Nations 2006). In 1963, again under pressure from active women, work was begun on devising a measure that would bring together a full statement of women's rights, resulting in 1967 in the adoption by the UN General Assembly of a Declaration on the Elimination of Discrimination against Women. This included a chapter (10) on employment, which proved to be one of the more controversial, so deeply are practices related to the employment of women embedded in the varying national cultures, societies and economies – in short, so entrenched are gender regimes. But this was merely a declaration, and the Commission on the Status of Women, beginning in 1974, initiated the process of preparing a more legally binding Convention. The Convention on the Elimination of All Forms of Discrimination against Women (CEDAW) was adopted by 130 votes to none (but 10 abstentions) in 1979 and signed by 64 countries at a formal ceremony in 1980. 183 states (in 2006) have now ratified it. The United States remains a signatory but without ratification. Whilst the Convention covers a wide range of rights, including a commitment to the elimination of prejudice and to political rights, articles 10 and 11 cover the removal of discrimination in economic life and equal employment, including equal remuneration for work of equal value.

UN work on the status of women is underpinned by the work of the Division for the Advancement of Women, located within the Department of Economic and Social Affairs. It has also been highlighted by world conferences on women, promoted by the UN Development Programme, for example in Mexico in 1975 (the year proclaimed International Women's Year by the UN) which designated 1976–85 the United Nations Decade for Women: Equality, Development and Peace. The end of the decade was marked by a conference in Nairobi, and in 1995 the Fourth World Conference was held in Beijing. This proved to be a particularly significant conference since it was preceded by intensive preparation by national delegations and accompanied by some measure of controversy (Hafner-Burton and Pollack 2002), especially in relation to women's reproductive rights. However, the outcome was both a declaration reaffirming the rights of women and a Platform for Action. A key feature of this platform was its commitment to what has become known as 'mainstreaming' – that is, the treatment of gender issues not as peripheral to or detached from other policy concerns, but as a central component of all policy discussions and formulation. The discourse of the Beijing conference was powerful and influential. However, the UN's commitment can apply only to its own agencies, and even when states have ratified the convention and approved the Platform for Action, the UN lacks enforcement capability, other than monitoring (all signatories to CEDAW are required to report at least once every four years on the actions they have taken to implement their obligations) and benchmarking, for example through the comments of a committee of experts on those reports.

The European Union is a unique international body because it contains within it a legal order of its own. As the nation-states of Europe pooled their sovereignty, the existence of equality as a principle in the constitutions of some of the member states had further repercussions. In the course of the 1956 and 1957 negotiations for the creation of the European Economic Community, it was realised that French industry might find itself not merely having to compete, but doing so on an unequal basis. The 1946 constitution had been followed up in France by legislation which said that agreements between employers and trade unions must incorporate equal pay and, in 1950, by a minimum wage with a single scale. But equal pay was not mandatory in other European countries. So labour costs in those countries, if women were employed, could potentially be structurally lower than in France, a point not lost on the Dutch where employers in some sectors, such as textiles, could gain advantages by employing women on low pay (Hoskyns 1996: 55). However, the negotiations were urgent and it was important to conciliate the French. So a little article was devised, along the lines of the ILO convention which four out of the six negotiating parties had ratified, and originally, and revealingly, allocated to a section on distortions to competition. It was finally slipped into a section of the draft treaty that dealt with social policy (Hoskyns 1996: 56; Guerrina 2005: 42). The concepts of social policy were limited, the focus narrowly economic, and no consideration at all was given to any broader issues of gender inequality (Guerrina 2005: 43). But the resultant Treaty of Rome did contain a specific reference to women as a category (Kaplan 1992: 29), for it included Article 119 (see Box 9.1).

However, 'Article 119 was not taken seriously by the member states' (Mazey 1989: 9). In the parliamentary debates on ratification the Dutch,

---

Box 9.1 Equal Rights in the EU Treaties

1958

Article 119 TEC (Treaty of Rome: came into force 1958)

1. Each Member State shall during the first stage ensure and subsequently maintain the application of the principle that men and women should receive equal pay for equal work.

1999

Article 3.2 TEC (as amended by the Treaty of Amsterdam: came into force 1999)

In all the activities referred to in this Article [i.e., the overarching activities of the European Community] the Community shall aim to eliminate inequalities, and to promote equality, between men and women.

Article 141 (ex 119) TEC (as amended by the Treaty of Amsterdam: came into force 1999)

1. Each Member State shall ensure that the principle of equal pay for male and female workers for equal work or work of equal value is applied.

   . . .

4. With a view to ensuring full equality in practice between men and women in working life, the principle of equal treatment shall not prevent any Member State from maintaining or adopting measures providing for specific advantages in order to make it easier for the under-represented sex to pursue a vocational activity or to prevent or compensate for disadvantages in professional careers.

Belgian and French governments all said it was only a declaration of intent, not an obligation (Vogel Polsky 1994: para. 1). In 1960, the European Commission produced a legal definition of equal pay, which simply said that when you were fixing pay levels you could not use the criterion of the sex of the worker to do so. And in 1961, when it became clear that the member states were not going to meet the 'during the first stage' deadline, which would be 31 December 1962, the Council of Ministers agreed to a Commission proposal and committed themselves to phased implementation. At the supra-national as well as at the national level, constitutional principles were liable to be vacuous until fleshed out by more specific provisions.

Grand designs: national blueprints for the position of women

The international principles discussed above are an example of provisions which underpin 'blueprint' policies (Mazur 2002: 47–61), setting out an overall design for a society in relation to the position of women. Since one of the functions of a constitution is precisely to lay out a general design for the operation of society, relevant principles will often be enunciated there and the renewal of a constitution has often provided an opening for the insertion of general principles of gender relations. This was so not only in the immediate post-war period but also, for example, in Spain in the 1970s following the downfall of fascism there. A package of constitutional reforms in Canada in 1982 saw the Constitution Act of 1982 entrench the Canadian Charter of Rights and Freedoms within the constitution. It contained an equality rights section with an anti-discrimination clause outlawing discrimination on a range of grounds, including sex. Similarly a general modernisation of the Dutch constitution in 1983 included the insertion of a general provision on non-discrimination on grounds of sex. However, first, not all developed industrial countries use their constitutions as a framework for an overall design within which equal employment policy can take its place. The Scandinavian and some East European countries do not have articles in their constitutions requiring equal employment and the United Kingdom does not have a codified constitution. In these countries more specific targeted legislation has been developed. Second, it is important to distinguish, as Mazur does (Mazur 2002: 49), between purely symbolic statements of pious intention, which often have minimal effect until they are operationalised by other actions or measures, and detailed and enforceable blueprints which are actually implemented.

Frameworks for national equal employment policy: legislation

The conditions which shape the relationships of men and women to employment and the labour market are nowhere the same. The differences between them arise from the prevailing gender regime within society. Moreover no modern society has been willing to tolerate a completely unregulated labour market. Because historical experience has clearly demonstrated that gender regimes within modern states will not result in free contracts producing equal employment opportunities, conditions and treatment between men and women, the achievement of such equality requires a legislative framework. This is a necessary but not sufficient condition. 'The design of equal employment policies still needs to recognize that inequities in the labour market are actually a product of forces outside of the labour market' (Mazur 2002: 80–1). Governments can provide incentives for practices to change through subsidies, tax breaks, education, training, information and attempts to change mindsets and attitudes. But alongside such carrots, the hard stick of enforceable legislation which protects rights is essential.

Equal employment legislation can be categorised as either negative – laws which forbid discrimination against either sex – or positive – laws which place requirements upon employers to promote equality of opportunity and treatment (Lovenduski 1986: 250; Randall 1987: 314). Negative legislation generally confers rights upon individuals and is used to ensure that concepts are translated into practice. The scope of domestic legislation structuring equal employment policy has tended to expand: starting, as the European Union did, with the regulation of equal pay and equal treatment, equal employment legislation at the start of the twenty-first century can comprise:

- provisions requiring equal pay for equal work;
- the extension of definitions of equal work to encompass work of equal value;
- provisions outlawing direct or indirect discrimination in access to employment or conditions of work;
- the regulation of part-time employment to ensure that employees on part-time contracts are no less favourably treated than full-timers;
- provisions requiring equality in arrangements for pensions (both public and private) and welfare benefits;
- the definition of a minimum wage.

However, progress towards so comprehensive a framework has been slow despite adherence to international conventions which, as Table 9.1 shows, in some cases took place at a quite early stage. Neither the post-war constitutions nor the European Community Treaty were initially translated into workable and precise provisions. Indeed, the United States, while bound neither by constitutional principles nor international obligations, was one of the first countries to introduce such legislation.

The European Union has now enacted legislation covering all the areas listed above except for the minimum wage, although by 2002 nine of the then fifteen EU member states did have minimum wage legislation, which tends to affect women more than men. In some cases and some areas, member states had developed appropriate legislation before the enactment of the EU directives. This did not always live up to the new

Table 9.1 Dates of first adoption/ratification of equal employment measures

	Constitution	CEDAW	ILO 100	Date of equal pay legislation	Sex discrimination/ equal treatment act
European Community/ Union	1958	n.a	n.a	1975	1976
Australia	No	1980	1974	1969[8]	1984
Belgium	1992[6]	1985	1952	1975[7]	1978 (economic orientation law)
Canada	1982 federal charter	1881	1972	1970s–80s[3]	–
Czech Republic	1993[1]	1993	1993	–	2000
France	1946	1983	1953	1972	1975/1983
Germany	1949	1985	1956	1955[8]/1980	1972
Hungary	No	1980	1956	2001/03	–
Italy	1948	1985	1956	1977	1977
Netherlands	1983	1991	1971	1975	1980
Norway	No	1981	1959	1978	1978

					Labour code amended 1996/2002
Poland	1997[2]	1980	1954	No	
Spain	1978	1984	1967	1988	Code of labour law 1995
Sweden	No	1980	1962	1979[4,5]	1979[5]
UK	No	1986	1971	1970	1975
USA	ERA not ratified	No	No	1963	1964

CEDAW = UN Convention on the Elimination of All Forms of Discrimination against Women 1979
ILO 100 = International Labour Organisation Convention on Equal Remuneration 1951
n.a.   = not applicable
ERA   = Equal Rights Amendment

Notes:

1   The constitutional charter of fundamental rights provides for 'fair' remuneration for everyone, but includes women with adolescents and handicapped persons as entitled to increased protection of health and special working conditions.
2   Based on wording of previous (1952 or Stalinist) constitution and 1992 interim constitution. See Polish women's rights centre at http://temida.free.ngo.pl/general.htm.
3   Different dates depending on province
4   Included within Equal Opportunities Act 1979
5   Amended and updated, 1991 and 2005 (equal pay) and 2003 (prohibition of discrimination)
6   Amendment explicitly guaranteeing equality
7   National collective agreement between unions and employers
8   Date of court ruling implementing general principle

Sources: Data from various sources including the websites of United Cities and Governments (UCLG), European Industrial Relations Observatory (EIRO), the International Labour Organisation (ILO) and the European Foundation for the Improvement of Living and Working Conditions.

standards, as the United Kingdom government discovered to its surprise as the result of a court ruling (see below).

Frameworks for equal employment policy: agreements between employers and trade unions

Whilst legislation is crucial, much policy change can also be achieved by collective agreements between employers and employees or their unions. Since equal employment policy has at its core – though not as its whole concern – the contractual relationship between an employer and an employee, collective agreements are in some countries, especially those with a tradition of industrial relations regulated between the 'social partners', an important mode of policy development. This was the case in Belgium, where over 80 per cent of the workforce is covered by collective bargaining mechanisms and equal pay was first introduced by a collective agreement (Bercusson 1996: 185). Similarly, in Sweden equal employment policies figured in collective agreements: 'in Sweden . . . [e]mployer reluctance [because of the costs of equality] and union protection of prerogatives led to their agreement that labour market matters were best settled by union and employer representatives' (Lovenduski 1986: 278–9) until a change of government in 1979 led to the passage of an act. Moreover, the European Union's social policy has always involved a substantial emphasis on the working together of the social partners. Hence its social policy provisions (contained within the 1992 Maastricht Treaty and adhered to by all member states since 1997) state that agreements reached at European level between employers and unions will be incorporated rather mechanically into EU law. This mechanism has been used for directives on both parental leave and the burden of proof.

Such agreements are highly dependent upon the willingness of the social partners, and especially the labour movement, to espouse concerns of equal employment and the role of collective bargaining has been important but ambivalent. When analysed closely with equal employment concerns in mind, apparently 'neutral' collective agreements – for example on pay scales or working time – may prove to have significant gender effects, and to incorporate indirect discrimination (Bercusson 1996: 183). Given that union activists in developed industrial democracies are often drawn from male, white, full-time workers, the values and issues embodied within collective agreements are liable to reflect their concerns and biases (Rees 1992: 107; see also Chapter 7).

Equal Employment Policy – Motivation and Machinery

In the developed industrial democracies, the achievement of equal employment legislation, both negative and positive, has largely been the culmination of a long process. Equal employment rights were for a long time, and perhaps slightly surprisingly, not a universal priority of feminist movements, though equally there has been little outright opposition (Randall 1982: 283): as one supporter of the United States' 1963 Equal Pay Act pointed out, opposition would be 'like being against motherhood' and an opponent said objecting was 'like opposing virtue' (quoted in Kessler-Harris 1990: 81). Nevertheless, the attitudes which in Poland produced laughter and ridicule when the Polish Women's Lobby attempted to introduce an equal opportunities bill in parliament (Einhorn 2005: 16) may not lie so far below the surface. Fairness for women who are in the labour market is rather uncontroversial even if the extent to which that should be achieved by legislation may be. But there is certainly opposition from proponents of 'family values', including women, to insistence on any requirement for women to undertake paid work (Bacchi 1999: 67). So here as elsewhere issues of equality and difference, and of differences between women, arise.

The range and complexity of motivations that have led to legislation are exemplified in Box 9.2. In most countries the Labour movement, specific women's groups, women MPs and the changing social environment have all contributed to it (Randall 1987: 163 and 287). Also, as the dates indicated in Table 9.1 suggest, many members of the European Community were impelled into the production of detailed legislation by the EC's 1975 and 1976 directives (see below) although, as in Ireland, this may have been only one influence, equal employment policy having often long been campaigned for by women's groups within the trade union movement and more widely (Galligan 1998: 71 and 79).

Equal employment policy comprises a number of elements, devised to meet the varied facets of employment that have been diagnosed as giving rise to problems. First, equal pay regulation responds to employer or public sector discrimination in both pay and pensions. Second, the extension of the definition to encompass work of equal value, as in the Australian ruling of 1972 and the EU legislation, addresses the devaluation of feminised work (Bacchi 1999: 73) and structural problems, for example, the immediate employer reaction to judicial rulings on equal pay in both Germany (1955) and Australia (1969) which consisted of the reclassification of types of work and increased segregation of the labour force, thus avoiding direct comparisons.

Box 9. 2   The Advent of Equal Employment Legislation in the USA

The United States 1963 Equal Pay Act and the subsequent 1964 Equal
Rights Act (which outlawed discrimination) were the product of a number
of converging factors:

- The status of women was rising, especially within the workforce. More
  women were graduating from higher education, a higher proportion
  was undertaking paid employment. Women were gradually moving
  into higher status professions and posts.
- Marital instability and the divorce rate were increasing. The notion that
  virtually all women would always be part of a family and hence supported
  by the family wage of a male breadwinner was no longer tenable.
- Modernisation and progress were on the agenda: 'high standards of
  living would help to justify America's claim to world leadership and
  legitimise the fight against Communism' (Kessler-Harris 1990: 102).
  Equal pay would, it was argued:
  - improve morale and productivity;
  - help to pull women into the workforce where they were needed;
  - result in higher consumption which, according to Keynesian
    economics, would speed economic growth.

The context was increasingly favourable:

- In line with the rhetoric of modernisation, President John Kennedy in
  1961 set up a President's Commission on the Status of Women.
- The Civil Rights movement was a movement in which black women
  were visible (not least the determined and iconic Rosa Parks) and had

Third, minimum wage legislation tackles issues of female inequality
since it tends to benefit women more than men. When a minimum wage
was introduced in Ireland in 2000, 7.3 per cent of women were estimated
to have received a pay increase. On the one hand, if women form a particularly high proportion of those receiving the minimum wage this may
indicate that they have at least been protected against even lower pay. In
the UK, 70 per cent of those on the minimum wage in 2000 were women.
On the other hand, if a high proportion of women receive the minimum
wage, this serves to emphasize that women may be disproportionately
badly paid. For example in France in 2001, 19.9 per cent of women
receive the minimum wage compared to 9.9 per cent of men (Rubery,
Grimshaw and Figueirido 2002: 103).

Fourth, regulation of part-time working also tackles unfairness by
employers. A high proportion of women work part-time (on average

→

since the mid-1950s been raising issues of democratic, civil and economic equality.

- The trade unions were supportive, and some had been lobbying for equal pay since the 1940s, if for ambivalent or negative reasons (Kessler-Harris 1990: 84):
  - to ensure that men were not undercut by women;
  - expecting that the obligation to pay equally would mean that employers would be unlikely to hire women. Ideology, social pressures and a gender segregated workforce were no longer proving sufficient to keep women out of male working domains.
- There were some organised women's groups, and women in Congress and in the administration who pushed the reform forward despite the absence of a widespread and vocal women's movement in favour. Esther Peterson, an experienced trade unionist appointed Assistant Secretary of Labour and Director of the Women's Bureau, collected information, organised lobbying and persuaded Kennedy to support the bill, to demonstrate his concern for his female electorate and to damp down what were seen as much more problematic demands for an Equal Rights Amendment to the constitution (Kessler-Harris 1990: 54).
- By the mid-1950s, 16 states and Alaska already had Equal Pay legislation.
- The advocates of equal pay and equal treatment succeeded in framing the arguments in terms that made opposition difficult. Moreover, in tactics that backfired, some Congressional opponents of the Civil Rights Act of 1964 were willing to support the inclusion in the bill of sex discrimination clauses on the grounds that this would increase the likelihood of the bill as a whole being thrown out (Hartmann 1989: 56).

across OECD countries 26 per cent, compared with less than seven per cent of men). In 1997, a directive on part-time working (EC 97/81) gave legislative force to an agreement between employers and unions at EU level to ensure that employees on part-time contracts are no less favourably treated than full-timers, and it was extended to the UK in 1998. A wider structural problem persists: '[p]art-time jobs are more likely to be found in lower-paid occupations that offer more limited opportunities for career advancement than full-time jobs . . . As a consequence, many women who seek part-time work end up "underemployed" as in order to find part-time work they have to accept less remunerative and less qualified work' (OECD 2002: 69).

Fifth, anti-discrimination legislation has accompanied or followed equal pay legislation. This tackles attitudes, though not perhaps the underlying structures of advantage and disadvantage (Bacchi 2004:

94ff). In both the UK and the USA, the treatment of specific groups within society came into focus in the 1960s. In both countries, legislation on discrimination on the basis of sex has owed some of its impetus to analogies with issues of race relations, and to the energetic substantive representation of women by a small number of female politicians. The European Community followed up its Equal Pay directive with an Equal Treatment directive, and this required member states to take action.

However, anti-discrimination and equal treatment legislation has posed notable problems for political systems. First, prejudice can affect both individuals (direct discrimination) and whole groups of people (indirect discrimination). Anti-discrimination law has in general been interpreted to cover both of these types of unfair treatment. However, '[d]iscrimination is essentially the overt expression of prejudice, which is irrational. Prohibiting in legislative terms acts which arise from emotions and providing adequate mechanisms [for enforcement] presents special problems for legislators' (Lovenduski 1986: 250). One response is the statutory duty imposed from 2007 on all public or quasi-public bodies in the UK, not merely not to discriminate on grounds of sex, but specifically to promote gender equality. On the whole, however, laws, do not change how people feel and think, and indirect discrimination, in particular, is likely to arise from deep-seated aspects of the gender regime in any society.

Second, proving the motivation of any action so as to demonstrate it was the result of prejudice or unequal treatment is difficult, since the perpetrator may simply deny this, and evidence is likely to be circumstantial. The EU has sought to remedy this to some extent by the 'burden of proof' directive, first proposed in 1984. This insists that if discrimination is alleged it is not the complainant who must prove that it was her (or, potentially, his) sex that was the cause of unfair treatment. Rather it is the defendant who must prove that they did not act unfairly. The directive was fiercely resisted as burdensome, and eventually achieved through the expression in law of an agreement between employers and unions under the Social Chapter of the Maastricht Treaty, from which the UK had opted out. With the change of government in the UK in 1997, a separate directive extended the measure to the UK.

Third, anti-discrimination legislation has been successfully used to block or prevent positive action on behalf of specific groups – treatment must not be detrimental, but specifically advantaging women, even on the basis that this compensates for a long history of structural and social disadvantage, can be argued to be detrimental to men. It was the Sex Discrimination Act that was invoked (see Chapter 5) to prevent the UK Labour Party's use of all-women shortlists, and the European Court of

Justice took a similar line in the *Kalanke* case in 1995 (see below). The EU has since attempted to counter this by the treaty article allowing for measures to redress the balance in favour of the under-represented sex.

Fourth, it is argued by a number of radical critics that reliance on legislation as a way of furthering equal employment policy is a weak and limited strategy (Mazey 1988). It relates only to waged employment relationships, and to strictly formal rights which do little to alter the actual conditions under which women operate within the waged labour market. Its aim is to ensure that women are dealt with as if they were men, with no acknowledgment of difference (Ward 1996: 378), and it does nothing to deal with the position of women in families and the domestic division of labour which is the major determinant of disadvantage for women.

Women's policy agencies: roles and dilemmas

Official bodies which have the mission of promoting the status and rights of women, known as women's policy agencies, were established in many states in the final decades of the twentieth century (Lovenduski et al. 2005: 3–4; Mazur and Stetson 1995: 3). The United Nations Commission on the Status of Women (see above) recommends that all governments create women's policy machinery, suggesting that its aims should be to improve women's status in relation to the needs identified in various situations. All advanced industrial democracies now have some machinery for advancing policy approaches which recognise women's interests (see Table 9.2). Causing governmental policy to meet those needs has been defined as 'state feminism'. Some agencies have a dual mission – thus the UK EOC has both a monitoring and enforcement role and a research, policy development and campaigning role. The characteristics and effectiveness of women's policy agencies vary a good deal across the states in which they exist, however. They vary in their structure, the range of their concerns and in their degree of marginalisation from the main centres where decisions are taken. They also vary in the levels of resourcing of their core funding, of their ability to fund internal and external programmes, of their staffing and of their autonomy and capacity to decide and regulate.

Some fundamental dilemmas arise in relation to women's policy agencies. First, structures pose problems. Agencies which take the form of more or less independent advisory commissions may play an important role in setting agendas; equally they may risk being marginalised or ignored if their advice does not chime in with what the political parties and the government of the day want to hear. Agencies which are structured as

Table 9.2 The establishment of women's policy agencies

Country	Women's policy agencies/mechanisms
Australia	1972 Women's advisor to the prime minister 1974 Office of the Status of Women
Belgium	1985 Junior ministerial portfolio (state secretary for social emancipation) 1986 (Advisory) Emancipation Council replaced 1993 by (advisory) Council on Equal Opportunities
Canada	1954 Women's bureau of the Ministry of Labour (concerned with women workers) 1971 Minister for the Status of Women with federal ministerial department (Status of Women Canada)
Czech Republic	2001 Advisory Government Council for Equal Opportunities for Men and Women
France	1965 Advisory Study and Liaison Committee on the problems of women's work 1974 Junior minister for the Condition of Women: 1981–86 Ministry for Women's Rights: 1986 onwards junior ministerial portfolio for equal opportunities under various names (from 2005 'for social cohesion and parity') 1995 (Consultative) Observatory of Parity between Men and Women 2000 Civil service division, 'service for women's rights and equality'
Germany	1986 Ministry for Health, Family and Youth became Ministry for Health, Family, Women and Young People. Since 1994, Ministry for Families, the Elderly, Women and Young People 1991–94 separate ministry for Women and Young People
Hungary	1995 Secretariat of Women's Policy, Ministry of Family and Social Affairs 1999 Council for Women's Issues
Italy	1983 National Committee for the implementation of the principles of equal treatment and opportunity between workers of both sexes (Ministry of Labour) 1984 National Committee for Equality and Equal Opportunities between men and women (Prime Minister's Office) 1996 Minister for Equal Opportunities with Ministry (now Department) of Equal Opportunities

211

Netherlands	1975–81 (Advisory expert) Emancipation Committee; 1981–97 Emancipation Council; 1998–2001 Temporary Expert Committee for Emancipation
	1978 Junior minister and official agency for equality policy in Ministry of Culture and Social Work. 1981 Moved to Ministry of Social Affairs
Norway	1972 Equal Status Council
Poland	2001 Government Plenipotentiary for Equal Status of Women and Men (in Prime Minister's office)
Spain	1983 Institute for Women (Ministry of Culture, then Ministry of Social Affairs)
Sweden	1972–6 Advisory Council to the Prime Minister on Equality between Men and Women
	1973 Assistant Minister of Labour 'with special responsibility for women's issues'
	1982 Minister for Gender Equality supported by Division of Gender Equality
UK	1969 Independent advisory (government-funded non-departmental public body) Women's National Commission
	1975 Equal Opportunities Commission (from 2007 amalgamating with Disability Rights Commission and 2009 with Commission for Racial Equality to form Commission for Equality and Human Rights)
	1986 Ministerial Group on Women's Issues, 1992 became Cabinet sub-committee
	1997 Ministerial portfolio as Minister for Women (always combined with another, larger portfolio) supported by an unpaid junior Minister for Women and Women's Unit
	2001 Women's Unit became Women and Equality Unit. Institutional location has followed portfolio of Minister holding portfolio for the time being
USA	1920 Women's Bureau in the Department of Labour
	1964 Equal Employment Opportunity Commission

Sources: Data from various sources including Mazur and Stetson 1995; Bundesministerium für Familie 2006; Noss 2005; Swedish Government 2007.

ministries or ministerial departments have a greater legitimacy in shaping policy development. But their incorporation as part of an 'official' machinery takes them out of the circuit of co-operation and information-sharing between non-governmental women's groups (Sawer 2003: 248) while within government they have often been envisaged as co-ordinating bodies, with no real policy clout and lacking staff and budgets. As newcomers they stand rather low in the hierarchy of prestige which helps to determine the strength of any ministry's input into policy debates. Location close to a prime minister may help: but when a prime minister's attention and priorities shift, impetus may be lost. For example, the women's policy agency in Canada was established within the central privy council office, but soon 'transferred to the periphery as a stand-alone agency ... As a result of its location, women's machinery in Canada has been hampered by a lack of both political clout and co-ordination capacity' (Chappell 2002: 87). Equally a lack of standing may make women's policy agencies very vulnerable to restructuring initiatives. The UK Women and Equality Unit has moved around the administrative structures (in 2006 from the Department of Trade and Industry to the Department for Communities and Local Government) following the assignment of the portfolio to different ministers at successive government reshuffles and there is no evident logic in the attachment of the portfolio to any particular minister. '[Ministers for Women] have been expected to combine a "proper" job with the women's job, thus reducing it to the status of political housework' (*The Economist*, 23 December 2000).

Sawer argues that in Australia the adoption of the managerial and efficiency-oriented approach of the New Public Management has been particularly damaging to the women's policy agencies,

- in the resulting increased volatility of administrative structures which has militated against long-term projects;
- in the devaluing of process, and of policy expertise, so that prior evaluation of proposed policy for its potential gender impact is impeded;
- in the levels of accountability, which tends in the new management structures to be achieved by target-setting and performance measurement, which does not necessarily incorporate gender-disaggregated measures.   (Sawer 2003: 250).

Second, leadership varies. While advisory bodies tend to have leaders identified for their commitment to the advancement of women, the receptivity of ministries for women to the demands of the women's movement and of feminists may depend to a considerable extent upon the personal orientation of the minister. When a very Conservative woman was appointed as minister assisting the prime minister for the status of women in Australia, budgets were cut and 'by 1999 operational funding was provided only to more conservative and less policy-active Non-Governmental Organisations' (Sawer 2003: 253). Moreover, posting into a women's policy agency can produce real difficulties for civil servants, especially if they are women (see Box 9.3).

Third, it is rare for women's policy agencies to be well funded: the Spanish Institute for Women which quite rapidly acquired a useful budget and substantial staff (Threlfall 1996: 124) is an unusual exception. More often such units have been continuously underfunded or particularly vulnerable to budget cuts in periods of financial stringency.

Type, proximity to the centres of power, administrative capacity and leadership (Lovenduski et al. 2005: 15) can all thus pose problems for women's policy agencies. The short-lived French Ministry for Women's Rights in the early 1980s illustrates many of the pitfalls (Reynolds 1988a, 1988b). Similarly, the women's policy machinery in Australia was in the early 1990s regarded as exemplary because of

- its location under the prime minister's portfolio in the main policy co-ordination centre of the government;
- its links into key points in other federal and state agencies;
- its encouragement of community representation on policy advisory bodies and its funding of advocacy as well as services for women;
- its incorporation amongst its employed officials of women who were specifically seeking to advance the position of women from within official structures (femocrats);
- its emphasis on gender budgeting – the disaggregation of the impact of 'mainstream' expenditure on women and men – and on gender auditing – the evaluation of out-turn in terms of its gendered effects.

However, these features turned out to be vulnerable to changing political and ideological context (Chappell 2002: 88 and 92). Since 1997, women's policy units in state and federal governments have been moved out of their central locations, accountability and gender auditing as policy tools have been devalued in the face of new managerial techniques, funding for women's community organisations has been cut, and women's views are sought in an unmediated fashion by market research techniques. Appointments to advisory bodies have been geared towards partisan loyalty while cuts in funding and staffing in many women's policy

---

Box 9.3   Femocrats

'Femocrat' is a term coined initially by Australian scholars to denote women employed within state institutions, especially within women's policy machinery. Originally carrying the connotation that femocrats have a background in the women's movement, and a clear agenda of combating discrimination against women and promoting the policy-making style and measures favoured by feminist collective ideologies, the term is sometimes applied to all women working within state bureaucracies. However, in some bureaucratic systems (for example, Canada) 'the idea that civil servants should adopt the role of internal lobbyists for women as a definable group was anathema' (Geller-Schwarz 1995: 49) and women's policy machinery has frequently been staffed by (often female) career civil servants, who risk being excoriated by the women's movement for not being lobbyists, and distrusted by their colleagues because they might be (Mazur and Stetson 1995: 35, 56–7, 105).

---

areas, for example the Human Rights and Equal Opportunities Commission and the Affirmative Action Agency, resulted in high staff turnover and reduced the openings for femocrats (Sawer 2003: 250–1, 257–8, and see Box 9.3).

A not dissimilar tale can be told of the women's committees established by local councils in the United Kingdom in the early 1980s (see Box 8.2). Women's policy agencies can thus play advisory roles in the formulation of policy measures, and their accountability and monitoring functions ensure more effective implementation of policy once it has been developed, but they also face substantial dilemmas in finding appropriate places within policy structures.

Interpreting policy provisions: the role of the courts

Where equal employment policy is underpinned by constitutional frameworks or by legislation, the decisions of the courts play a key role in its interpretation and implementation. 'Equality before the law' arguments which have been reinforced by judicial action have often served as 'a foundation stone for future developments' (Shaw 1999). Examples can be cited in both Germany and Australia. In West Germany in 1955 the federal labour court, referring to Article 3 of the basic law which specified equality between men and women, ruled that pay settlements could not specify differential rates with a standard percentage deduction for women (Kolinsky 1989: 55). In Australia in 1969, the Australian Council of Trade Unions took a case to the Commonwealth Court of Conciliation and Arbitration which produced a ruling requiring equal pay (see Table 9.1), and another case in 1972 expanded the principle to rule that pay must be equal for work of equal value. The notion of equal value was also enforced by court rulings in the EU. In the United Kingdom when the Equal Pay Act was debated in 1970, the government rejected the notion of equal value (Ellis 1996: 8, fn 2). It was a judgement by the European Court of Justice that compelled the UK government to introduce amending legislation in 1983. The framework provisions of Article 119 of the Treaty of Rome (see Box 9.1) provided the basis for judgements by the European Court of Justice (ECJ) which had a very substantial impact in stimulating more detailed legislation and ensuring its application throughout the member states. In the European Union the treaties convey rights on individuals, but cases on behalf of a disadvantaged individual must be brought in the national courts of the member state in the first instance. It is only in cases where the scope and application of the law may not be firmly established that a ruling is sought from the European Court of Justice. But the case of Gabrielle Defrenne was so referred (see Box 9.4) and, in the lengthy period while the legal processes unrolled, came together with a range of other pressures to induce the production of specific legislation.

Court judgements are based upon the substance of the law. But court rulings, especially those of the European Court of Justice which has taken a broad view of its role in furthering the aims of the EU treaties, can serve to highlight the limits of the law, and thus stimulate further changes. This occurred, for instance, when the ECJ, in the *Kalanke* case in 1995, interpreted the directives so as to rule unlawful a positive action provision in the German *Land* of Bremen which automatically gave preference to a woman if there were two equally qualified candidates for a public service post. As both Hoskyns (Hoskyns 1996: 158–9 and 198) and Guerrina (Guerrina 2005) have argued, in the hands of judges 'equality can be a harsh principle' (Hoskyns 1996: 198) and a limited one, when hard judicial reasoning limits it to narrow applications of procedure, rather than outcome. A similar comment has been made in relation to the Canadian courts in their application of the equality provision of the 1982 Canada Charter of Rights and Freedoms (Bashevkin 1998; Gingras 1995; Mazur 2002: 53), alleging that it was being used as a mechanism for men to limit women's rights. However, this can in itself prompt changes. The *Kalanke* case prompted the addition to the treaty allowing for measures to overcome disadvantage (see Box 9.1). The *Kalanke* judgement was ill-received, especially by women's policy

Box 9.4　The Defrenne Cases

The late 1960s was a period of growing awareness and action amongst women. One of the events was an equal pay strike at a Belgian weapons factory, which at its peak involved 3,000 women workers (Hoskyns 1996: 67). Some of the strikers had placards calling for the application of Article 119 of the Treaty of Rome (see Box 9.1). A young woman lawyer called Eliane Vogel-Polsky wrote an article arguing that it was possible that Article 119 might give individuals rights in their national courts even if the national government had not specifically made the necessary provisions. What was needed was a test case. Working with another lawyer, Marie-Thérèse Cuvelliez, she found one. The air hostesses of Sabena airlines were professional women, working alongside, and doing jobs identical to, the male stewards of the airline. But while the retirement age for the stewards was 55, theirs was 40. They lost status and salary, had a much reduced pension and had to look for new work in mid-career. In 1968 Gabrielle Defrenne, who had worked for Sabena since 1951, reached 40 and had to retire. She agreed to allow Vogel-Polsky and Cuvelliez to take the case forward.

The case opened in 1968, and shortly thereafter a second case, linked to Sabena's pension scheme, which was generous to everyone except, explicitly, air hostesses, was also opened. Both cases were eventually referred by the Belgian courts to the European Court of Justice for its ruling on the applicability and meaning of the law. The first ruling, in fact on the second case, came in 1971, the second in 1976. In the second ruling the Court accepted that Article 119 gave rise to direct rights that had both economic and social significance and that formed 'part of the foundations of the Community'. In failing to implement equal pay the member states had been failing to observe the treaty (see Hoskyns 1996).

agencies and groups, and the women's movement 'demonstrated an enviable capacity to translate its objections to the *Kalanke* judgment . . . into concrete proposals then adopted at the highest level in the EU' (Shaw 1999).

Policy enforcement by the courts can also exact a personal cost. Looking back upon one of the leading cases on sex discrimination in the USA (Eveleth Mines), one of the lawyers involved remarked with sadness upon the toll it had taken: there had been great victories but, on the other hand, 'there was the great cost, and that great cost actually was paid by the women, the plaintiffs. As a lawyer in the case, the case took years, and I saw part of what the toll was on the women' (Boler 2004).

Monitoring and Enforcing Policy

The efficacy of legislation and the role of the courts depend upon

- the willingness of individuals, sometimes with wider support, to contest what they see as illegal actions by employers;
- and/or the vigilance of institutions, agencies and NGOs in monitoring the application of, and compliance with, the legislation and ensuring it is enforced.

In a number of cases, equal employment legislation also included within it a mechanism for monitoring its enforcement. In the United States, the Equal Employment Opportunity Commission was created in 1964. It receives and investigates complaints of unfair treatment in a number of fields, particularly racial discrimination, but '[i]n the first year after enactment, one-third of charges filed with the EEOC alleged sex discrimination . . . The unexpected inclusion of sex in the statute quickly led women workers and the newly emerging women's movement of the late 1960s to take advantage of the opportunity to pursue equality in the courts' (EEOC 2004). The American experience was one of the factors which prompted the setting up of the Equal Opportunities Commission in the United Kingdom, and the Equal Employment Agency in the Republic of Ireland. In the UK the EOC experienced a hesitant start in monitoring the law, not least because it was operating in what became, during the 1980s, a hostile political environment (Lovenduski and Randall 1993: 185). However, '[g]radually the Commission was persuaded that using the law and the courts would be faster and more effective than chipping away at government opinion' (Lovenduski and Randall 1993: 188) and it began to take judicial review proceedings against the government as well as supporting key cases brought by individuals. Similarly in Canada in the 1980s, the government provided funds to support legal defence organisations taking cases to court (Mazur 2002: 53).

The institutional merging of concerns for women's rights with other human rights concerns (a feature of the EEOC in the USA from the start) is becoming more common. This will occur in the UK and has already done so in Norway, with the creation on 1 January 2006 of the office of an anti-discrimination Ombudsperson, and an Equality and Anti-discrimination Tribunal, and in France in early 2005 when the office for combating discrimination and promoting equality – the *Haute Autorité de Lutte contre Les Discriminations et pour l'Egalité* (HALDE) – was set up. Such mergers have been a cause of concern for feminists, who fear the watering down of a specific focus on gender issues.

Within the European Union, the European Commission, which has an overall duty to ensure compliance with EU law, has played an important role in ensuring that the equal employment policy directives were adequately transposed into national law. For example, the United Kingdom initially took no action in respect of the 1975 and 1976 equal pay and equal treatment directives on the grounds that the objectives of the directives were already met by existing legislation. The Commission eventually took the UK before the ECJ and in a 1982 judgement the court ruled that the UK was not compliant with the requirement that equal pay should cover work of equal value (Ellis 1996: 9–10). UK law was consequently changed. Similarly, the Commission initiated proceedings against Italy (Guerrina 2005) and West Germany (Kolinsky 1989: 64). In Ireland after the passage of the Equal Pay Act, the government faced strong pressure to delay its implementation, both from within its own services and from private industry where, in both cases, the cost of implementation was a concern, while some sections of the labour movement were concerned by the possibility of a loss of male jobs. The European Commission ruled against the delay and directed the Irish government to give immediate effect to the law (Galligan 1998: 79). However, the Commission's monitoring of compliance can only extend as far as ensuring that the necessary national measures have been introduced. Enforcement of the detailed measures must depend upon the national courts, which can act only if there are allegations that an individual's rights have been infringed.

Equal Employment Policy: Outcomes

Operating through the frameworks described above, all advanced industrial states now have official equal employment policies and provisions. But how effective have they been in (a) objectively ensuring employment equality and (b) in subjectively changing attitudes and lessening the likelihood that discrimination will occur?

Reducing employment inequality

Equal employment has resulted, in advanced industrialised democracies, in the creation of well-developed frameworks of legislation which have allowed women to pursue complaints and, in some cases, seek redress for instances of blatant discrimination through the courts. Paradoxically, the post-Communist countries, which had a particularly strong ideological commitment to gender equality under the Communist regimes, have been notably slow to set up gender policy machinery. A major impetus seems to have been the existence of UN and EU benchmarking. The requirement to report periodically to the UN on progress in implementing obligations under the CEDAW convention has been one spur to action, as has the need to implement existing EU legislation on accession. But there is in all countries something of a gap between formal frameworks and the habits and actions of society. Employers' organisations have been markedly unwelcoming towards gender equality legislation which they consider 'counterproductive', and gender equality has not been high on the collective bargaining agenda of the trade unions (EFILWC 2006b: 8–9). As Chapter 1 suggests, specific and material changes have been slow to come. There is still a gender pay gap, and marked occupational segregation, both vertical and horizontal (see Chapter 1). In the 27 EU member states in the first decade of the twenty-first century, 'a woman has a significantly higher chance of falling into the lower income category, and a significantly lower chance of falling into the higher income category than has a man with a similar occupation, full-time status, tenure etc.' (EFILWC 2006b: 7).

Changing attitudes

Whilst (disappointing) changes induced by the legislation in terms of specific outcomes can be measured, it is inevitably a great deal harder to measure the changes in attitudes and social reflexes which anti-discrimination legislation is also often charged with producing. Critics of such legislation may object to the level of 'social engineering' which is involved but, as with quotas for representation (see Chapter 5), it is implied that such legislation will eventually become virtually redundant, since the behaviour it requires will become ingrained.

That this is far from being the case is suggested by the number of cases referred to monitoring bodies or taken before the courts. Moreover, statistical studies in the European Union have found that in most of the EU countries a proportion of the gender pay gap can be explained by differences in the characteristics of men and women in the workforce. But another proportion (and in one estimation and one country (Italy) the whole of the gap) has to be ascribed to differences in the extent to which society is prepared to reward those characteristics. For many commentators (though not all) those differences amount quite simply to discrimination, in other words an irrational undervaluing of

what women do (Beblo et al. 2003). This is not necessarily overt or deliberate, as we saw in Chapter 6 in relation to women in senior positions, but
it is nevertheless pervasive and persistent.

Further evidence of failure to shift attitudes as opposed to ensuring
compliance with regulation comes from the differences between public
and private sector employment. Public sector employers have by and
large to be careful about, and accountable for, compliance with legal
requirements. They tend (but see above, p. 4 for the effects of the new
public management) to have relatively transparent recruitment and
promotion procedures and pay scales. It is therefore unsurprising that on
the whole gender pay gaps and 'vertical' segregation are less apparent in
public sector employment.

Many feminists would suggest that it is futile to expect equal employment policy, even when it goes to the lengths, as it does for UK public
service employers, of requiring not merely the avoidance of discrimination but the promotion of gender equality, by itself to disrupt the patriarchal patterns of behaviour that surround and condition women's
employment. 'Employment on the same terms as men is neither a viable
nor a desirable goal for women as long as those terms remain unchanged'
(Bryson 1999: 143). Such a disruption, they argue, must be dependent
upon ending the gendered division of all labour, not just waged employment, but also household maintenance and caring. This too requires
policy and legislative frameworks, for example on working hours, on
parental and caring leave and on child and elder care. Some advanced
industrial democracies have moved in this direction. But none has been
willing to tackle the division of labour within the private sphere head-on.
'Although changes in employment practices are a necessary condition for
men's increased domestic role, they are not sufficient' (Bryson 1999:
134).

Conclusion

A number of pessimistic conclusions could be drawn from the discussion
in this chapter. First, equal employment is fraught with almost irreconcil-
able conflicts and dilemmas. If the reference point for equality is the male
worker, with his combination of autonomy and dependence upon female
support, then equal employment policy will continue to ignore the private
sphere. The outcome is that many women carry a double burden of
employment and care, with all the limitations that places on them,
combined with some degree of outsourcing of caring to a largely female,

usually poorly paid workforce. But creating a new reference benchmark currently seems not to be in any way envisaged by the legislative or policy frameworks.

Linked to this dilemma is the conflict between protection and equality. Women, perhaps in part because they have so frequently been an oppressed group, have often been envisaged as requiring special protection, for example through the prohibition of night work or special arrangements during pregnancy and lactation. But such protection emphasises difference, and may work to disadvantage women in seeking employment. The modern version, however, is the policies, for example in the UK, which speak in gender neutral terms of assisting 'work–life balance' but which, when unpacked, in both rhetoric and substance are directed largely towards women. They are aimed at assisting women to embrace the limitations imposed by their double burden, trading pay (and often, in practice, career advancement opportunities) for private time (Kodz, Harper and Dench 2002). Moreover, this intersects with other social divisions.

> In some important respects [class differences] grew more acute during the 1990s. Any sensible approach to work–life policies cannot ignore the intractable phenomenon of occupational class in the amount of access and take-up of work–life balance entitlements. Women in managerial and professional jobs with higher incomes and benefits are in a much better position to achieve a balance than their much lower-paid and insecure counterparts employed, for example, in the retail trade and textiles.   (Taylor 2001)

Third, the movement towards equal employment has resulted in the commercialisation of many of the previously unpaid services provided by women. As women go out of the home to paid employment, jobs are created for child carers, homecare nurses, cleaners, producers of convenience foods and similar personnel. Such services may also become available through the 'black' or illegal economy. But such jobs are still viewed as 'women's work', often poorly paid, and, if they fall into the illegal economy – being filled, for example, by illegal immigrants – risk appalling exploitation. They are seldom a path to true economic autonomy for women. Women's movement into relatively poorly paid employment of this kind helps to explain why gender pay gaps persist even in the most 'egalitarian' societies, as in Scandinavia.

A final conflict has been between compliance with the letter of the law, often against the grain of social expectation and habit, and deep-rooted social attitudes. In a number of countries, neo-liberal or conservative ideologies which emphasize individualism and fail to challenge underlying structures have become more prevalent (Einhorn 2006: 167–9; Taylor 2001: 8). Forbes argues that they represent a fight-back by privileged groups (especially white, middle-class, professional males) who have found their interests challenged by the implementation of equal employment policies (Forbes 1996: 168). Change can seem glacially slow.

Set against this pessimism must be some more optimistic observations. Equal employment policy is strongly underpinned by international conventions and, in the EU, transnational legislation. Equal employment legislation is a necessary condition of non-discrimination and is very widely present in advanced industrial democracies. It is nowhere under serious challenge, even if rather little advantage is being taken of the EU Treaty provisions allowing for measures 'providing for specific advantages'. The comparative work of feminist scholars has drawn attention to the diversity of practice and the lessons to be drawn from differing national practices, and activists are self-conscious about the roots of their beliefs and the extent of diversity amongst women in terms of class or ethnicity.

Conclusion

This book concludes on a note of cautious optimism. In general, as Chapter 1 illustrated, women's economic position, status and power in the societies of OECD countries at the start of the twenty-first century fail to measure up to that of men. Those who wish to see these enhanced recognise that much remains to be achieved. But there have been very substantial changes over the last 40 years, and younger people today can and do make everyday assumptions about women's position that would have seemed at best highly radical and at worst unimaginable only a few decades ago. Such optimism is grounded in the recognition that women have been demonstrating their autonomy in their use of their votes, and become a constituency which the political parties cannot afford to ignore (Chapter 3). Women have moreover been taking their place within the political decision-making elites, to the extent that two of the major political contests of the first decade of the twenty-first century include a woman (Hillary Clinton in the USA and Ségolène Royal in France) amongst their frontrunners. There is increasing recognition that activity outside the formal political institutions offers scope for women to shape and influence the binding collective decisions that are made within a society which shape people's lives (Chapter 7). But formal institutions remain crucial not only in shaping decisions but also in implementing, enforcing and monitoring them (Chapter 9). The part that women have played in political life has vindicated the assertion by the suffragettes of more than a century ago that political action and social change are reciprocal and reinforcing. However, despite undoubted progress, not least in the extent to which the presence of women, combined with legislative frameworks, has in many countries made the public and formal expression of prejudice unacceptable, optimism can only be cautious. Paradoxes and dilemmas persist.

First, the theme of equality and difference has run throughout this book, and the dilemmas it presents are far from fully resolved. While many would agree that millennia of male dominance currently justify the continued recognition of difference, the nature of the 'equal person' that might emerge if equality (which cannot simply mean the extension of male rights to women (Bryson 1999: 204)) were to be achieved is far from clear. That this person would not simply conform to the stereotypical model of the (male) political and economic actor is widely recognised. But what would he/she be like?

A related dilemma is the question of care and provision for human needs (see Box 4.2). The 'abstract individual' of traditional political science cannot exist, since no human being can escape from being the recipient of care – at least as babies all require it and all normally continue to do so at different stages throughout their lives (Sevenhuijsen 1998: 846). But how and by whom should it be provided? What is an appropriate balance of reward, esteem and resourcing within society between wealth creation and caring, in their widest senses? And even could such a balance be discerned, how is it to be arrived at? Some aspects of the policy of the European Union epitomise this problem: on the one hand the so-called Lisbon Agenda of 2000 set a target for increasing the average participation rate of women in the labour force from 51 to over 60 per cent over the following decade, and on the other hand much of their social legislation seeks explicitly 'to take into account that women predominantly carry the burden of having to reconcile family and professional life' (European Commission 2000). There is always the risk that so-called 'family-friendly' measures are in fact targeted specifically at women with the implication that only women require 'concessions' to a caring role to be undertaken. Thus in January 2007 the UK government announced a 'Quality Part-Time Work Fund' to assist, in the words of the press release, the creation and retention of more part-time jobs *for women* [my emphasis] at a senior level (news release of 30 January 2007).

A further dilemma is how presence at political level can be transformed into social change more widely. Only in Norway and Spain has a commitment to female presence in political life resulted in similar commitment to ensuring female presence in other sectors of decision-making. A quota has been imposed for the boards of public companies, resulting, in Norway, in well over one-third of board positions in the top 50 publicly quoted companies being held by women (European Union 2006). In Sweden, which has higher levels of female representation in parliament, the proportion is some ten percentage points lower. In the Fortune 500 top companies in the United States in 2006, 13.6 per cent of board members are female, compared with 16.2 per cent of the membership of the House of Representatives.

Optimism has thus to be tempered by caution, given the continuing dilemmas, and the slow rate of progress. Moreover, change in the position of women takes many different forms. Where a particular pattern of behaviour was the consequence of a more or less imposed ideology (as was the case for the role of women under communism in Europe), changes in the political and ideological regime rapidly revealed the extent to which it had not been underpinned by social attitudes. Interestingly, the reverse position may be observed in Spain: there coercive fascism imposed the oppression rather than the forced 'emancipation' of women and the end of that regime has seen rapid progressive advance. They now constitute half of the government's ministers.

One conclusion must therefore be – and this too has a been a theme throughout this book – that even among autonomous and active women there is no consensus about the type of emancipation that is desirable or the nature of their interests. Women start from hugely varied points, in their ethnicity, in the types of society in which they live, in their levels of social advantage, and in religion, and political conviction. The cross-cutting of these attributes with their gender produces both theoretical and practical division. Examination of the role of women within politics illuminates the extent of these divisions, and suggests that 'progress' may take markedly different forms and directions.

Some outcomes of women's campaigning seem well embedded. The return of a majority of a different political hue did not result in the repeal of the French parity law. However, while the constitutional amendment that permitted it seems as solid as the constitution, the law itself is time-limited and far from secure. Similar observations could be made, for example, about abortion rights which, though an almost archetypal symbol of feminist progress despite disagreements even among feminists about their morality, have been greatly restricted in East Germany and Poland and have come under question elsewhere.

The slowness of change and the continued male domination of formal institutions seem daunting and discouraging to those who wish to see women's position enhanced. The trajectories of Angela Merkel and Nancy Pelosi, for example, suggest that women are increasingly permeating the formal positions of power. Pessimists may argue that that they are doing so precisely at the point when globalisation from above and decentralisation from below are removing the scope for policy action by the formal bodies of the nation-state. On the other hand, first, a very great deal of power remains with these bodies, and the increasing presence of women within them is a cause for optimism, and equally, in so far as power is fragmenting, it may be moving into areas of issue politics and of local activism and participation where women can and do readily play a major role. There is much to be lost if vigilance is relaxed and progress taken for granted. Women both can and should be deeply concerned and involved with understanding and explaining the discourse and behaviour of the individuals and groups who participate in collective decision-making. They can be and are widely engaged in creating and reshaping the strategies for handling conflict which constitute politics.

Further Reading

Both Vicky Randall and Joni Lovenduski have produced very useful surveys of the trends in feminist thought and its impact on political science (Randall 1991; Lovenduski 1998; Randall 2002). Their own early surveys of the area of women and politics are still well worth reading for the wisdom and insight they contain (Randall 1987; Lovenduski 1986).

The field of women's history has grown very rapidly. Anderson and Zinsser (1990) provide a good general overview, while Reynolds (1996) is a model of how to write the history of a particular country and period with an emphasis on women.

Women are almost entirely absent from the standard textbooks on comparative politics such as Hague and Harrop (2004) and recent overviews of the place of women and politics across a range of countries are few and far between. However, Nelson and Chowdhury (1994) cover 43 countries. While some of the information is a little out of date, the background and analysis is still extremely wide ranging and very pertinent. Wendy Stokes has produced a useful study which also incorporates surveys of developments across a number of other countries although its main emphasis is on the United Kingdom (Stokes 2005). Readers of French are well served by two books by Catherine Achin and her colleagues (Achin and Lévêque 2006; Achin 2007).

There is more information on individual regions and countries. Ruth and Simon Henig brought together information about Western Europe (Henig and Henig 2001) and Karen Beckwith's forthcoming book promises to be both up-to-date and comprehensive (Beckwith forthcoming). On Scandinavia there is the collection edited by Bergqvist (1999), and on Eastern Europe that edited by Matland and Montgomery (2003a) is an admirable start. There is now an immense literature on women and politics in the United States, much of it positivist and behaviourist in orientation. Some of the key contributions of the last three decades have been brought together by O'Connor and her colleagues (O'Connor et al. 2006), while for a general overview of development I suggest you start with Dolan et al. (Dolan, Deckman and Swers 2006) and with Tremblay and Trimble (2003) for Canada.

Notions of gender and their implications are comprehensively discussed by Connell (1987) and Kimmel (2000). The implications for political ideas are explored in Judith Squires's indispensable study (1999). Jane Freedman provides a very accessible introduction to feminism (2001). Some of the key concepts discussed throughout the book and now much used in feminist political analysis derive from Rosabeth Moss Kanter (1993) and from Carol Gilligan (1982). Both deserve to be read directly rather than filtered through the discussions of others. Anne Phillips's anthology (1998a) brings together some of the classic writings of feminist theory and political thought and her own work (Phillips 1991, 1995, 1999) is indispensable.

Lister (2003) and Einhorn (2006) provide very stimulating insights on notions of citizenship, and Friedman has edited an up-to-date theoretical discussion (Friedman 2005). Any consideration of the concept of representation has to start with the work of Hanna Pitkin (1972). On the political orientation and behaviour of women around the world and over time see Inglehart and Norris (2003). The best resource on voter turnout by gender is the work of the International Institute for Democracy and Electoral Assistance available on their website (http://www.idea.int/gender/). Rosie Campbell (2006) surveys women's voting behaviour in the UK, while Norris considers the current state of knowledge in the USA (2003). On the outcomes and strategies for improvement, including quotas and parity, see Lovenduski (2005a), the thorough discussion by Mateo Diaz (2005) and recent work by one of the pioneers, Drude Dahlerup (2006). The processes of policy change in this area are the focus of a recent collection (Lovenduski 2005a). Squires (forthcoming) looks both at inputs and outcomes. As the numbers of women representatives increase, they can be more widely studied. The work of Childs (2004) and Dodson (2006) is splendidly showing the way. Footitt (2002), Puwar (2004) and Kathlene (2001, 2005) illuminate the ways in which women speak and operate within assemblies, and Stivers looks at public administration (1993).

The nature and growth of the women's movement is considered by the contributors of the collections edited by Threlfall (1996) and Marsh et al. (2000), while the implications of current changes to the nature of the state are covered by the contributors to Banaszak et al. (2003).

The Research Network on Gender Politics and the State has produced valuable studies of policy and policy-making in areas of particular feminist concern (see Mazur and Stetson 1995; Mazur 2001; Stetson 2001; Mazur 2002; Outshoorn 2004). On the European Union see Guerrina (2005) and Rossilli (2000a).

References

Abelès, Marc (2000) *Un Ethnologue à l'assemblée* (Paris: Odile Jacob).

Achin, Catherine (2007) *Sexes, genre et politique* (Paris: Economica).

Achin, Catherine and Sandrine Lévêque (2006) *Femmes en Politique* (Paris: La Découverte).

Agacinski, Sylviane (2000) *Politique des Sexes, Précédé de mise au point sur la Mixité* (Paris: Seuil: Collection Points).

Alban-Metcalfe, Beverly and Michael A. West (1991) 'Women Managers'. In *Women at Work*, ed. Jenny Firth-Cozens and Michael A. West (Buckingham: Open University Press), pp. 154–71.

Alimo-Metcalfe, Beverly (1995) 'An Investigation of Female and Male Constructs of Leadership and Empowerment'. *Women in Management Review* 10, no. 2: 3–8.

Allison, Maggie (2000) 'Women and the Media'. In *Women in Contemporary France*, ed. Abigail Gregory and Ursula Tidd (Oxford: Berg), pp. 65–87.

Allwood, Gill and Khursheed Wadia (2000) *Women and Politics in France* (London: Routledge).

Almond, Gabriel A. and Sidney Verba (1963) *The Civic Culture: Political Attitudes and Democracy in Five Nations* (Princeton, NJ: Princeton University Press).

Amar, Micheline, ed. (1996) *Le Piège de la Parité – Arguments pour un débat* (Paris: Hachette).

Andersen, Kristi (1996) *After Suffrage: Women in Partisan and Electoral Politics before the New Deal* (Chicago, ILL: University of Chicago Press).

Anderson, Bonnie S. and Judith P. Zinsser (1990) *A History of their Own* (London: Penguin Books).

Apfelbaum, E. and M. Hadley (1986) 'Leadership Ms-Qualified: 11 Reflections on Initial Case-Study Investigation of Contemporary Women Leaders'. In *Changing Conceptions of Leadership*, ed. Carl F. Graumann and Serge Moscovici (New York and Berlin: Springer-Verlag), pp. 199–221.

Apter, Terri (1985) *Why Women Don't Have Wives: Professional Success and Motherhood* (Basingstoke: Macmillan).

Australian Bureau of Statistics (2000/6) *6302.0 Average Weekly Earnings 16 November 2000 and 18 May 2006*; accessed 10 July 2006.

Australian Public Service Commission (2004–5) *Statistical Bulletin*, available at http://www.apsc.gov.au/stateoftheservice/0405/statistics/mainfeatures.htm#ses; accessed 13 April 2006.

Bacchi, Carol Lee (1999) *Women, Policy and Politics: The Construction of Policy Problems* (London: Sage).

Bacchi, Carol Lee (2004) 'Policy and Discourse: Challenging the Construction of Affirmative Action as Preferential Treatment'. *Journal of European Public Policy* 11, no. 1: 128–46.

Badinter, Elisabeth (1996) 'Non aux Quotas des Femmes'. In *Le Piège de la Parité: Arguments pour un Débat*, ed. Micheline Amar (Paris: Hachette), pp. 18–22.

Baer, Denise L. (2003) 'Women, Women's Organizations and Political Parties'. In *Women and American Politics*, ed. Susan J. Carroll (Oxford: Oxford University Press), pp. 111–45.

Banaszak, Lee Ann (2003a) 'When Power Relocates: Interactive Changes in Women's Movements and States'. In *Women's Movements Facing the Reconfigured State*, ed. Lee Ann Banaszak, Karen Beckwith and Dieter Rucht (Cambridge: Cambridge University Press), pp. 1–29.

Banaszak, Lee Ann (2003b) 'The Women's Movement Policy Successes and the Constraints of State Reconfiguration'. In *Women's Movements Facing the Reconfigured State*, ed. Lee Ann Banaszak, Karen Beckwith and Dieter Rucht (Cambridge: Cambridge University Press), pp. 141–68.

Banaszak, Lee Ann, Karen Beckwith and Dieter Rucht eds. (2003) *Women's Movements Facing the Reconfigured State* (Cambridge: Cambridge University Press).

Bashevkin, Sylvia B. (1998) *Women on the Defensive: Living through Conservative Times* (Toronto: University of Toronto Press).

Baudino, Claudie (2005) 'Gendering the Republican System: Debates on Women's Political Representation in France'. In *State Feminism and Political Representation*, ed. Joni Lovenduski (Cambridge: Cambridge University Press), pp. 85–105.

BBC News (1999) Evelyn Parker: 'Greenham Women Succeeded'. BBC, Wednesday, 10 November 1999, 17:44 p.m.

BBC (2003) *Women's Party to Fight On*. Available from http://news.bbc.co.uk/1/hi/northern_ireland/3299125.stm; accessed 11 January 2007.

Beblo, Miriam, Denis Beninger, Anja Heinze and François Laisney (2003) 'Measuring Selectivity-corrected Gender Wage Gaps in the EU'. In *Equal Pay in Europe Seminar* (held in Manchester on 12 December 2003; available at http://www.mbs.ac.uk/vesearth/european-employment/conference-seminars/documents/DP_2ew.pdf; accessed 31 March 2007).

Beckwith, Karen (2000) 'Beyond Compare? Women's Movements in Comparative Perspective'. *European Journal of Political Research* 37, no. 4: pp. 438–61.

Belloubet-Frier, Nicole (1997) 'Sont-Elles Différentes?' *Pouvoirs*, no. 82: pp. 59–75.

Bendix, John (1994) 'Women and Politics in Germany and Switzerland'. *European Journal of Political Research* 25, no. 4: 413–438.

Bennie, Lynn (2002) *Survey of Political Studies 2002*. Available from http://www.psa.ac.uk/psanews/0210/survey.htm; accessed 20 November 2006.

Benoit, Kenneth and Jacqueline Hayden (2004) 'Institutional Change and Persistence: The Evolution of Poland's Electoral System, 1989–2001'. *The Journal of Politics* 66, no. 2: 396–427.

Bercusson, Brian (1996) 'Equality Law in Context: Collective Bargaining'. In *Sex Equality Law in the European Union*, ed. Tamara Hervey and David O'Keefe (Chichester: John Wiley), pp. 179–200.

Bergqvist, Christine (ed.) (1999) *Equal Democracies? Gender and Politics in Nordic Countries* (Oslo: Scandinavian University Press).

Bird, Karen (2003) 'Who are the Women? Where are the Women? And What Difference can they Make? Effects of Gender Parity in French Municipal Elections'. *French Politics* 1, no. 1: 5–38.

Bird, Karen (2004) 'Who Needs Women? Gender Parity in French Elections'. In *The French Presidential and Parliamentary Elections of 2002*, ed. J. Gaffney (Aldershot: Ashgate).

Boler, Jean (2004) EEOC panel, available at http://www.eeoc.gov/abouteeoc/40th/panel/40thpanels/panel2/transcript.html; accessed 31 March 2007.

Bono, Paola and Sandra Kemp (eds) (1991) *Italian Feminist Thought: A Reader* (Oxford: Blackwell).

Boothroyd, Betty (2002) *The Autobiography* (London: Arrow Books).

Borrelli, Mary Anne (2000) 'Gender Politics and Change in the United States Cabinet: The Madeleine Korbel Albright and Janet Reno Appointments'. In *Gender and American Politics: Women, Men, and the Political Process*, ed. Sue Tolleson-Rinehart and Jyl J. Josephson (Armonk, NY: M. E. Sharpe), pp. 185–204.

Boston, Sarah, (ed.) (1987) *Women Workers and the Trade Unions* (London: Lawrence & Wishart).

Bouchier, David (1983) *The Feminist Challenge* (London: Macmillan).

Bourque, Susan. C. and Jean Grossholtz (1984) 'Politics an Unnatural Practice: Political Science Looks at Female Participation'. In *Women and the Public Sphere*, ed. Janet Siltanen and Michelle Stanworth (London: Hutchinson), pp. 103–21.

Box-Steffensmeier, Janet. M., Suzanna De Boef and Tse-Min Lin (2004) 'The Dynamics of the Partisan Gender Gap'. *American Political Science Review* 98, no. 3: 515–28.

Bredin, Frédérique (1997) *Députée: journal de bord* (Paris: Fayard).

Brimelow, Elizabeth (1981) 'Women in the Civil Service'. *Public Administration* 59, no. 3: 313–35.

Bronfenbrenner, Kate (2005) *Union Organizing among Professional Women Workers*, DPE Conference on Organizing Professionals in the 21st Century, Crystal City, Virginia; available at http://digitalcommons.ilr.cornell.edu/cgi/viewcontent.cgi?article=1024&context=cbpubs; accessed 7 August 2006.

Brown, A., T. B. Donaghy, F. MacKay and E. Meehan (2002) 'Women and Constitutional Change in Scotland and Northern Ireland', *Parliamentary Affairs* 55, no. 1: 71–84.

Bryson, Valerie (1999) *Feminist Debates: Issues of Theory and Political Practice* (Basingstoke: Macmillan).

Buckley, Mary (1997) 'Adaptation of the of the Soviet Women's Committee: Deputies' Voices from "Women of Russia" '. In *Post-Soviet Women: From the Baltic to Central Asia*, ed. Mary Buckley (Cambridge: Cambridge University Press), pp. 157–85.

Budgeon, Shelley (2001) 'Emergent Feminist Identities: Young Women and the Practice of Micropolitics'. *European Journal of Women's Studies*, 8, no. 1: 7–28.

Buffotot, Patrice and David Hanley (1998) 'Chronique d'une défaite anoncée: Les élections legislatives des 25 mai et 1er juin 1997'. *Modern and Contemporary France* 6, no. 1: 5–20.

Bundesministerium für Familie, Senioren, Frauen und Jugend (2006) *Geschichte des Ministeriums*. Available from http://www.bmfsfj.de/bmfsfj/generator/ Kategorien/Ministerium/geschichte.html; accessed 28 January 2007.

Burns, Nancy, Kay Lehman Schlozman and Sidney Verba (2001) *The Private Roots of Public Action: Gender, Equality, and Political Participation* (Cambridge, MA: Harvard University Press).

Burrell, Barbara (2004) *Women and Political Participation: A Reference Handbook* (Santa Barbara, CA: ABC-CLIO).

Bussemaker, Jet and Kees van Kersbergen (1999) 'Contemporary Social-Capitalist Welfare States and Gender Inequality'. In *Gender and Welfare State Regimes*, ed. Diane Sainsbury (Oxford: Oxford University Press), pp. 15–46.

Campbell, Rosie (2002) *Gender and Voter Turnout in the 2001 British General Election*. Available from http://www.essex.ac.uk/ECPR/events/jointsessions/paperarchive/turin/ws22/Campbell; accessed 7 December 2005.

Campbell, Rosie (2004) 'Gender, Ideology and Issue Preference: Is there such a Thing as a Political Women's Interest in Britain?'. *British Journal of Politics and International Relations* 6, no. 1: 20–44.

Campbell, Rosie (2006) *Gender and the Vote in Britain* (Colchester, Essex: ECPR Press).

Carroll, Susan J. (1988) 'Women's Autonomy and the Gender Gap: 1980 and 1982'. In *The Politics of the Gender Gap: The Social Construction of Political Influence*, ed. Carol M. Mueller (Newbury Park, CA: Sage), pp. 236–57.

Carroll, Susan J. (1994) *Women as Candidates in American Politics* (Bloomington, IN: Indiana University Press).

Carroll, Susan J. (2004) *Gender Gap Persists in 2004 Election*. Available from http://www.cawp.rutgers.edu/Facts/Elections/GG2004Facts; accessed 6 December 2005.

Caul, M. (2001) 'Political Parties and the Adoption of Candidate Gender Quotas: A Cross-National Analysis', *Journal of Politics* 63, no. 4: 1214–29.

Center for American Women and Politics (2005a) *Women's Vote 2004*. Available at http://www.cawp.rutgers.edu/Facts/Elections/Womensvote2004.html; accessed 10 April 2006.

Center for American Women and Politics (2005b) *Archives: Did You Know?* Available at http://www.cawp.rutgers.edu/factoidarchive; accessed 23 April 2006.

Center for American Women and Politics (2005c) *Women who Succeeded Their Husbands in Congress*. Available at http://www.cawp.rutgers.edu/Facts/ Officeholders/widows; accessed 23 April 2006.

Center for American Women and Politics (2006a) *Officeholders*. Available at http://www.cawp.rutgers.edu/Facts/Officeholders/fedcab; accessed 1 May 2006.

Center for American Women and Politics (2006b) *Women Officeholders: Fact Sheets and Summaries*. http://www.cawp.rutgers.edu/Facts/Officeholders/ mayors-curr; accessed 28 January 2007.

Center for Reproductive Rights (2007) *Female Genital Mutilation: Legal Prohibitions Worldwide*. Available at http://www.reproductiverights.org/ pub_fac_fgmicpd.html; accessed 27 March 2007.

Chaney, Paul (2004) 'Women and Constitutional Change in Wales', *Regional and Federal Studies* 14, no. 2: 281–303.

Chappell, Louise A. (2002) 'The "Femocrat" Strategy: Expanding the Repertoire of Feminist Activists', *Parliamentary Affairs* 55, no. 1: 85–98.

Charles, Nickie (2000) *Feminism, the State and Social Policy* (Basingstoke: Palgrave Macmillan).

Childs, Sarah (2001) ' "Attitudinally Feminist"? The New Labour Women MPs and the Substantive Representation of Women'. *Politics* 21, no. 3: 178–85.

Childs, Sarah (2002) 'Hitting the Target: Are Labour Women MPs "Acting for" Women?' *Parliamentary Affairs* 55, no. 1: 143–53.

Childs, Sarah (2004) *New Labour's Women MPs: Women Representing Women* (London: Routledge).

Childs, Sarah and Mona Lena Krook (2006) 'The Substantive Representation of Women: Rethinking the "Critical Mass" Debate'. Political Studies Association Conference at Reading, UK, April 2006. Available at http://www.psa.ac.uk/ Journals/pdf/5/2006/Childs.pdf; accessed 31 March 2007.

Childs, Sarah, Joni Lovenduski and Rosie Campbell (2005) *Women at the Top 2005: Changing Numbers, Changing Politics* (London: Hansard Society).

Childs, Sarah and J. Withey (2004) 'Women Representatives Acting for Women: Sex and the Signing of Early Day Motions in the 1997 British Parliament'. *Political Studies* 52, no. 3: 552–64.

Chiva, Cristina (2005) 'The Nation and Its Pasts: Gender, History and Democratisation in Romania'. In *Nation and Gender in Contemporary Europe*, ed. Vera Tolz and Stephenie Booth (Manchester: Manchester University Press), pp. 80–95.

CIA (2006) *World Factbook*. http://www.odci.gov/cia/publications/factbook/ index; accessed 14 February 2006.

Clift, Eleanor and Tom Brazaitis (2000) *Madam President: Shattering the Last Glass Ceiling* (New York: Scribner).

Coalition of Labor Union Women (2006) *History Timeline*; available at http://www.cluw.org/about-historytimeline.html; accessed 8 August 2006.

Collins, James and Val Singh (2006) 'Exploring Gendered Leadership'. In *Women in Leadership and Management*, ed. Duncan McTavish and Karen Miller (Cheltenham: Edward Elgar Publishing), pp. 11–31.

Connell, Robert W. (1987) *Gender and Power: Society the Person and Sexual Politics* (Cambridge: Polity Press).

Conover, Pamela Johnston (2006) 'Feminists and the Gender Gap', reprinted from 1988 in *Gendering American Politics: Perspectives from the Literature*, ed. Karen O'Connor, Sarah Brewer and Michael Philip Fisher (New York: Pearson Longman), pp. 111–20.

Cook, Elizabeth Adell and Clyde Wilcox (2006) 'Feminism and the Gender Gap: A Second Look', reprinted from 1991 in *Gendering American Politics: Perspectives from the Literature*, ed. Karen O'Connor, Sarah Brewer and Michael Philip Fisher (New York: Pearson Longman), pp. 121–6.

Council of European Municipalities and Regions (2005) *Women's Political Participation in CEMR Members*. Available at http://www.ccre.org/news_detail_en.htm?ID=456; accessed 28 January 2007.

Cowley, Philip and Sarah Childs (2003) 'Too Spineless to Rebel? New Labour's Women MPs', *British Journal of Political Science* 33, no. 3: 345–65.

Curtin, Jennifer. (1997) *The Gender Gap in Australian Elections*. Available from http://www.aph.gov.au/library/pubs/rp/1997-98/98rp03; accessed 9 November 2005.

Dahlerup, Drude (1984) 'Overcoming the Barriers: an Approach to How Women's Issues are Kept from the Political Agenda'. In *Women's Views of the Political World of Men*, ed. Judith Stiehm (Dobbs Ferry, NY: Transnational Publishers), pp. 31–66.

Dahlerup, Drude (1988) 'From a Small to a Large Minority: Women in Scandinavian Politics'. *Scandinavian Political Studies* 11, no. 4: 257–98.

Dahlerup, Drude (1992) 'Confusing Concepts, Confusing Reality: a Theoretical Discussion of the Patriarchal State'. In *Women and the State*, ed. Anne Showstack-Sassoon (London: Routledge), pp. 93–127.

Dahlerup, Drude (ed.) (2006) *Women, Quotas and Politics* (New York: Routledge).

Dahlerup, Drude and Lenita Freidenvall (2005) 'Quotas as a "Fast Track" To Equal Political Representation for Women: Why Scandinavia is no Longer the Model'. *International Feminist Journal of Politics* 7, no. 1: 26–48.

Darcy, R., Susan Welch and Janet Clark (1994) *Women, Elections and Representation* (Lincoln: University of Nebraska Press).

Dauphin, Sandrine and Jocelyne Praud (2002) 'Debating and Implementing Gender Parity in French Politics', *Modern and Contemporary France* 10, no. 1: 5–11.

Davidson, Marilyn J. and Ronald J. Burke, eds (2000) *Women in Management Current Research Issues*, vol. 2 (London: Sage).

Davies, C. (1999) 'The Masculinity of Organisational Life'. In *Women and Public Policy: The Shifting Boundaries between Public and Private Spheres*, ed. S. Baker and A. Van Doorne Huiskes (Aldershot: Ashgate), pp. 35–56.

Del Carmen Feijoó, Maria (1994) 'From Family Ties to Political Action, Women's Experiences in Argentina'. In *Women and Politics Worldwide*, ed. Barbara J. Nelson and Najma Chowdhury (New Haven, CT: Yale University Press), pp. 60–72.

Della Porta, Donatella, Hanspeter Kriesi, and Dieter Rucht (1999) *Social Movements in a Globalizing World* (New York: St Martin's Press).

Delmar, Rosalind (1986) 'What is Feminism?' In *What is Feminism?*, ed. Juliet Mitchell and Ann Oakley (Oxford: Basil Blackwell), pp. 8–33.

Dex, Shirley, Holly Sutherland and Heather Joshi (2000) 'Effects of Minimum Wages on the Gender Pay Gap'. *National Institute Economic Review*, no. 173: 80–8.

Diamond and Nancy Hartsock (1998) 'Beyond Interests in Politics: A Comment on Virginia Sapiro's "When are Interests Interesting?" The Problem of Political Representation of Women'. In *Feminism and Politics*, ed. Anne Phillips (Oxford: Oxford University Press), pp. 193–202.

Diem-Wille, Gertraud and Judith Ziegler (2000) 'Traditional or New Ways of Living'. In *Gendering Elites: Economic and Political Leadership in 27 Industrialised Societies*, ed. Mino Vianello and Gwen Moore (Basingstoke: Palgrave Macmillan), pp. 169–76.

Dietz, Mary G. (1998) ' "Context is All": Feminism and Theories of Citizenship'. In *Feminism and Politics*, ed. Anne Phillips (Oxford: Oxford University Press), pp. 378–400.

Dodson, Debra L. (2005) 'Making a Difference: Behind the Scenes'. In *Women and Elective Office: Past, Present, and Future*, ed. Clyde Wilcox and Sue Thomas (New York: Oxford University Press), pp. 129–51.

Dodson, Debra L. (2006) *The Impact of Women in Congress* (Oxford: Oxford University Press).

Dolan, Julie A., Melissa M. Deckman and Michele L. Swers (2006) *Women and Politics: Paths to Power and Political Influence* (Upper Saddle River, NJ: Pearson Prentice Hall).

Dolan, Kathleen (2005) 'How the Public Views Women Candidates'. In *Women and Elective Office: Past, Present, and Future*, 2nd edn, ed. Clyde Wilcox and Sue Thomas (New York: Oxford University Press), pp. 41–59.

Drew, Eileen, Gwen Moore, Renata Siemienska and Mino Vianello (2000) 'A Theoretical Framework'. In *Gendering Elites: Economic and Political Leadership in 27 Industrialised Societies*, ed. Mino Vianello and Gwen Moore (Basingstoke: Palgrave Macmillan), pp. 3–10.

Duchen, Claire (1994) *Women's Rights and Women's Lives in France, 1944–1968* (London: Routledge).

236   *References*

Duerst-Lahti, Georgia (1998) 'The Bottleneck: Women becoming Candidates'. In *Women and Elective Office: Past, Present and Future*, 1st edn, ed. Sue Thomas and Clyde Wilcox (New York: Oxford University Press), pp. 15–25.

Duerst-Lahti, Georgia and R. M. Kelly, eds (1995) *Gender Power, Leadership and Governance* (Ann Arbor, MI: University of Michigan Press).

Duerst-Lahti, Georgia and Dayna Verstegen (1995) 'Making Something of Absence: The "Year of the Woman" and Women's Political Representation'. In *Gender, Power, Leadership and Governance*, ed. Georgia Duerst-Lahti and Rita Mae Kelly (Michigan, MI: University of Michigan Press), pp. 213–38.

Duncan, Simon (1996) 'The Diverse Worlds of European Patriarchy'. In *Women of the European Union*, ed. Maria Dolors Garcia-Rowan and Janice Monk (London: Routledge), pp. 74–110.

EEOC (2004) Equal Employment Opportunity Commission, USA *Celebrating the 40th Anniversary of Title VII*; available at http://www.eeoc.gov/abareeoc/40th/parcel/expanding.html; accessed 31 March 2007.

EFILWC (European Foundation for the Improvement of Living and Working Conditions) (2006a) *Fourth European Working Conditions Survey*. Available at http://eurofound.europa.eu/pubdocs/2006/78/en/1/ef0678en.pdf; accessed 18 January 2007.

EFILWC (European Foundation for the Improvement of Living and Working Conditions) (2006b) *The Gender Pay Gap: Background Paper*. Available at http://eurofound.europa.eu/pubdocs/2006/101/en/1/ef06101en.pdf; accessed 18 January 2007.

Einhorn, Barbara (1992) 'German Democratic Republic: Emancipated Women or Hard-Working Mothers?' In *Superwomen and the Double Burden*, ed. Chris Corrin (London: Scarlet Press), pp. 125–54.

Einhorn, Barbara (2005) 'Citizenship, Civil Society and Gender Mainstreaming: Contested Priorities in an Enlarging Europe'. In conference on '*Gendering Democracy in an Enlarged Europe*', Prague 20 June 2005; available at http://qub.ac.uk/egg/ accessed 31 March 2007.

Einhorn, Barbara (2006) *Citizenship in an Enlarging Europe* (Basingstoke: Palgrave Macmillan).

Eisenstein, H. (1996) *Inside Agitators: Australian Femocrats and the State* (Philadelphia, PA: Temple University Press).

Elections (2003) *Parties and Elections*. http://www.parties-and-elections.de/nireland2; accessed 11 January 2007.

Ellis, Evelyn (1996) 'Equal Pay for Equal Work: The United Kingdom's Legislation Viewed in the Light of Community Law'. In *Sex Equality Law in the European Union*, ed. Tamara Hervey and David O'Keefe (Chichester: John Wiley), pp. 8–19.

Epstein, Michael J., Eichard G. Niemi and Linda W. Powell (2005) 'Do Women and Men State Legislators Differ?' In *Women and Elective Office: Past, Present, and Future Second Edition*, ed. Clyde Wilcox and Sue Thomas (New York: Oxford University Press), pp. 94–109.

Equal Opportunities Commission (2005) *Submission to the Women and Work Commission: Part One: Occupational Segregation.* Available at http://www.eoc.org.uk/pdf/WWC_occ_seg.pdf; accessed 12 January 2007.

Esping-Andersen, Gøsta (1999) *Social Foundations of Postindustrial Economies* (Oxford and New York: Oxford University Press).

European Commission (2000) *Commission Communication concerning a Community Framework Strategy on Gender Equality, 2001–05.* Com (2000) 325.

European Commission (2003) *Commission Staff Working Paper: Gender Pay Gaps in European Labour Markets.* SEC (2003) 937.

European Commission (2006) *Press Release IP/06/493 of 12 April 2006*

European Industrial Relations Observatory (2006) *Pay Developments 2005.* Available at http://www.eiro.eurofound.eu.int/2006/06/update/tn0606101u.html; accessed 18 January 2007.

European Union (2006) *Database on Men and Women in Decision-Making.* Available at http://europa.eu.int/comm/employment_social/women_men_stats/out/measures_out4211_en.htm; accessed 13 April 2006.

Eurostat (2005) *Comparable Time Use Statistics: National Tables from 10 European Countries 2005 Edition.* Available at http://www.uni-mannheim.de/edz/pdf/eurostat/05/KS-CC-05-001-EN.pdf; accessed 31 March 2007.

Eurostat (2006a) News release 59/2006 May.

Eurostat (2006b) *EU Labour Force Survey – Principal Results 2005.* Available at http://epp.eurostat.ec.europa.eu/; accessed 1 October 2006.

Evans, Judith (1981) 'USA'. In *The Politics of the Second Electorate*, ed. Joni Lovenduski and Jill Hills (London: Routledge), pp. 33–51.

Eveline, Joan (2005) 'Woman in the Ivory Tower: Gendering Feminised and Masculinised Identities'. *Journal of Organizational Change Management* 18, no. 6: 641–58.

Ezekiel, Judith (2002) 'Open Forum le Women's Lib: Made in France'. *European Journal of Women's Studies* 9, no. 3: 345–61.

Fairhall, David (2006) *Public and Private: The Dichotomies of Citizenship* (London: I.B. Tauris).

Fawcett, Millicent Garrett (1925) *What I Remember* (London: T. F. Unwin).

Fawcett Society (2004) *Women and the Criminal Justice System* (London: The Fawcett Society). Available at http://www.fawcettsociety.org.uk/index.asp?PageID=95; accessed 15 March 2006.

Fearon, Jane (2002) *Northern Ireland Women's Coalition: Institutionalizing a Political Voice and Ensuring Representation.* Available from http://www.c-r.org/accord/peace/accord13/nor.shtml accessed 11 January 2005.

Federation of Canadian Municipalities (2005) *Women in Municipal Politics.* Available from http://www.fcm.ca/english/policy/women.html; accessed 28 January 2007.

Ferguson, K. E. (1984) *The Feminist Case against Bureaucracy* (Philadelphia: Temple University Press).

Fletcher, J. K. (1999) *Disappearing Acts* (Cambridge, MA: MIT Press).

Flexner, Eleanor (1976) *Century of Struggle: The Women's Rights Movement in the United States* (Cambridge, MA: Belknap Press of Harvard University Press).

Fogarty, Michael P., Isobel Allen and Patricia Walters (1981) *Women in Top Jobs 1968–1979* (London: Heinemann).

Footitt, Hilary (2002) *Women, Europe and the New Languages of Politics* (London: Continuum).

Forbes, Ian (1996) 'The Privatisation of Equality Policy in the British Employment Market for Women'. In *Sex Equality Policy in Western Europe*, ed. Frances Gardiner (London and New York: Routledge), pp. 161–79.

Fox, Richard L. and Jennifer L. Lawless (2004) 'Entering the Arena? Gender and the Decision to Run for Office'. *American Journal of Political Science* 48, no. 2: 264–80.

Fox, Richard L. and Jennifer L. Lawless (2006) 'Family Structure, Sex Role Socialization and the Decision to Run for Office'; reprinted from 2003 in *Gendering American Politics*, ed. Karen O'Connor, Sarah Brewer and Michael Philip Fisher (New York: Pearson Longman), pp. 87–95.

Frader, Laura L. (1998) 'Doing Capitalism's Work: Women in the Western European Industrial Economy'. In *Becoming Visible: Women in European History*, 3rd edn, ed. Renate Bridenthal, Susan Mosher Stuard and Merry E. Wieser (New York: Houghton Mifflin Company), pp. 295–326.

Frazer, Elizabeth and Kenneth Macdonald (2003) 'Sex Differences in Political Knowledge in Britain', *Political Studies* 51, no. 1: 67–83.

Freedman, Jane (1997) *Femmes Politiques: Mythes et Symboles* (Paris: L'Harmattan).

Freedman, Jane (2001) *Feminism* (Milton Keynes: Open University Press).

Freeman, Jo (2000) *A Room at a Time: How Women Entered Party Politics* (New York: Rowman and Littlefield).

Friedan, Betty (1965) *The Feminine Mystique* (Harmondsworth: Penguin Books).

Friedman, Milton and Rose D. Friedman (1980) *Free to Choose: A Personal Statement* (Harmondsworth: Penguin Books).

Galbi, Douglas (1993) International Aspects of Social Reform in the Interwar Period: Center for Population and Development Studies (Cambridge, MA: Harvard University). Available at http://www.galbithink.org/isr.pdf; accessed 15 June 2006).

Galligan, Y. (1998) *Women and Politics in Contemporary Ireland: From the Margins to the Mainstream* (London: Pinter).

Garcia, Ada and Isabella Dumont (2003) *Women in Trade Unions: Making the Difference* (European Trade Union Confederation). Available at http://www.etuc.org/a/234; accessed 7 August 2006.

Geddes, Andrew (2003) *The Politics of Migration and Immigration in Europe* (London: Sage).

Geller-Schwarz, Linda (1995) 'An Array of Agencies: Feminism and State Institutions in Canada'. In *Comparative State Feminism*, ed. Amy Mazur and Dorothy M. Stetson (Thousand Oaks, CA: Sage Publications), pp. 40–58.

Gilligan, Carol (1982) *In a Different Voice* (Cambridge, MA: Harvard University Press).

Gingras, François-Pierre (1995) *Gender and Politics in Contemporary Canada* (Toronto: Oxford University Press).

Githens, Marianne (2003) 'Accounting for Women's Political Involvement: the Perennial Problem of Recruitment'. In *Women and American Politics*, ed. Susan J. Carroll (Oxford: Oxford University Press), pp. 33–52.

Glen, Nancy E. and Meredith Reid Sarkees (2001) 'Foreign Policy Decision-Makers: the Impact of Gender'. In *The Impact of Women in Public Office*, ed. Susan J. Carroll (Bloomington: Indiana University Press), pp. 117–48.

Goldin, Claudia (1990) *Understanding the Gender Gap: An Economic History of American Women* (New York: Oxford University Press).

Goot, Murray and Elizabeth Reid (1975) 'Women: if not Apolitical, then Conservative'. In *Women and the Public Sphere*, ed. Janet Siltanen and Michelle Stanworth (London: Hutchinson), pp. 122–39.

Gosnell, Harold Foote (1930) *Why Europe Votes* (Chicago, IL: University of Chicago Press).

Green, Manda (2004) 'Women and the National Assembly in France: an Analysis of Institutional Change and Substantive Representation with Special Reference to the 1997–2002 Legislature', unpublished thesis, University of Stirling.

Greenfield, Lawrence A. and Tracy L. Snell; Bureau of Justice Statistics: Special Report (1999) *Women Offenders*. Available at http://www.ojp.usdoj.gov/bjs/pub/pdf/wo.pdf; accessed 15 March 2006.

Grimshaw, Damian and Jill Rubery (1997) *The Concentration of Women's Employment and Relative Occupational Pay:A Statistical Framework for Comparative Analysis*. Organisation for Economic Co-operation and Development, OCDE/GD(97)186. Available at http://www.olis.oecd.org/OLIS/1997DOC.NSF/LINKTO/OCDE-GD(97)186; accessed 12 November 2006.

Grimshaw, Damian and Jill Rubery (2001) *The Gender Pay Gap: A Research Review* (Manchester: Equal Opportunities Commission).

Guerrina, Roberta (2005) *Mothering the Union: Gender Politics in the EU* (Manchester: Manchester University Press).

Guigou, E., P. Favier and M. Martin Roland (2000) *Une Femme au Coeur de l'Etat* (Paris: Fayard).

Hafner-Burton, Emilie and Mark A. Pollack (2002) 'Mainstreaming Gender in Global Governance'. *European Journal of International Relations* 8, no. 3: 339–73.

Hague, Rod and Martin Harrop (2004) *Comparative Government and Politics*, 6th edn (Basingstoke: Palgrave Macmillan).

Hakim, Catherine (2004) *Key Issues in Women's Work: Female Diversity and the Polarisation of Women's Employment* (London and Portland, OR.: GlassHouse).

Halford, Susan and Pauline Leonard (2001) *Gender, Power and Organisations* (Basingstoke: Palgrave Macmillan).

Harford, Barbara and Sarah Hopkins (1984) *Greenham Common: Women at the Wire* (London: Women's Press).

Hartmann, Susan M. (1989) *From Margin to Mainstream: American Women and Politics since 1960* (Philadelphia: Temple University Press).

Hartsock, Nancy (1998) 'The Feminist Standpoint Revisited'. In *The Feminist Standpoint Revisited and Other Essays*, ed. Nancy Hartsock (Boulder, CO: Westview Press).

Heath, Mary (2005) *The Law and Sexual Offences against Adults in Australia*, Australian Centre for the Study of Sexual Assault, Issue 4. Available at http://www.aifs.gov.au/acssa/pubs/issue/i4.html; accessed 20 March 2005.

Held, David (1996) *Models of Democracy* (Cambridge: Polity).

Heldman, Caroline, Stephanie Olson and Susan J. Carroll (2000) 'Gender Differences in Print Media Coverage of Presidential Candidates: Elizabeth Dole's Bid for the Republican Nomination'. American Political Science Association annual confference, 31 August–3 September 2000. Available at http://cawp.futgefs.edu/research/report/dole.pdf; accessed 31 March 2007. (Washington DC).

Hernes, Helga M. (1992) 'Women and the Welfare State: the Transition from Private to Public Dependence'. In *Women and the State,* ed. Anne Showstack Sassoon (London: Routledge), pp. 72–92.

Henig, Ruth and Simon Henig (2001) *Women and Political Power: Europe since 1945*. London: Routledge.

Heywood, Andrew (1994) *Political Ideas and Concepts* (London and Basingstoke: Macmillan).

Hilden, Patricia (1986) *Working Women and Socialist Politics in France* (Oxford: Oxford University Press).

Højgaard, Lis (2002) 'Tracing Differentiation in Gendered Leadership: an Analysis of Differences in Gender Composition in Top Management in Business, Politics and the Civil Service'. *Gender, Work and Organization* 9, no. 1: 15–35.

Holli, Anna Maria and Johanna Kantola (2005) 'A Politics for Presence: Finland'. In *State Feminism and Political Representation*, ed. Joni Lovenduski (Cambridge: Cambridge University Press), pp. 62–84.

Home Office (United Kingdom) (2005) 'Criminal Statistics 2004'. *Home Office Statistical Bulletin 19/05*. Available at http://www.homeoffice.gov.uk/rds/pdfs05/host1905.pdf; accessed 27 March 2007.

Hoskyns, Catherine (1996) *Integrating Gender: Women, Law and Politics in the European Union* (London: Verso).

IDEA (Institute for Democracy and Electoral Assistance) (2006) *Global Database of Quotas for Women*. Available at http://www.quotaproject.org/; accessed 14 February 2006.

Inglehart, R. and Pippa Norris (2003) *Rising Tide: Gender Equality and Cutural Change around the World* (Cambridge: Cambridge University Press).

Institute for Women's Policy Research (2005) *Fact Sheet: The Gender Pay Ratio*; available at http://www.iwpr.org/pdf/C350.pdf; accessed 10 July 2006.

International Labour Organisation (2006) *History*. Available at http://www. ilo.org/public/english/about/history.htm; accessed 15 June 2006.

Inter-Parliamentary Union (2000) *Politics: Women's Insight* (Geneva: Inter-Parliamentary Union). Available at http://www.ipu.org/PDF/publications/womeninsight_en.pdf; accessed 23 January 2006.

Inter-Parliamentary Union (2006) *Women in Parliament on 31 January 2001*; available at http://www.ipu.org/wmn-e/arc/classif300101.htm; accessed 9 January 2006.

Jenson, Jane and Mariette Sineau (1995) *Mitterrand et les Françaises* (Paris: Presses de la Fondation Nationale des Sciences Politiques).

Jones, Kathleen B. (1993) *Compassionate Authority: Democracy and the Representation of Women* (New York: Routledge).

Judt, Tony (2005) *Postwar* (London: William Heinemann).

Kanter, Rosabeth Moss (1993) *Men and Women of the Corporation*, new edn (New York: HarperCollins: Basic Books).

Kaplan, Gisela (1992) *Contemporary West European Feminism* (London: UCL Press).

Kaplan, Temma (1997) *Crazy for Democracy: Women in Grassroots Movements* (New York: Routledge).

Kathlene, Lyn (2001) 'Words that matter: Women's Voices and Institutional Bias'. In *The Impact of Women in Political Office*, ed. Susan T. Carroll (Bloomington, IN: Indiana University Press), pp. 22–48.

Kathlene, Lyn (2005) 'In a Different Voice: Women and the Policy Process'. In *Women and Elective Office: Past, Present, and Future Second Edition*, ed. Clyde Wilcox and Sue Thomas (New York: Oxford University Press), pp. 213–29.

Katzenstein, Mary Fainsod (2003) 'The Reconfigured US State and Women's Citizenship'. In *Women's Movements Facing the Reconfigured State*, ed. Lee Ann Banaszak, Karen Beckwith and Dieter Rucht (Cambridge: Cambridge University Press), pp. 203–18.

Kaufmann, Karen M. and John R Petrocik (1999) 'The Changing Politics of American Men: Understanding the Sources of the Gender Gap'. *American Journal of Political Science* 43, no. 3: 864–87.

Keith, Kristen and Paula Malone (2005) 'Housework and the Wages of Young, Middle-Aged, and Older Workers'. *Contemporary Economic Policy* 23, no. 2: 224–41.

Kenworthy, Lane and Melissa Malami (1999) 'Gender Inequality in Political Representation: a Worldwide Comparative Analysis'. *Social Forces* 78, no. 1: 235–69.

Kessler-Harris, Alice (1990) *A Woman's Wage: Historical Meanings and Social Consequences* (Lexington, KY: University Press of Kentucky).

Kimmel, Michael S. (2000) *The Gendered Society* (Oxford: Oxford University Press).

Kingham, Tess (2001) 'Comment & Analysis: Cheesed Off by Willy-Jousters in a Pointless Parliament'. *Guardian*, 20 June, 16.

Klugman, Barbara (1994) 'Women in Politics under Apartheid: A Challenge to the New South Africa'. In *Women and Politics Worldwide*, ed. Barbara J. Nelson and Najma Chowdhury (New Haven: Yale University Press), pp. 640–58.

Kodz, J., H. Harper, and S. Dench (2002) *Work–Life Balance: Beyond the Rhetoric* (Falmer, Brighton: Institute for Employment Studies IES Report 384).

Kolinsky, Eva (1989) *Women in West Germany* (London: Berg).

Kolinsky, Eva (1993) 'Party Change and Women's Representation in West Germany'. In *Gender and Party Politics*, ed. Joni Lovenduski and Pippa Norris (London: Sage), pp. 113–46.

Kostadinova, Tatiana (2003) 'Women's Legislative Representation in Post-Communist Bulgaria'. In *Women's Access to Political Power in Post-Communist Europe*, ed. Richard E. Matland and Kathleen A. Montgomery (Oxford: Oxford University Press), pp. 304–20.

Krupavičius, Algis and Irmina Matonytė (2003) 'Women in Lithuanian Politics: from Nomenklatura Selection to Representation'. In *Women's Access to Political Power in Post-Communist Europe*, ed. Richard E. Matland and Kathleen A. Montgomery (Oxford: Oxford University Press), pp. 81–104.

Kruse, Lenelis and M. Wintermantel (1986) 'Leadership Ms.-Qualified: the Gender Bias in Everyday and Scientific Thinking'. In *Changing Conceptions of Leadership*, ed. Carl F. Graumann and Serge Moscovici (New York: Springer-Verlag), pp. 171–97.

Kymlicka, Will (2000) 'Introduction'. In *Citizenship in Diverse Societies*, ed. Will Kymlicka and Wayne Norman (Oxford: Oxford University Press), pp. 99–123.

Kymlicka, Will (2002) *Contemporary Political Philosophy* (Oxford: Oxford University Press).

Lubier, Claire (ed.) (1990) *The Condition of Women in France, 1945 to the present: A Documentary Anthology* (London: Routledge).

Lawrence, Elizabeth (1994) *Gender and Trade Unions: Gender and Society* (London: Taylor & Francis).

Leijenaar, Monique (1993) 'A Battle for Power: Selecting Candidates in the Netherlands'. In *Gender and Party Politics*, ed. Joni Lovenduski and Pippa Norris (London: Sage), pp. 204–30.

Levine, Philippa (1987) *Victorian Feminism, 1850–1900* (London: Hutchinson).

Levy, Darline Gay, Harriet Branson Applewhite and Mary Durham Johnson (1979) *Women in Revolutionary Paris, 1789–1795: Selected Documents* (Urbana, ILL: University of Illinois Press).

Levy, Roger and Anne Stevens (2006) 'Gender in the European Commission'. In *Women in Leadership and Management: A European Perspective*, ed. Karen Miller and Duncan McTavish (Cheltenham: Edward Elgar Publishing), pp. 204–20.

Lewis, Jane (2001) 'The Decline of the Male Breadwinner Model: Implications for Work and Care'. *Social Politics*, Summer: 152–69.

Lister, Ruth (2003) *Citizenship: Feminist Perspectives*, 2nd edn (Basingstoke: Palgrave Macmillan).

Lobby, European Women's (2006) *Working Towards Parity Democracy in Europe*. Available at http://www.womenlobby.org/site/1abstract.asp?DocID=183&v1ID=&RevID=&namePage=&pageParent=&DocID_sousmenu=&parentCat=16; accessed 21 September 2006.

Lovenduski, Joni (1986) *Women and European Politics* (Brighton: Harvester Wheatsheaf).

Lovenduski, Joni (1998) 'Gendering Research in Political Science'. *American Review of Political Science* 1: 335–56.

Lovenduski, Joni (2005) *Feminizing Politics* (Cambridge: Polity).

Lovenduski, Joni ed. (2005a) *State Feminism and Political Representation* (Cambridge: Cambridge University Press).

Lovenduski, Joni and Pippa Norris eds. (1993a) *Gender and Party Politics* (London: Sage Publications).

Lovenduski, Joni and Pippa Norris (1993b) 'Gender and Party Politics in Britain'. In *Gender and Party Politics*, ed. Joni Lovenduski and Pippa Norris (London: Sage Publications), pp. 35–59.

Lovenduski, Joni and Pippa Norris (2003) 'Westminster Women: the Politics of Presence'. *Political Studies* 51, no. 1: 84–102.

Lovenduski, Joni and Vicky Randall (1993) *Contemporary Feminist Politics* (Oxford: Oxford University Press).

Lovenduski, Joni, C. Baudino, M. Guadagnini, P. Meier and D. Sainsbury (eds) (2005) *State Feminism and the Political Representation of Women* (Cambridge: Cambridge University Press).

Lovenduski, Joni, Pippa Norris and Rosie Campbell (2004) *Gender and Political Participation* (London: Electoral Commission); available at http://www.electoralcommission.org.uk/templates/search/document.cfm/9470; accessed 1 February 2006.

Lowndes, V. (2004) 'Getting On or Getting By? Women, Social Capital and Political Participation'. *British Journal of Politics and International Relations* 6, no. 1: 45–64.

Lucas, Jeffrey W. (2003) 'Status Processes and the Institutionalization of Women as Leaders'. *American Sociological Review* 68, no. 3: 464–80.

Ludi, Regula (2005) 'Gendering Citizenship and the State in Switzerland after 1945'. In *Nation and Gender in Contemporary Europe*, ed. Vera Tolz and Stephenie Booth (Manchester: Manchester University Press), pp. 53–79.

Lukes, Steven (1974) *Power: A Radical View* (London and Basingstoke: Macmillan).

Lyon, Dawn and Alison E. Woodward (2004) 'Gender and Time at the Top: Cultural Constructions of Time in High-Level Careers and Homes'. *European Journal of Women's Studies* 11, no. 2: 205–21.

MacInnes, John (1995) 'Analysing Patriarchy Capitalism and Women's Employment in Europe'. *Innovation: The European Journal of Social Sciences* 11, no. 2: 227–48.

Mackay, Fiona (2001) *Love and Politics: Women Politicians and the Ethics of Care* (London and New York: Continuum).

Mackay, Fiona (2004) 'Gender and Political Representation in the UK: The State of the Discipline'. *British Journal of Politics and International Relations* 6, no. 1: 99–120.

Maddock, S. and D. Parkin (1993) 'Gender Cultures: Women's Choices and Strategies at Work'. *Women in Management Review* 8, no. 2: 3–9.

Mansbridge, Jane (1998) 'Feminism and Democracy'. In *Feminism and Politics*, ed. Anne Phillips (Oxford: Oxford University Press), pp. 142–58.

Mansbridge, Jane (1999) 'Should Blacks Represent Blacks and Women Represent Women? A Contingent "Yes".' *Journal of Politics* 61, no. 3: 628–57.

Mansbridge, Jane (2000) 'What Does a Representative Do? Descriptive Representation in Communicative Settings of Distrust, Uncrystallized Interests and Historically Denigrated Status'. In *Citizenship in Diverse Societies*, ed. Will Kymlicka and Wayne Norman (Oxford: Oxford University Press), pp. 99–123.

Mansbridge, Jane (2006) 'Why We Lost the ERA.' In *Gendering American Politics*, ed. Karen O'Connor, Sarah Brewer and Michael Philip Fisher (New York: Pearson Longman), pp. 33–42.

Marchbank, Jen (2005) 'Power, Non-Decision Making and Gender', unpublished paper for Economic and Social Research Council Workshop, Edinburgh University 8 June 2005.

Marshall, T. H. and Tom Bottomore (1992) *Citizenship and Social Class* (London: Pluto).

Marx Ferree, Myra (1995) 'Making Equality: the Women's Affairs Offices in the Federal Republic of Germany'. In *Comparative State Feminism*, ed. Amy Mazur and Dorothy M. Stetson (Thousand Oaks, Calif.: Sage Publications), pp. 95–113.

Mason, Bertha (1912) *The Story of the Women's Suffrage Movement* (London: Sherratt and Hughes).

Mateo Diaz, Mercedes (2005) *Representing Women? Female Legislators in West European Parliaments* (Colchester: ECPR Press).

Matland, Richard E. (2003) 'Women's Representation in Post-Communist Europe'. In *Women's Access to Political Power in Post-Communist Countries*, ed. Richard E. Matland and Kathleen A. Montgomery (Oxford: Oxford University Press), pp. 321–42.

Matland, Richard and Kathleen Montgomery (eds) (2003a) *Women's Access to Political Power in Eastern Europe* (Oxford: Oxford University Press).

Matland, Richard E. and Kathleen A. Montgomery (2003b) 'Recruiting Women to National Legislatures: a General Framework with Applications to Post-Communist Democracies'. In *Women's Access to Political Power in Post-Communist Europe*, ed. Richard E. Matland and Kathleen A. Montgomery (Oxford: Oxford University Press), pp. 19–42.

Mazey, Sonia (1988) 'European Community Action on Behalf of Women: the Limits of Legislation'. *Journal of Common Market Studies* 27, no. 1: 63–84.

Mazey, Sonia (1989) *Women and the European Community: Polytechnic of North London European Dossier Series* (London: The PNL Press).

Mazur, Amy G. (2001) *State Feminism, Women's Movements and Job Training: Making Democracies Work in a Global Economy* (London and New York: Routledge).

Mazur, Amy G. (2002) *Theorizing Feminist Policy* (Oxford: Oxford University Press).

Mazur, Amy G. and Dorothy M. Stetson (1995) *Comparative State Feminism* (Thousand Oaks, CA: Sage Publications).

McLaughlin, Janice (2003) *Feminist Social and Political Theory* (Basingstoke: Palgrave).

Meehan, Elizabeth (1993) *Citizenship and the European Community* (London: Sage).

Meinhof, U. H. (1986) 'Subversion and its Media Representation'. In *Women, State and Revolution*, ed. Siân Reynolds (Brighton: Harvester Wheatsheaf), pp. 141–60.

Melucci, Alberto (1996) *Challenging Codes: Collective Action in the Information Age* (Cambridge: Cambridge University Press).

Merriam, Charles Edward and Harold Foote Gosnell (1924) *Non-Voting: Causes and Methods of Control* (Chicago, IL: University of Chicago Press).

Meyer, David (2003) 'Restating the Women Question: Women's Movements and State Restructuring'. In *Women's Movements Facing the Reconfigured State*, ed. Lee Ann Banaszak, Karen Beckwith and Dieter Rucht (Cambridge: Cambridge University Press), pp. 275–94.

Michels, Robert (1958) *Political Parties: A Sociological Study of the Oligarchial Tendencies of Modern Democracy* (Illinois: Free Press).

Mill, John Stuart (1985) *The Subjection of Women* (London: Dent Everyman).

Miller, Arthur H., Patricia Gurin, Gerald Gurin and Oksana Malanchuk (1981) 'Group Consciousness and Political Participation'. *American Journal of Political Science* 25, no. 3: 494–511.

Molyneux, Maxine (1986) 'Mobilization without Emancipation: Women's Interests, State and Revolution'. In *Transition and Development: Problems of Third World Socialism*, ed. Richard R. Fagen, Carmen Diana Deere and José Luis Coraggio (Boston, MA: Monthly Review Press), pp. 283–4.

Molyneux, Maxine (1996) 'Women's Rights and the International Context in the Post-Communist States'. In *Mapping the Women's Movement*, ed. Monica Threlfall (London: Verso), pp. 232–59.

Montgomery, Kathleen A. (2003) 'Introduction'. In *Women's Access to Political Power in Post-Communist Europe*, ed. Richard E. Matland and Kathleen A. Montgomery (Oxford: Oxford University Press), pp. 1–18.

Moser, Robert G. (2003) 'Electoral Systems and Women's Representation: the Strange Case of Russia'. In *Women's Access to Political Power in*

Post-Communist Europe, ed. Richard E. Matland and Kathleen A.
. Montgomery (Oxford: Oxford University Press), pp. 153–95.

Mossuz-Lavau, Janine (1997) 'L'Évolution du Vote Des Femmes'. *Pouvoirs*, no.
82: 35–44.

Mossuz-Lavau, Janine (1998) *Femmes/Hommes: Pour La Parité* (Paris: Presses
de Sciences Po.).

Mossuz-Lavau, Janine and Mariette Sineau (1983) *Enquête sur les Femmes et la
Politique en France* (Paris: Presses Universitaires de France).

Mueller, Carol M. and John D. McCarthy (2003) 'Cultural Continuity and
Structural Change: the Logic of Adaptation by Radical, Liberal and Socialist
Feminists to State Reconfiguration'. In *Women's Movements Facing the
Reconfigured State*, ed. Lee Ann Banaszak, Karen Beckwith and Dieter Rucht
(Cambridge: Cambridge University Press), pp. 219–41.

Munro, Anne (1999) *Women, Work, and Trade Unions* (New York: Mansell).

Nash, K. (2002) 'A Movement Moves . . . is there a Women's Movement in
England Today?' *European Journal of Women's Studies* 9, no 3: 311–28.

National Assembly, France (2006) Available at http://www.assemblee-
nationale.fr/connaissance/delegation-femmes.asp; accessed 7 June 2006.

Nelson, Barbara J. and Najma Chowdhury (eds) (1994) *Women and Politics
Worldwide* (New Haven, CT: Yale University Press).

Nelson, Barbara J., Najma Chowdhury, Kathryn Carver, Nancy J. Johnson, and
Paula O'Loughlin (1994) 'Redefining Politics: Patterns of Women's
Engagement from a Global Perspective'. In *Women and Politics Worldwide*,
ed. Barbara J. Nelson and Najma Chowdhury (New Haven: Yale University
Press), pp. 3–24.

Newman, Janet (1996) 'Gender and Cultural Change'. In *Gender, Culture and
Organizational Change: Putting Theory into Practice*, ed. Catherine Itzin and
Janet Newman (London; New York: Routledge), pp. 11–29.

Norris, Pippa (1996a) 'Legislative Recruitment'. In *Comparing Democracies :
Elections and Voting in Global Perspectives*, ed. Lawrence LeDuc, Richard
G. Niemi and Pippa Norris (Thousand Oaks, CA: Sage Publications), pp.
184–215.

Norris, Pippa (1996b) 'Women Politicians: Transforming Westminster?' In
Women in Politics, ed. Joni Lovenduski and Pippa Norris (Oxford: Oxford
University Press), pp. 91–104.

Norris, Pippa (1996c) 'Mobilising the Women's Vote: the Gender-Generation
Gap in Voting Behaviour'. *Parliamentary Affairs* 49, no. 2: 333–42.

Norris, Pippa (1997a) *Electoral Change in Britain since 1945* (Oxford:
Blackwell).

Norris, Pippa (1997b) 'Women Leaders Worldwide: a Splash of Colour in the
Photo-Op?' In *Women, Media, and Politics*, ed. Pippa Norris (New York, NY
and Oxford: Oxford University Press), pp. 149–65.

Norris, Pippa (ed.) (1997c) *Women, Media, and Politics* (New York, NY and
Oxford: Oxford University Press).

Norris, Pippa (2002) 'Women's Power at the Ballot Box'. In *Voter Turnout Since 1945: A Global Report*, ed. Rafael López Pintor and Maria Gratschew (Stockholm: International Institute for Democracy and Electoral Assistance (International IDEA).

Norris, Pippa (2003) 'The Gender Gap: Old Challenges, New Approaches'. In *Women and American Politics: New Questions, New Directions*, ed. Susan J. Carroll (Oxford: Oxford University Press), pp. 146–70.

Norris, Pippa (2004) *Electoral Engineering: Voting Rules and Political Behaviour* (New York: Cambridge University Press).

Norris, Pippa and Joni Lovenduski (1995) *Political Recruitment: Gender, Race and Class in the British Parliament* (Cambridge: Cambridge University Press).

Norris, Pippa and Ronald Inglehart (2005) 'Women as Political Leaders Worldwide: Cultural Barriers and Opportunities'. In *Women and Elective Office: Past, Present, and Future. Second Edition*, ed. Clyde Wilcox and Sue Thomas (New York: Oxford University Press), pp. 244–63.

Noss, Cecilie Ostensen and Venice Commission Council of Europe (2005) *Gender Equality in Norway*. Available at http://www.venice.coe.int/docs/2006/CDL-JU(2006)028-e.asp; accessed 12 November 2006.

Nowotny, Helga (1981) 'Women in Public Life in Austria'. In *Access to Power: Cross National Studies of Women and Elites*, ed. Cynthia F. Epstein and R. L. Coser (London: Allen and Unwin), pp. 147–56.

nzhistorynet. Available at http://www.nzhistory.net.nz/politics/suffrage-briefhistory; accessed 21 December 2006.

Oakley, Ann (1997) 'A Brief History of Gender'. In *Who's Afraid of Feminism? Seeing Through the Backlash*, ed. Ann Oakley and Juliet Mitchell (London: Hamish Hamilton), pp. 29–55.

O'Connor, Sandra, Sarah Brewer and Michael Philip Fisher (eds) (2006) *Politics: Perspectives from the Literature* (New York: Pearson Longman).

O'Donovan, Katherine (1985) *Sexual Divisions in Law* (London: Weidenfeld & Nicolson).

O'Donovan, Katherine (1993) *Family Law Matters* (London: Pluto Press).

OECD (Organisation for Economic Cooperation and Development) (2002) *OECD Employment Outlook 2002 – Surveying the Jobs Horizon*; available at http://www.oecd.org/home/0,2605,en_2649_201185_1_1_1_1_1,00.html; accessed 30 July 2006.

Offen, Karen (1998) 'Contextualising the Theory and Practice of Feminism in Nineteenth-Century Europe'. In *Becoming Visible: Women in European History*, 3rd edn, ed. Renate Bridenthal, Susan Mosher Stuard and Merry E. Wieser (New York: Houghton Mifflin), pp. 327–55.

Olsson, Su and Judith K. Pringle (2004) 'Women Executives: Public and Private Sectors as Sites of Advancement'. *Women in Management Review* 19, no. 1: 29–9.

Ondercin, Heather L. and Susan Welch (2005) 'Women Candidates for Congress'. In *Women and Elective Office: Past Present and Future*, 2nd edn, ed. Sue Thomas and Clyde Wilcox (Oxford: Oxford University Press), pp. 60–80.

Opello, Katherine A. R. (2006) *Gender Quotas, Parity Reform and Political Parties in France* (Lanham, MD: Lexington Books).

Orloff, Ann (1996) 'Gender in the Welfare State'. *Annual Review of Sociology* 22: 51–78.

Oshagbemi, Titus and Roger Gill (2003) 'Gender Differences and Similarities in the Leadership Styles and Behaviour of UK Managers'. *Women in Management Review* 18, no. 6: 288–98.

Oswald, Andrew and Nattavudh Powdthavee (2005a) 'Daughters and Left-Wing Voting', University of Warwick paper. Available at http://www2. warwick.ac.uk/fac/soc/economics/research/phds/n.powdthavee/ daughtersospowd2005.pdf, accessed 16 December 2005.

Oswald, Andrew and Nattavudh Powdhavee (2005b) 'Further Results on Daughters and Left-wing Voting: Germany, 1985–2002' University of Warwick paper. Available at http://www2.warwick.ac.uk/fac/soc/economics/ research/phds/n.powdthavee/daughtersospowd2005.pdf. Accessed 20 January 2006.

Outshoorn, Joyce (ed.) (2004) *The Politics of Prostitution:Women's Movements, Democratic States and the Globalisation of Sex Commerce* (Cambridge: Cambridge University Press).

Parry, Geraint (1969) *Political Elites*, Studies in Political Science no. 5 (London: Allen & Unwin).

Pateman, Carole (1994) 'Three Questions about Womanhood Suffrage'. In *Suffrage and Beyond: International Feminist Perspectives*, ed. Carol Daley and Melanie Nolan (Auckland NZ: Auckland University Press), pp. 17–31.

Paxton, Pamela (1997) 'Women in National Legislatures: a Cross-National Analysis'. *Social Science Research* 26: 442–64.

Paxton, Pamela and Sheri Kunovitch (2003) 'Women's Political Representation: the Importance of Ideology'. *Social Forces* 82, no. 1: 87–114.

Pedersen, Susan (1993) *Family, Dependence and the Origin of the Welfare State: Britain and France, 1914–1945* (Cambridge: Cambridge University Press).

Penn, Shana (2005) *Solidarity's Secret* (Ann Arbor, MI: University of Michigan Press).

Pfall Effinger, Birgit (1998) 'Gender Cultures and the Gender Arrangement – A Theoretical Framework for Cross-National Gender Research'. *Innovation: The European Journal of Social Sciences* 11, no. 2: 147–66.

Phillips, Anne (1991) *Engendering Democracy* (Cambridge: Polity Press).

Phillips, Anne (1995) *The Politics of Presence* (Oxford: Oxford University Press).

Phillips, Anne (ed.) (1998a) *Feminism and Politics* (Oxford: Oxford University Press).

Phillips, Anne (1998b) 'Democracy and Representation'. In *Feminism and Politics*, ed. Anne Phillips (Oxford: Oxford University Press), pp. 224–40.

Phillips, Anne (1999) *Which Equalities Matter?* (Cambridge: Polity).

Phillips, Anne (2002) 'Multiculturalism, Universalism and the Claims of Democracy'. In *Gender Justice, Development and Rights*, ed. Maxine Molyneux and S. Razavi (Oxford: Oxford University Press), pp. 115–39.

Pitkin, Hanna F. (1972) *The Concept of Representation* (Berkeley, CA: University of California Press).

Public Service Human Resources Management Agency of Canada (2003–04) *Employment Equity in the Federal Public Service*: Available at http://www.hrma-agrh.gc.ca/reports-rapports/dwnld/EE03-04_e.pdf; accessed 13 April 2006.

Putnam, Robert D. (2002) *Democracies in Flux: The Evolution of Social Capital in Contemporary Society* (Oxford: Oxford University Press).

Puwar, N. (2004) 'Thinking about Making a Difference'. *British Journal of Politics and International Relations* 6, no. 1: 65–80.

Radcliff, Pamela Beth (2001) 'Imagining Female Citizenship in the "New Spain": Gendering the Democratic Transition, 1975–1978' *Gender and History* 13, no. 3, pp. 498–525.

Randall, Vicky (1982) *Women and Politics: An International Perspective* (London: Macmillan).

Randall, Vicky (1991) 'Feminism and Political Analysis', *Political Studies* 39, no. 3: 513–32.

Randall, Vicky (1987) *Women and Politics: An International Perspective*, 2nd edn (London: Macmillan).

Randall, Vicky (2002) 'Feminism'. In *Theory and Methods in Political Science*, ed. David Marsh and Gerry Stoker (Basingstoke: Palgrave Macmillan), pp. 109–30.

Rawls, John (1999) *A Theory of Justice*, rev. edn (Oxford: Oxford University Press).

Rees, Theresa (1992) *Women and the Labour Market* (London and New York: Routledge).

Rees, Theresa (1998) *Mainstreaming Equality in the European Union: Education, Training and Labour Market Policies* (London and New York: Routledge).

Reinalda, Bob (1996) '*Deus ex Machina* or the Interplay between National and International Policy-Making: A Critical Analysis of Women in the European Union'. In *Sex Equality Policy in Western Europe*, ed. Frances Gardiner (London and New York: Routledge), pp. 197–215.

Reynolds, Siân (1986) 'Marianne's Citizens? Women, the Republic and Universal Suffrage in France'. In *Women, State and Revolution*, ed. Siân Reynolds (Brighton: Harvester Wheatsheaf), pp. 102–22.

Reynolds, Siân (1988a) 'The French Ministry of Women's Rights, 1981–1986'. In *France and Modernisation*, ed. John Gaffney (Aldershot: Brookfield CT: Ashgate), pp. 149–69.

Reynolds, Siân (1988b) 'Whatever Happened to the French Ministry of Women's Rights?' *Modern and Contemporary France* 33, pp. 4–9.

Reynolds, Siân (1996) *France between the Wars: Gender and Politics* (London: Routledge).

Robinson, O. F. (1988) 'The Historical Background'. In *The Legal Relevance of Gender*, ed. Sheila McLean and Noreen Burrows (London: Macmillan), pp. 40–60.

Rosanvallon, Pierre (1992) *Le Sacre du Citoyen, Histoire du Suffrage Universel en France* (Paris: Gallimard).

Rosenthal, Cindy Simon (2005) 'Women Leading Legislatures: Getting There and Getting Things Done'. In *Women and Elective Office: Past, Present, and Future*, 2nd edn, ed. Clyde Wilcox and Sue Thomas (New York: Oxford University Press), pp. 197–212.

Ross, Karen (2002) 'Women's Place in Male Space: Gender and Effect in Parliamentary Contexts'. *Parliamentary Affairs* 55: 189–201.

Rossi, Alice S, ed. (1974) *The Feminist Papers* (New York: Bantam Books).

Rossilli, Mariagrazia (2000) 'Introduction: The European Union's Gender Policies'. In *Gender Policies in the European Union*, ed. Mariagrazia Rossilli, (New York: Peter Lang).

Rossilli, Mariagrazia (ed.) (2000) 'Gendered Rationality? A Geneaological Exploration of the Philosophical and Sociological Conception of Rationality, Masculinity and Organisation'. *Gender Politics in the European Union* (New York: Peter Lang), pp. 1–21.

Ross-Smith, Anne and Martin Kornberger (2004) *Gender, Work and Organization* 11, no. 3, 280–305.

Rubery, Jill, Damian Grimshaw and Hugo Figueirido (2002) *The Gender Pay Gap and Gender Mainstreaming Pay Policy in EU Member States* (Manchester: Manchester School of Management, UMIST).

Rucht, Dieter (2006) 'Political Participation in Europe'. In *Contemporary Europe*, 2nd edn, ed. Richard Sakwa and Anne Stevens (Basingstoke: Palgrave Macmillan), pp. 110–37.

Ryan, Michelle K. and S. Alexander Haslam (2005) 'The Glass Cliff: Evidence that Women are Over-Represented in Precarious Leadership Positions'. *British Journal of Management* 16: 81–90.

Sainsbury, Diane (1999) 'Gender and Social Democratic Welfare States'. In *Gender and Welfare State Regimes*, ed. Diane Sainsbury (Oxford: Oxford University Press), pp. 15–46, 245–75.

Sanbonmatsu, Kira (2002) 'Political Parties and the Recruitment of Women to State Legislatures'. *Journal of Politics* 64, no. 3: 791–801.

Sapiro, Virginia (1998) 'When Are Interests Interesting?' In *Feminism and Politics*, ed. Anne Phillips (Oxford: Oxford University Press), pp. 161–92.

Sawer, Marian (2002) 'The Representation of Women in Australia: Meaning and Make-Believe'. *Parliamentary Affairs* 55, no. 1: 5–18.

Sawer, Marian (2003) 'Women's Policy Machinery in Australia'. In *Mainstreaming Gender, Democratising the State: Institutional Mechanisms for the Advancement of Women*, ed. Shirin M. Rai (Manchester: Manchester University Press), pp. 243–63.

Sawer, Marian and Marian Simms (1993) *A Woman's Place: Women and Politics in Australia* (North Sydney: Allen & Unwin).

Sawer, Marian, Manon Tremblay, and Linda J. Trimble (2006) 'Introduction: Patterns and Practice in the Parliamentary Representation of Women'. In *Representing Women in Parliament: A Comparative Study*, ed. Marian Sawer, Manon Tremblay and Linda J. Trimble (London: Routledge), pp. 1–24.

Schlozman, Kay Lehman, Nancy Burns, Sidney Verba and Jesse Donahue (1995) 'Gender and Citizen Participation: Is There a Different Voice?' *American Journal of Political Science* 39, no. 2: 267–83.

Schnabel, Claus and Joachim Wagner (2005) *Determinants of Union Membership in 18 EU Countries: Evidence from Micro Data, 2002/03*. Available at ftp://repec.iza.org/RePEc/Discussionpaper/dp1464.pdf; accessed 26 July 2006.

Schreiber, Ronnee (2006) 'Injecting a Woman's Voice: Conservative Women's Organisations, Gender Consciousness and the Expression of Women's Policy Preferences'. Reprinted from 2002 in *Gendering American Politics: Perspectives from the Literature* (2002), ed. Karen O'Connor, Sarah Brewer and Michael Philip Fisher (New York: Pearson Longman), pp. 141–50.

Schwartz, Paula (1989) 'Partisanes and Gender Politics in Vichy France'. *French Historical Studies* 16, no. 1.

Scott, J. W. (2005) 'French Universalism in the Nineties'. In *Women and Citizenship*, ed. Marilyn Friedman (New York and Oxford: Oxford University Press), pp. 35–51.

Sevenhuijsen, Selma (1998) *Citizenship and the Ethics of Care* (London: Routledge).

Shaw, Jo (1999) 'Gender and the Court of Justice'. Conference paper; available at http://eucenter.wisc.edu/conferences/Gender/shaw.htm; accessed 4 July 2006.

Siaroff, A. (2000) 'Women's Representation in in Legislatures and Cabinets in Industrial Democracies'. *International Political Science Review* 21, no. 2: 197–215.

Siim, B. (2000) *Gender and Citizenship: Politics and Agency in France, Britain, and Denmark* (Cambridge: Cambridge University Press).

Simms, Marian (1981) 'Australia'. In *The Politics of the Second Electorate*, ed. Joni Lovenduski and Jill Hills (London: Routledge), pp. 83–111.

Simms, Marian (1993) 'Two Steps Forward, One Step Back: Women and the Australian Party System'. In *Gender and Party Politics*, ed. Joni Lovenduski and Pippa Norris (London: Sage), pp. 16–34.

Sineau, Mariette (1997) 'Les Femmes Politiques sous La Ve République'. *Pouvoirs* 82: 45–57.

Sineau, Mariette (2001) *Profession: Femme Politique: Sexe et Pouvoir sous la Cinquième République* (Paris: Presses de Sciences P.).

Skjeie, Hege (1993) 'Ending the Male Political Hegemony: the Norwegian Experience'. In *Gender and Party Politics*, ed. Joni Lovenduski and Pippa Norris (London: Sage), pp. 231–62.

Sloat, Amanda (2005) 'The Rebirth of Civil Society: the Growth of Women's NGOs in Central and Eastern Europe'. *European Journal of Women's Studies* 12, no. 4: 437–52.

Smith, D. (1999) *Writing the Social: Critique, Theory and Investigations* (Toronto: University of Toronto Press).

Sones, Boni (2005) *The New Suffragettes* (London: Politico's).

Squires, Judith (1999) *Gender in Political Theory* (Cambridge: Polity).

Squires, Judith and Mark Wickham-Jones (2001) *Women in Parliament: A Comparative Analysis* (Manchester: Equal Opportunities Commission). Available at www.eoc.org.uk/research; accessed 15 September 2005.

Stacey, Margaret and Marion Price (1981) *Women, Power and Politics* (London and New York: Tavistock Publications).

Stanford, Jane H., Barbara R. Oates and Delfina Flores (1995) 'Women's Leadership Styles: a Heuristic Analysis'. *Women in Management Review* 10, no. 2: 9–19.

Statistics Canada (2003) *Fact Sheet on Unionization*. Available at http://www.statcan.ca/english/freepub/75-001-XIE/75-001-XIE2003108.pdf; accessed 16 January 2007.

Statistics Canada (2006a) *Average Earnings by Sex and Work Pattern*. Available at http://www40.statcan.ca/l01/cst01/labor01b.htm; accessed 10 July 2006.

Statistics Canada (2006b) *Labour Force 2005*. Available at http://www.statcan.ca/english/reference/professional.htm; accessed 5 October 2006.

Stephenson, M. A. (1998) *The Glass Trapdoor: Women, Politics and the Media during the 1997 General Election* (London: Fawcett Society).

Stetson, D. M. (2001) *Abortion Politics, Women's Movements, and the Democratic State: A Comparative Study of State Feminism* (Oxford: Oxford University Press).

Stevens, Anne (1986) 'Women Politics and Government in Contemporary Britain, France and Germany'. In *Women State and Revolution*, ed. Siân Reynolds (Brighton: Harvester Wheatsheaf), pp. 123–40.

Still, Leonie (2006) 'Where are the Women in Leadership in Australia?' *Women in Management Review* 21, no. 3: 180–94.

Stivers, Camilla (1993) *Gender Images in Public Administration* (London: Sage Publications).

Stokes, Wendy (2005) *Women in Contemporary Politics* (Cambridge: Polity).

Studlar, D. T. (2002) 'Electoral Systems and Women's Representation: a Long-Term Perspective'. *Representation* 39, no. 1: 3–14.

Studlar, Donley and Richard E. Matland (2004) 'Determinants of Legislative Turnover: a Cross National Comparison'. *British Journal of Political Science* 34, no. 1: 87–108.

Studlar, D. T. and I. McAllister (2002) 'Does a Critical Mass Exist? A Comparative Analysis of Women's Legislative Representation since 1950'. *European Journal of Political Research* 41, no. 2: 233–54.

Swedish Government (2007) *Factsheet: Equality Between Men and Women.* Available at http://www.sweden.se/templates/cs/BasicFactsheet_4123.aspx; accessed 28 January 2007.

Swers, Michele L. and Carin Larson (2005) 'Women in Congress: Do They Act as Advocates for Women's Issues?' In *Women and Elective Office: Past, Present, and Future*, 2nd edn. ed. Clyde Wilcox and Sue Thomas (New York: Oxford University Press), pp. 110–28.

Taylor, Robert (2001) *The Future of Work-Life Balance: Economic and Social Research Council.* Available at http://www.esrcsocietytoday.ac.uk/ESRCInfoCentre/about Corporate Information: Corporate Publications: Research Publications; accessed 10 July 2006.

Thomas, Sue (2005) 'Introduction'. In *Women and Elective Office: Past, Present, and Future*, 2nd edn, ed. Clyde Wilcox and Sue Thomas (New York: Oxford University Press), pp. 3–25.

Threlfall, Monica (1996) 'Feminist Politics and Social Change in Spain'. In *Mapping the Women's Movement: Feminist Politics and Social Transformation*, ed. Monica Threlfall (London: Verso), pp. 115–51.

Tremblay, Manon and Linda J Trimble, eds (2003) *Women and Politics in Canada* (New York: Oxford University Press).

Trimble, Linda J. (2006) 'When Do Women Count? Substantive Representation of Women in Canadian Legislatures'. In *Representing Women in Parliament: A Comparative Study*, ed. Marian Sawer, Manon Tremblay and Linda J. Trimble (London: Routledge), pp. 120–33.

Trimble, Linda and Jane Arscott (2003) *Still Counting: Women in Politics across Canada* (Peterborough Ontario: Broadview Press).

Tronto, Joan C. (1993) *Moral Boundaries: A Political Argument for an Ethic of Care* (New York and London: Routledge).

Turner, Bryan S. (1990) 'Outline of a Theory of Citizenship'. *Sociology* 24, no. 2: 189–217.

UNDAW (United Nations Division for the Advancement of Women) (2006) *Short History of Cedaw Convention.* Available at http://www.un.org/womenwatch/daw/cedaw/history.htm; accessed 18 January 2007.

UNECE (United Nations Economic Commission for Europe) (2006) *Statistical Database: Gender and Social Statistics: Families and Households*; available at http://w3.unece.org/pxweb/Dialog/statfile1_new.asp; accessed 5 October 2006.

UNESCAP (United Nations, Economic and Social Commission for Asia and the Pacific) (2001) *Country Reports on the State of Women in Urban Local Government: Australia.* Available at http://www.unescap.org/huset/women/reports/australia.pdf; accessed 13 March 2007.

United Nations Statistics Division (2006) *Demographic and Social Statistics.* Available at http://unstats.un.org/unsd/demographic/default.htm consulted on 5 October 2006.

US Department of Labor (2006) *Bureau of Labor Statistics*; available at http://www.bls.gov/news.release/union2.t01.htm; accessed 16 January 2007.

United States Office of Personnel Management (2004) 'Federal Civilian Workforce Statistics the Fact Book'. Available at http://www.opm.gov/feddata/factbook/2004/factbook.pdf; accessed 10 April 2006.

Valiente, Celia (2003) 'The Feminist Movement and the Reconfigured State in Spain (1970s–2000)'. In *Women's Movements Facing the Reconfigured State*, ed. Lee Ann Banaszak, Karen Beckwith and Dieter Rucht (Cambridge: Cambridge University Press), pp.30–47.

Vianello, Mino (2000) 'Exercising Power'. In *Gendering Elites: Economic and Political Leadership in 27 Industrialised Societies*, ed. Mino Vianello and Gwen Moore (Basingstoke: Palgrave Macmillan), pp. 141–54.

Visser, Jelle (2006) 'Union Membership Statistics in 24 Countries'. *Monthly Labour Review*, January 2006: pp. 38–49.

Voet, Rian (1998) *Feminism and Citizenship* (London: Sage).

Vogel-Polsky, Eliane (1994) 'Les Impasses de l'égalité ou Pourquoi les Outils Juridiques Visant à l'égalité des Femmes et des Hommes Doivent être Repensés en Termes de Parité'. *Parité-Infos*, May 1994.

Vogel-Polsky, Eliane (1999) *Interiew*. Available at http://www.eurplace.org/other-half/interviste/eliane.html; accessed 5 March 2004.

von Wahl, Angelika (2005) 'Liberal, Conservative, Social Democratic or . . . European? The European Union as Equal Employment Regime'. *Social Politics – International Studies in Gender State and Society* 12, no. 1: 67–95.

Walby, Sylvia (1997) *Gender Transformations* (London: Routledge).

Ward, Ian (1996) 'Beyond Sex Equality: the Limits of Sex Equality Law in the New Europe'. In *Sex Equality Law in the European Union*, ed. Tamara Hervey and David O'Keefe (Chichester: John Wiley and Sons), pp. 369–82.

Weitz, Margaret Collins (1995) *Sisters in the Resistance: How Women Fought to Free France, 1940–1945* (New York: J. Wiley).

Wilcox, Clyde, Beth Stark and Sue Thomas (2003) 'Popular Support for Electing Women in Eastern Europe'. In *Women's Access to Political Power in Post-Communist Europe*, ed. Richard E. Matland and Kathleen A. Montgomery, pp. 43–62.

Williams, Beryl (1986) 'Kollontai and After: Women in the Russian Revolution'. In *Women, State and Revolution*, ed. Siân Reynolds (Brighton: Harvester Wheatsheaf), pp. 60–80.

Wollstonecraft, Mary (1975) *Vindication of the Rights of Woman*, reprinted from 1792 (London: Penguin Books).

Woodward, Alison E. and Dawn Lyon (2000) 'Gendered Time and Women's Access to Power'. In *Gendering Elites: Economic and Political Leadership in 27 Industrialised Societies*, ed. Mino Vianello and Gwen Moore (Basingstoke: Palgrave Macmillan), pp. 91–103.

Yeatman, Anna (1990) *Bureaucrats, Femocrats, Technocrats: Essays on the Contemporary Australian State* (Boston, MA: Allen and Unwin).

Young, Iris Marion (1998) 'Polity and Group Difference: a Critique of the Ideal of Universal Citizenship'. In *Feminism and Politics*, ed. Anne Phillips (Oxford: Oxford University Press), pp. 401–29.

Young, Iris Marion (2000) *Inclusion and Democracy* (Oxford: Oxford University Press).

Index

activism by women 143, 145, 146, 154
  in environmental groups 163–4
  in non-institutionalized groups 161–7
  in Trade Unions 154–61
Adams, Abigail (1744–1818) 26
affirmative action *see* positive action
Albright, Madeleine 127, 141
Alliot-Marie, Michèle 141
all-women shortlists (United Kingdom)
    109, 111, 208
ambition, political 86, 89, 91
Anselmi, Tina 169–70
anti-discrimination legislation 31, 43, 44,
    193, 200–4, 207–9, 219–20
  prevents preference for women 109–10,
    111
  see also Kalanke case
Argentina, women's groups in 166
aspiration to elective office 86–92
Astor, Nancy (1879–1964) 79
Aung San Suu Kyi 124
Australia
  barriers to women's political
    participation 86
  Commonwealth Court of Conciliation
    and Arbitration ruling on equal pay
    215
  equal pay 205
  gender gap in voting behaviour 54
  Human Rights and Equal Opportunities
    Commission 214
  impact of women in parliament 184–5
  Labour Party *see* Australian labour
    party
  local government, female representation
    78
  marriage bar 42
  rape victims in criminal justice system
    29
  women in public services 125
  women's parties 100
  women's policy unit 213

Australian Labour Party, women in party
    structures 101
Austria,
  constitution 196
  partisan preferences of women 57
  voting rights for women 37
autonomy 6–7, 23, 25

Beauvoir, Simone de (1908–1986) 147
Bebel, Auguste (1840–1913) 35
Beckett, Margaret 134, 141
Beijing Conference (4th United Nations
    International Conference on Women)
    112–13, 197–8
Belgium
  candidate lists 94
  electoral law 94–5
  levels of female representation 81
  quotas 110
  women in parliament 81
  women in parliamentary committees
    186
Bhutto, Benazir 170
'Blair's babes' 139
Boothroyd, Betty 172, 178
bourgeois (liberal) feminism *see* feminism
Bredin, Frédèrique 135
burden of proof 208
bureaucracy 125, 131–3
Burrow, Sharan 158

cabinet ministers (women) 128, 139–41
Campbell, Kim 129
Canada
  Charter of Rights and Freedoms 200
  Constitution Act 1982 200
  equal employment enforcement 217
candidate selection
  mechanisms of 84, 93
  obstacles for women 93–4
  in United Kingdom 94
carer–earner regime in welfare state 41